A R C H I B A L D   M A C   L E I S H

D0936475

MacLeish at work in his studio, August 1972.
Photograph © 1985 by Jill Krementz

Archibald MacLeish
R E F L E C T I O N S

Edited by

Bernard A. Drabeck and

Helen E. Ellis

Foreword by Richard Wilbur

The University of Massachusetts Press

Amherst, 1986

Copyright © 1986 by The University of Massachusetts Press
Printed in the United States of America
Second printing
Set in Linoterm Trump Medieval at The University of Massachusetts Press
Printed by Cushing-Malloy and bound by John H. Dekker & Sons

Library of Congress Cataloging-in-Publication Data
MacLeish, Archibald, 1892–
    Archibald MacLeish: reflections.

    Includes index.
    1. MacLeish, Archibald, 1892–   —Interviews.
2. Poets, American—20th century—Interviews.
3. Poetry. I. Drabeck, Bernard A. II. Ellis, Helen E.
III. Title.
PS3525.A27Z465   1986   811'.52   85-28912
ISBN 0-87023-511-7

Acknowledgment is made for permission to reprint poems by
Archibald MacLeish:

Houghton Mifflin Company for "Companions," "The Silent Slain,"
"Definitions of Old Age," "You, Andrew Marvell," "End of the World,"
"Invocation to the Social Muse," "Lines for an Interment," "Critical
Observations," "The Revenant," "Years of the Dog," "The Young Dead
Soldiers," and "Night Watch in the City of Boston," from *New and Collected
Poems, 1917–1976*, copyright © 1976 by Archibald MacLeish. Reprinted by
permission of Houghton Mifflin Company.

Equity Magazine, published by Actors' Equity Association, for "Brooks
Atkinson," published 1960. Reprinted by permission.

C O N T E N T S

ILLUSTRATIONS

ACKNOWLEDGMENTS

This book would not have been possible without the vision, encouragement, support, and assistance of many people: the late Lewis O. Turner who, as president of Greenfield Community College, provided the opportunity to begin the series of interviews of which this book is composed; Greenfield Community College, which gave each of us a sabbatical to complete the manuscript; Lynne Morris, Eleanor Stebbins, and Marilyn O'Brien, who transcribed and typed; the MacLeish Committee, which aided and comforted; the staff of the college library, especially Margaret Howland and Norma Hillier, and the members of the Media Center, who gave professional assistance; members of the MacLeish family, especially Bill and Bruce MacLeish and Ellen MacLeish Zale, who provided photographs and information; Richard McAdoo, who served as consulting editor; Roy Winnick, Alex Rossmann, Frederick Ellis, and Carolyn Nims, who offered suggestions and advice; and finally our colleagues, whose direct and indirect contributions taught us that "colleague" can mean "friend."

F O R E W O R D

Archie (as he asked to be called, as one thought of him always) did not want to write his autobiography. In his later years at Conway he wanted to devote himself to poems or plays, should any ask to be written, and to his beloved wife, Ada, whose presence is captured in such poems as "Late Abed" and "Poem in Prose," and whose charm, pluck, and talent are so often evoked in this book of good talk. Had Archie undertaken a full account of his life, it would have been too vast and engrossing a task, involving too much verification and research; what poet ever led so many lives, in so many milieux, and encountered so many people high or humble? But it is good that he could find time for these interviews. What moved him to grant them is made plain both in the Drabeck-Ellis introduction and in the text: it was not to settle scores, not to magnify himself, but to get the essential facts straight.

Written autobiography tends to choose a plot and style and enwrap memory within them. Talked autobiography, prompted by questions, can, as in this case, present the man more variously, in all his selves and voices. Here we have Archie being forthright and downright, slipping into jocularity and wordplay, relishing a memory as it comes to him, being frankly forgetful, abruptly expressing affections and detestations, mixing slang and eloquence. In one voice we hear him saying, "Haven't you ever wanted to kill a man?"; in another—the voice of the capable public servant—we hear him fully and lucidly outlining his reorganization of the Library of Congress. Nowhere does he sound lofty, but what transpires from the plain facts of his life, from his choices and acts and behaviors, is that he was a naturally high-minded man—a man, as Yeats said of Hugh Lane, of the "passionate serving kind." Another thing made clear is that he had little of that dividedness or inconsistency so often ascribed to the patrician liberal or leftist: he was not pious about Yale and "Bones"; the kind of thing he wrote for Henry Luce's *Fortune* did not align him with "the arrogant rich"; he saw Antigua's Mill Reef Club as having its share of privileged "horse's asses." He comes across, early and late, as a patriot of broad social sympathies, who felt that his country had been plundered by the greedy, yet never ceased to hope that free minds and institutions could fulfill it.

Like most poets, Archie did not greatly care to explain or expound his poems, but in these interviews a number of arresting self-interpretations do escape him, as when he tells how his epic *Conquistador* was first conceived as a "metaphor of the American situation." What he more readily discloses are the circumstances that attended some job of writing, or its presentation. It is most interesting to see, in his description of the Gypsy circuses which worked the Normandy coast in the summer of 1924, the elements of his well-known poem, "The End of the World." It is fascinating to learn that his finest poem, "You, Andrew Marvell," was struck off in two or three hours of a single day, with an unaccustomed speed which he attributes to the fact that the poem is one long, additive sentence. Readers unaware or forgetful of the *engagé* theater of the thirties will relish Archie's account of the Broadway production of his anticommunist play *Panic,* which featured Martha Graham and Orson Welles, and which on its third night was performed for a largely communist audience admitted at fifty cents a head. Amongst so much else they will relish too the related story of *The Fall of the City,* which was the first verse play for radio to be broadcast in America, and but one instance of its author's adventurous versatility.

There is no self-importance in these interviews, but they are full of a well-balanced self-respect. When Archie says, "I was a pretty good lawyer," it does not sound like a boast. When he says that it was he whose long efforts got Ezra Pound out of the madhouse, he is only stating a truth which has been somewhat obscured by others. If he regrets the current neglect of *Conquistador,* and calls it "quite good! . . . very good!" he is as ready to judge that his *Einstein* was a failure. A man who has earned his own respect need not insist on his dignity: the tale of Archie's struggle to discover what Harvard expected of him as Boylston Professor is a comic one, and he is part of the comedy, but he tells the tale. In the many pages that follow, the note of personal resentment is very rare; he rose above that. His blunt negative words about Gertrude Stein or Edward Stettinius are free of spite. Consider the tone of this sentence: "I was pegged as a Fascist by John Strachey, who was an extremely well-born, intellectual, agreeable, nice, big, tall Englishman, who had turned Communist the way a lot of people did." What I hear in that is detachment, amusement, mild mockery, and a wish to be fair. Archie took guff from such difficult characters as Hemingway and Pound, and did not cease to honor them for their achievements. Though Louise Bogan had lately given him a "zinger" of a negative review in the *New Yorker,* he appointed her to the Chair of Poetry at the Library of Congress because she seemed "the best qualified person available." A generous man, a magnanimous man, whose voice it is good to hear again.

RICHARD WILBUR
Cummington

ARCHIBALD MACLEISH

INTRODUCTION

Over a six-year period (1976–1981), we drew from Archibald MacLeish what he called "the autobiography of my professional life." It was his chance to speak, and he decided to take it even though he knew that by agreeing to the telling, he would be making a commitment that would take many of his hours over several years.

There is a story in the way the interviews came about. Initiating them took two years, and during that time what we hoped to do changed almost as often as we talked to him about the project.

It all began in 1974 with the establishment of a MacLeish Collection at Greenfield Community College. Lewis O. Turner, president of the college, asked the faculty to suggest projects the newly established Greenfield Community College Foundation might support. We thought of acquiring a collection of the works of Archibald MacLeish, who lived in our area and was, without question, the most distinguished artist we could claim for "our own." Realizing that we would need his permission and his cooperation if the collection were to amount to anything, we made an appointment to see him at his home in Conway. He liked the idea and gave us some of his books to get started.

We also wanted to do some interviews with him. He said some interviews might be a good idea and he'd see, maybe in a few months. But he said that if he did agree, he would want to proceed without a subject. "No matter where the interview starts," he added, "it is bound to get to the perennial and perpetual problem of the name and nature of poetry. The relationship between poetry and reality is a problem . . . and a theme I am always working toward."

But, as everyone who has worked with it knows, oral history, which is what we were really talking about, is not as simple as it may seem. Good answers require good questions, and both take time to prepare and to execute. That's why he hesitated as long as he did before he finally permitted us to journey into his past. We thought of every reason we could to persuade him to do the project, and we repeated those reasons every time we saw him. At first, because we thought he might like to both see and hear himself, we talked about videotapes we could do in various settings. He wasn't really enthusiastic about that prospect, and we ourselves were unsure of how the technical side might be handled. We concentrated instead on getting an overview of his life on audiocassette. In April 1975 we thought we were making progress when he admitted that tapes might indeed have some value. Perhaps, he said, he should think of the process in relation to some of his colleagues. He wondered, "If I had known that Hemingway had only two years to live, what would I most have wanted to ask him?" He liked his question, and he said he should do the interviews because he might have something of value to say. After all, he had lived so long and his years had not been spent in lonely isolation either. He was in Paris during the 1920s; he worked as an editor for *Fortune* during the Great Depression; he was in Washington as Librarian of Congress during World War II; he was involved in the formation of UNESCO; and he knew almost everybody. He was also an artist who struggled with his art all his life. Writing was what he had wanted to do, and he did it, in spite of odds and opposition, both at the start and during the years that followed. The honors he received (Pulitzer prizes, the Bollingen Prize, and the National Medal for Literature, among others) he valued mostly as they confirmed his goal of becoming and being a poet. We thought we were on our way and were delighted—he had agreed and even suggested an outline for the series.

We were delayed for a year while we tried to get funding, learning after submitting a proposal and negotiating with the National Endowment for the Humanities that they did not (at that time) fund projects on living authors. They finally said they were willing to pay for equipment and tapes, but that was all they could do, and in exchange they wanted copies of the tapes. We did not like that idea much and MacLeish did not like it at all. He was worried about control of the material, and what he was reading in the papers about other writers did not ease his doubts. We made an ardent appeal to President Turner, who said we should proceed without any grant funding, that the college would give what help it could (as well as release each of us from one class for the year). We were ready to begin.

Of course, during that year we had, working out the NEH proposal with MacLeish, agreed on the objectives and procedures of the project; but MacLeish continued to vacillate. Three days before we submitted the proposal he called us to say he had changed his mind but had come up with something that would be easier on him and still help us. A letter would follow. This is what he wrote:

2 May 1975

Dear Helen:

Tossing notions in my sleep I've come more or less to the conclusion that the trouble lies in the relation between your proposal and me. I am the subject, not to say the object, and the consequence could be embarrassment to me and irritation to the bureaucrats, all of which, or most of which, would disappear if I were made the means and if the object were learning, broadly defined. Meaning not "research" into *me* but into certain aspects of human experience over the past fifty years with which I have been involved and which *my* experience might illuminate.

Why *me*? For two reasons: because I happened to be caught up one way or another in several critical aspects of those years, and because I am still alive. To which I should perhaps add a third consideration: that I have, throughout this period, and regardless of whatever else I undertook, labored at the art of poetry which is the art of attempting to make sense of human experience. I have left, in other words, a record of sorts behind me—a record which might, occasionally, have something to say.

Let me be specific as to these aspects of experience. I was born into an entirely different America from the one we live in, and I began writing in an awareness of that America. I knew the First World War at first hand: a year in France in the field artillery—and I wrote some very bad and a few still readable poems that belong peculiarly to that war. Thereafter I was a spy in the camps of the Egyptians—a teacher of law and a practising lawyer and therefore a small and insignificant figure on the frontier where the new American system and the beginnings of "modern poetry" met each other: there are lines about that—quite a lot of them. Then I dropped everything, took my small family and my non-income to Paris and lived there for five or six years in a world which seems for some reason to excite the insatiable curiosity of the contemporary young. What was important about all that was not the "expatriates" (I never met one) or the "lost" generation (we were no more lost than any other) but the extraordinary burst of creative energy in Paris with young artists and composers and poets and writers from all over the world, some of whom I knew. After that when the economic collapse hit us all I had almost a decade as an "editor" of *Fortune* spending most of my time on trips all over the country and abroad to Asia and Europe and South America—an unusual graduate course in the Depression, in the beginnings of fascism, in Marxist economics—most of all in the Republic itself, its kind, its true quality, its underlying nature—all of which left its record not only in *Fortune* but in verse—a rather lengthy record.

That ended with seven or eight years of public service beginning with the Library of Congress of which I was director (Librarian of Congress) for five years during which the entire library was reorganized. This involved a war of words with the professional librarians who were, at first, violently opposed to my appointment for very understandable reasons, and then a continuing struggle, with the professional librarians on my side, to re-shape the institution and, to some degree, the profession. There is, need-less to say, no record of this in poems but there is an extended record in speeches, articles etc., etc. (*Champion of a Cause*) which raises a great many issues which are still unfinished business in our, if you will pardon the expression, civilization.

Early in this period we entered the Second World War and I was in-structed by the President to take on additional duties (work on speeches in the White House, beginnings of a ministry of information (Office of Facts and Figures)) which produced, again, a body of speeches and articles and involved me in ructions with the America Firsters, the Chicago Tribune, the Fulton Lewises and so on down the line. There is, however, a long poem at the end, when FDR died and I resigned as Assistant Secre-tary of State, which tries to put all this into a perspective of sorts. Also, during this period (no, before Pearl Harbor) I published *The Irresponsibles* which took the academic community and many of my friends among the writers, to task for their failure to see that the Second World War was not the First all over again and that Fascism *had* to be stopped. This precipi-tated a real verbal war of which the record is scattered over the next many years. The issue, in fact, is still very much alive.

After that, and after the war ended, I was appointed Chairman of the American Delegation to the London U.N. Conference which established UNESCO and wrote the preamble to the Constitution of Unesco. Here too there is a body of prose pieces dealing with issues which are still very much with us.

Then comes my appointment as Boylston Professor at Harvard and the work which took me into literary criticism—specifically *Poetry and Experience* etc.

What this all comes down to is that there is a considerable body of material in prose and, more importantly, in verse dealing with aspects of poetic and political and economic and moral issues which are by no means of merely historic interest, and that there is, still alive and in really good shape, an old character over here on a hill, who might well be willing to discuss points of difficulty with scholars young or old who had mastered the written materials and wanted to push the discussion farther. How much time he could give would depend on how busy he was (and he plans to be good and busy) but something could certainly be worked out.

Now all this seems to me to make sense. You collect the materials, the materials attract the interested, and the interested have an opportunity (within reason) to consult the old codger when they know enough about the record to put the right questions.

But how this translates into a project to be *funded* I simply don't know. There would be materials to buy or secure copies of and there would perhaps be some recording to do but beyond that I have no inklings. Certainly I wouldn't want recompense for occasional conversations: all I would demand would be the intervention of some person or persons who would see to it that my work wasn't interfered with—because I plan to go on working full time as long as I can keep it up. Too much to DO!

best,
A MacL

We can still recall the dismay and disappointment we felt when we received the call and the letter. It seemed as if the whole process had broken down and that he had backed away from the interviews entirely; so we drove to Conway and begged him to reconsider. We said the endowment would not fund a collection as such and we repeated every argument we could think of. He did reconsider, and we finally set a date for the first interview, which we called "Reflections in the Bicentennial Year." It really wasn't an interview because he did not need questions ("It has to come out of me," he said). He talked about what he had been doing to observe the two-hundredth anniversary of American Independence. Although he was at that time eighty-four years old, he had been hopping all over the country giving readings and attending performances of his play *The Great American Fourth of July Parade* and had even appeared on television as part of the CBS official observance of the Fourth. We met him in the music room of the house (the wing added to the original house for his wife). He took an easy chair and we sat with our little portable tape recorder on a coffee table between us. He appeared to be very relaxed and composed, but we were nervous about dealing with the equipment and about how the session would go. It went very well. He was obviously very professional, he was used to questions, and he knew exactly what he wanted to say.

There was one gaffe, however. He had told us he would at some point discuss a talk at Bread Loaf which included reading and commentary on several of his poems. We had decided that we would have with us a copy of his *New and Collected Poems* which Helen could refer to as he read. So she did just that, and as she looked at the printed page we were horrified to hear him say, with a small sound of disappointment, that it would help if she looked at him.

> The reason I loved my interview with Bill Moyers was that Bill Moyers would ask you a question, then he wasn't thinking about something else. He really cared about what you were going to say. . . . So you could talk to him.

And then he went on as if nothing had happened, but we were mortified. As we drove home, we first thought we should erase that part of the tape and of course we wanted to explain to him why we had done as we had so he would know it was not from lack of interest or courtesy. And that is what we did the next time we saw him—at the second interview, one we called "The Taping Project" (September 28, 1976), where we made it a matter of record what we would do and how we would proceed. We would establish a basic chronology for the series and set an approximate timetable. At the conclusion of each interview we would decide on the topic for the next meeting and then all use the time before it to do our homework, he to brush up on dates and names and we to read what we had to and prepare questions. He also made it clear in that session that he wished to retain control over the use made of the tapes. What he wanted to provide, he said, was "certain basic true information which would make it a little difficult to do the sort of thing that they're now doing to my poor friend Hemingway." But he also wanted an agreement with the college that would provide him with "sort of veto power over what is done with the materials." We agreed that his lawyer and one for the GCC Foundation might work out a satisfactory contract, and before we left we set a date to begin the series proper. He wanted to start with "The Library of Congress Years," and that was what he talked about in December 1976. Helen had to do that one alone—it was the only time he offered a drink before, during, or after an interview—and that was it for a while, because he was going away on his winter trip to Antigua and we would not see him until late spring. From June to October 1977 we got together for five more interviews, and we completed the years in government, those in Paris, and the 1930s.

There was another lapse of time, partly because of his schedule, partly because of ours, and we met again in June 1978, for four more sessions, covering the radio verse plays, other media productions, and the stage plays. A half-hour of the fourth session was devoted to his years at Harvard, but we had to do that part of the interview twice. The first time was difficult and poignant. MacLeish was quite ill from a bout with intestinal flu, and he answered our questions lying down on the big sofa in the music room. We suggested postponing, but he would not hear of it. He was eager to finish, so we went ahead. He did not seem to be affected by his condition, except that his physical being seemed contained. It was not the end, however, because the taping equipment malfunctioned. We learned this when Helen played through the tape that evening (our standard practice was for Helen to take the tape home with her and play it through) and found a half-hour stretch of silence where words about Harvard ought to have been. We were afraid to tell him but he was not upset when we did; malfunctions were to be expected from things mechanical, he said. He made another date with us for September and we covered the material that did not get taped before, but this time we had *two* tape recorders going as we talked. (We did the same for the next two interviews.) In fact, we felt the second time around was even better than the first, because we had a two-hour session on the Harvard years to replace the half-hour that was lost.

After that, we made only three more tapes. We did two updates, in 1980 and 1981. The updates were our idea. We thought they would offer him an opportunity to amplify material we had already covered or perhaps open new ground for him to move over. Besides, we wanted to find out what he had been doing: at eighty-eight and eighty-nine he was still very active, but he was coping with health matters (his own and Ada's) which had slowed him down. He felt frustrated by this, but not defeated. We also wanted to see him because we had decided to throw a grand ninetieth birthday party for him at the college in the form of a MacLeish Symposium set for May 1982. So at the 1981 update we asked him if we could return for an interview in November with some photographers. We would take pictures and ask him questions about his house and workplace and we would put together a slide-tape we would show at the symposium. And that is what we did. The photographers took shots in color and in black and white of the inside and outside of his house while we chatted with him about its history, its furnishings, and the memorabilia. Then we settled in the music room and he talked about his family, especially his father and his brother Kenneth, and he was close to tears as he recalled Kenneth's death in World War I more than sixty years earlier. One of the photographers asked him some questions about his work habits and his approach to writing a poem, which we thought he might find redundant, but he did not mind at all, and what he said was both old and new and it was from the vantage point of eighty-nine years. We had been a little apprehensive about the session because we were unsure of how he would react to the photographers and the questions, and to moving around and posing. We worried for nothing, because he appeared to love it all, showing off his house and talking about his life and family there. He did set some limits, however. Ada was not in the pictures, nor would she be. But he seemed to enjoy the outing and even provided himself with a Scottish bonnet which he told Helen he would wear when we went outside (the day was a bright but nippy 32°) because he no longer had "the protection most males had." It was a good day and he had been in fine form. It was also, as it turned out, the last time we saw him.

So it all began, as most large things do, with a small idea that grew because we were interested and we interested him. He was nearly dragged into it, and even after we began he fidgeted and chafed under the burden of so little time and so much to do: readings and public appearances and lectures and receiving awards. But even as he talked of these, it was with a sense of impatience because he wanted to get back to poetry. Always that was his theme and his concern. Even publishing *Riders on the Earth*, a collection of essays, did not satisfy finally because "if you pull off and go to work at prose, it takes an awful long time for the slow streams to work their way through the silt." For the same reason, he was not entirely pleased to be working on an edition of *Six Plays*, which was published in 1980, because he had to rewrite (particularly *Nobodaddy*) and provide new prefaces. He was also involved, if only as a consultant, with their projected performance on WGBH.

There were also things he really did not want to talk about. We knew from the beginning that family matters were essentially private. And we learned that there were also aspects of his art he would rather not go into. During one of the interviews on Paris, for instance, he spoke at length about the writing of "End of the World." He was obviously delighted to be able to tell us about the circumstances leading to its composition, and we thought a similarly happy experience for him would be commenting on other poems from that period. Thus we read through *Streets in the Moon* and *Poems, 1924–1933* and compiled questions about particulars in many of the individual works. We were dismayed to learn that we had made a tactical error. While he did not leave our questions unanswered, his tone made us very aware that he considered some of them inappropriate. But the tape was made and he did not disallow it; both what he says so reluctantly and the obvious discomfort he feels about saying it are mutually revealing. It was, however, an experience he did not want repeated. At the penultimate session in the series, we asked if he would do another tape about poetry and poems. We had not yet, we said, talked "about *Pot of Earth*; we talked briefly about *The Hamlet*, but we haven't gone beyond." This was his answer:

> I wonder if talking about individual poems and so forth is what we ought to do with this. What we've been doing is making sense of the vagaries of a life that has touched too many different places perhaps, and sort of related them to each other. I don't like talking about my own poems very much. . . . They either do their job as poems or they don't. Nothing I can say will help that.

Some problems we faced were practical ones. He seemed frequently to be rushing from one demand on his time to another, especially in the last years. Once after we came in he told us that he had just gotten a call from Vice-President Mondale asking for his thoughts on an issue. We said that he must be flattered but he shook his head. It was, he said, just another distraction from the real work he wanted to do. Also his hearing weakened in later years, and sometimes he would latch onto a word or a phrase and launch into an answer without grasping the whole question.

In spite of the problems we encountered, individually or collectively, we would not have foregone the experience. For him, the project had some merit or he would not have done it at all. He really wanted a chance to speak "for the record." His publisher had in fact asked him if he would simply talk into a tape recorder by himself, or with Ada, when he could or would; but that project had no appeal. We, on the other hand, offered opportunity and a demonstrated resolve, which he may have recognized as useful commodities in such an undertaking. We also felt that he trusted us to respect his limits and to take good care of what he shared with us.

We derived some personal benefits from the project. Talking to Mr. MacLeish was an altogether happy and exciting time. He was articulate—often eloquent. He was thoughtful. He was not stand-offish. He was a true professional. And he was as eager to please us as we were to be helpful partners in the process.

The principal value of what we did, however, lay in the content. What he gave us was both informative and important. Because his career spanned the course of twentieth-century American literature and thought and because of his involvement with so many aspects of letters and life, he was uniquely qualified to comment on what he had done, what he had seen, and what he thought of both.

Except for some editorial emendations, omissions of repeated material, and rearrangement of information to more nearly approximate a chronology, the text is a verbatim transcript.

BERNARD A. DRABECK AND HELEN E. ELLIS

The
Paris
Years

1892	Born in Glencoe, Illinois, May 7 to Andrew and Martha Hillard MacLeish.
1907–11	Attended Hotchkiss School in Lakeville, Connecticut.
1915	A.B., Yale University. A leaflet containing his "Class Poem 1915" was distributed to the class-day audience. *Yale University Prize Poem, 1915, Songs for a Summer's Day*. Yale University Press.
1916	Married Ada Hitchcock of Farmington, Connecticut, June 21.
1917	*Tower of Ivory* (poetry). Yale University Press.
1917–18	Stationed in France with the United States Army.
1919	LL.B., Harvard University.
1919–23	Taught at Harvard College.
1921–23	Practiced law in the Boston firm of Choate, Hall & Stewart.
1923	Moved with his family to Paris.
1924	*The Happy Marriage and Other Poems*. Houghton Mifflin Co.
1925	*The Pot of Earth* (poetry). Houghton Mifflin Co.
1926	*Nobodaddy* (verse play). Dunster House. *Streets in the Moon* (poetry). Houghton Mifflin Co.
1927	Bought the Arms family farmhouse in Conway, Massachusetts.
1928	Returned to America to live in the Conway house. *The Hamlet of A. MacLeish* (poetry). Houghton Mifflin Co.

The first thirty years of your life were ones of great conflict. There was on the one hand your study of law, and on the other the call of poetry pulling you in a different direction. Could you comment on your experiences with poetry during your years at Yale, or did they begin even before that?

Before that, of course. My mother[1] was one of the great North American women, no question about that. She was the daughter of a Congregational clergyman, later in this town[2] in the late 1880s; a member of one of the first classes at Vassar; a professor at Vassar (they called everybody professors in those days!). Almost immediately after graduation she taught there for two or three years. Then at the age of twenty-six she was invited to go to Rockford College in western Illinois, which is famous as being the college of Jane Addams and Julia Lathrop[3]—all the women in that great period, the women that saved Chicago from itself. My mother was president of Rockford Female Seminary for some four or five years. And she married my father,[4] two of whose daughters by an earlier wife had been students of hers at Vassar. My father saw the light when he saw her.

She had a tremendous interest in child education. She was one of the first people in the country who really was excitedly interested in the kindergarten movement, which comes by way of Germany—Italy via Germany. I had a sister first, who died in infancy; then an older brother, Norman; then me; then my brother Kenneth; and then my sister Ishbel, who is Mrs. Campbell now.[5]

When Norman was, I think, a little over six she began reading to him. She had a marvelous voice and a real understanding of the innards of poetry; she understood the relation between intellectual rhythm and verbal rhythm. She began reading fairly obvious choices, like Kingsley's *Water Babies* (I *lived* those days!) and she became an immediate success. I begged to be included; Kenny was a little bit too young. She then moved to stories from the Bible, in the King James version, no paraphrasing but very careful selection, always something that had narrative quality, except the psalms and things of that sort, which have something better than narrative quality. That worked so well that she then moved to Shakespeare—being again selective but never paraphrasing, never explaining anything. Then she got to Dante. She took the *Inferno* head on. We had a huge folio of Dante with the Doré illustrations. I can remember lying on the floor with that thing under my nose. She very wisely used the beautiful prose translation by, I think, Carlyle's brother.[6] By the time I was twelve or fourteen, although my passionate interest in life was raising chickens, I had read a lot more than most college undergraduates read now.

Naturally, when you get hooked that way, you begin doing it yourself; she knew that would happen. My older brother, Norman, used to write fantasies about the Ice King on Lake Michigan: the water freezes and it builds up little mountains on the shallow part of the lake where the warmer water underneath can't protect it. I thought this was nonsense, but that didn't stop me from a flagrant imitation of Dante. That was something no man would have gall enough to do! And it began coming out seriously when I went to a high school nearby called New Trier. It's quite a good high school now; I think it was probably pretty good then, but it had no "cultural interest" whatsoever, if the phrase may be forgiven me. I was then sent to the Hotchkiss School,[7] which was about as cultural at that time as an institution can be. It had a huge Englishman, whose name is stuck in my mind, a Mr. Stevens; black hair, 6 foot 4 inches; a man with a passionate love of Swinburne. Mr. Stevens would read me Swinburne; I read Swinburne to Mr. Stevens, and Mr. Stevens would get fake Swinburne from me. You can imagine how awful fake Swinburne would be when the original is what it is. So by the time I went down to Yale I was already writing perfectly dreadful verses but writing a great many of them.

Yale was pretty discouraging at that time; I mean from that point of view. The whole emphasis in the English department was made by Chauncey Tinker, who was, as you know, an eighteenth-century scholar and a very good one—a man who believed that Johnson wrote poetry. The rest of the flavor of the English department was given by Billy Phelps, a very nice, pleasant, gentlemanly, commercial type, who taught a famous course for people who had no other experience with the art of poetry which he called "Tennyson and Browning." I avoided that. He taught another on metaphysical poets in which he completely miscomprehended Donne. He killed Donne for me, if you could believe that. It took me years to get back to him. Yale was really pretty close to the bottom (I was there in the "blue sweater" era, class of 1915), with very little distinction but a lot of warm human relationships and some pretty good undergraduates—the Elizabethan Club started while I was there. I was chairman of the literary board.[8] I wrote verse through Yale and won all the prizes that you can win. Anybody could get a prize at Yale by producing a couple of lines.

I don't want to be too bitter about it. I loved Yale deeply, love it, but it wasn't an educational institution. It lacked the sort of thing that I felt at once when I went to the Harvard Law School and would occasionally cross over to the Yard.

But I imagine what you had in mind in your question is the bridge between New Trier High School and Hotchkiss School, Yale and the Harvard Law School, and Paris. Well, I think this is something that I've puzzled about too. And I think the answer is the war. By the time I got through the law school, I really discovered something about the intellectual life—having been laid out, drawn and quartered the first day I ever appeared in a Harvard Law School class! Joey Beal was the most caustic of all the caustic users of the Socratic method. My misfortune was he was drawn to my face and began talking to me. I, at that time, thought rather well of myself—I had graduated from Yale Phi Beta Kappa, the key prominently displayed. By the time he got through with me, I was hiding my Phi Beta Kappa key and wondering if I'd ever come back to a class again. The law school was an extraordinary intellectual experience and I discovered early that I was quite good at it. In fact, I graduated with the Fay Diploma,[9] which they give one of every year. I was an editor of the *Harvard Law Review* and all that that implies. But at the same time I had gone on writing verse. The *Yale Review* had published one poem when I was an undergraduate and there were some other publications in other magazines. I was putting them together and trying to prepare them for some kind of publication—working at this fairly hard and fairly consistently and assuming, as nearly as I can re-create my state of mind, that that was what I was going to do. I was also assuming that the reason I was in the law school was that I knew that I was going to have to support myself somehow. I had already met my wife, Ada,[10] as she now is, and I knew I was going to marry her no matter what she said about it. Therefore, the law to me was a means to livelihood, but what I hadn't counted on was that it was a very exciting intellectual discipline. Also the law is *the* great gateway to history. It is the one contemporary study which carries with it, by virtue of its nature, a conception of the tradition of the mind. At Harvard Law School, as in all law schools, I assume, the teaching is in the common law. You don't teach statute law to anybody; just open the statute book and there it is. The work is all on the common law: common law cases—one case stands on another's shoulders. You see a tradition building itself up. It is a very enlarging experience. Best indoor sport in the world, I think!

I think that I was assuming that I was going to earn our keep by practicing law and that I would write immortal lines between clients. This was, by me, an unexamined idea. This all seemed extremely pleasant because the law was so interesting—although you didn't make the fortune that lawyers now make. Then suddenly the war came on. Ada and I got married at the end of the first year of law school, my father having said it was up to me whether I wanted to use the allowance he was giving me for myself or if I wanted to see if what they say is true—that two can live as cheaply as one, and that was the basis on which we proceeded. At the end of my second year, the war came along; our son Kenneth had been born in February.[11] The examinations were moved up into May. I took my examinations and was on my way to France within two weeks.

I was associated in the beginning with an ambulance outfit. The ambulance outfit was shipped to France ahead of Pershing. When I got there I was able to get free from the ambulance outfit and join the field outfit. This was the kind of experience which calls for a great deal of reexamination of your situation, of what you're doing, what you believe (what you *really* believe). Ada and I had been married for just about a year and I didn't see her again for over a year and then only briefly. That's quite a lot to think about. It meant reexamining the assumptions, and the more I reexamined them, the more I kept pushing them out of my mind. It seemed to me that logically it made perfectly good sense: I'd practice law, earn our keep that way, and write as I could. But I had a strong intimation even then (this is hard to talk about now) that there was something very wrong with this idea, that it was sort of like dividing horses by apples; that the law as a profession is not something you can deal with, divide, multiply, add, subtract, on the same basis that you would use in dealing with the art of poetry. One is a means of earning a living, and probably having a pretty good intellectual time doing it; the other is something that involves your entire being. And they just don't blend. I kept pushing this out of my mind but it was constantly there.

I remember at Saumur, the field artillery school where I started and spent the brutally cold winter of 1917–18, I would go out on the hard frozen roads beside the Loire and try to figure this thing out and decided, just for the sake of my sanity, to stop thinking about it.

Well, I came back to this country after the second battle of the Marne to a new outfit, to train a new regiment in hundred and fifty-five millimeter *grand puissant fusil*, which is a rifle. I saw Ada briefly. The new regiment had its sailing orders and then the armistice came along. So eventually, after several months of fooling around one place and another (it takes an awful long time to get out of the army), I did get released and went back to Cambridge.[12]

And the law school put on a special term for people who were in my situation, a really very generous thing for them to do! All the teachers lost their summer vacation.

I got my degree and passed my bar examinations in the fall of that year, 1919, and it was then that I came face to face with this. And I found myself doing some things that I'd never really decided to do. I had some justification in what I'm about to tell you because by the time we were graduated, as I recall it, it was September or October 1919 (it was quite late in the year) and I had offers from law offices—one good one in New York and several in Boston. I found myself turning them down and taking a job teaching constitutional law in Harvard College, not in the law school. The department of government had never had a course in constitutional law or if they had, not for some time, and they wanted it taught. So I was asked to do this and they'd pay me a stipend that would enable us to eat. I also assisted Professor Wilson[13] in international law, a subject about which I knew nothing and cared less.

I think if I had done a little more walking up and down the roads by the Loire, I might have realized what was going on. I just wasn't able to put myself in a law office even with good law offices to go into, so I taught constitutional law and I taught international law. This didn't provide enough money, so I taught a night-school course in legal procedure at Northeastern, which was then beginning as an educational institution. And that didn't work really well enough so I began writing the educational column of *Time* magazine, which was then starting. I got paid ten dollars a week for that—very useful.

This went on for two or three years. During that time I was writing. I forgot to say that while I was abroad, all my Yale stuff, and other stuff just after leaving Yale, had been published under the very appropriate title of *Tower of Ivory* by a young professor at Yale named Lawrence Mason, published through the Yale University Press. While I was doing all this, I was working on what turned into *The Happy Marriage*, which Houghton Mifflin not too hesitantly agreed to publish. The *Tower of Ivory* included my class poem at Yale, the poem from the *Yale Review*, and a sonnet sequence which won a Yale prize. *The Happy Marriage* was all new stuff, written while I was in law school. Also in this period I was writing a verse play that Maurice Firuski at the Dunster House Book Shop published—Dunster Press—called *Nobodaddy*, Blake's name for God. It was Adam and Eve in the Garden of Eden.

What happened was that these various attempts to keep out of practicing law—keep somewhere near the academic world where at least my poor little swallow's nest could hang to the wall—well, they simply didn't add up to enough money to live on. That's the plain and simple whole truth of it! I believe in the year 1921 I finally went to Mr. Choate,[14] who had been asking me to work for Choate, Hall & Stewart, and said I would do so but that I wanted to keep on with my constitutional law course at Harvard. He didn't like that, but he said if I could stand it, he could. And so for two years the thing that I had thought previously I was not going to do, and had great hesitancy about doing, was being done. I was practicing law. I was also teaching constitutional law, and I was writing *The Happy Marriage* and that's just about it.

And the poetry was becoming what you were doing least, probably.

Yes, less and less. Less and less time for it. And it was an impossible situation. I backed myself into the stall the wrong way around. I couldn't get at the oats and I couldn't kick. There wasn't anything I could do. I'd made a real mess. This was in 1923. And in 1923 I was thirty-one years old. I was much too old to be fooling around with my life. But something came over me after two years of very active practice of law—in court all the time everywhere, all over the country, carrying Mr. Choate's briefcase and trying some cases by myself. And it came over me one afternoon in February, in a very brief space of time, that I would either get out of law then, or I never would. Because I was a pretty good lawyer, which was the difficulty. I mean it was quite clear that I was going to be a good operating lawyer. This hit me at the end of the afternoon, a very tiring afternoon. Now the ordinary method of getting home to Cambridge from 30 State Street was to walk to Park Street Under and take the subway to Harvard Square and to walk out to Coolidge Hill. On this night I came out opposite the Common approaching Park Street Under and there in the icy, absolutely clear sky was the new moon with the old moon in its arms. I started down the subway steps, met the fetid air, and realized I wasn't going there. I would not take the subway; I would walk home, which I did. I walked the whole length of Commonwealth, out to Massachusetts Avenue and then the whole length of Massachusetts Avenue to the Square, and on out past the Square another mile and a half to where we lived.

It was fairly late and I was due home before I started. By the time I got there, Ada was terribly worried and therefore very angry. So it was the worst possible atmosphere to discuss anything. We discussed it; we discussed it all night long and she agreed. It became perfectly clear that I had been running away from a decision that I should have made. I'd thought I'd made it, and discovered I hadn't made it, and discovered that it wasn't a decision anyway, discovered that I didn't know anything about what I was doing.

Then things happened very, very rapidly. I arrived late. Ada was very much concerned and after we got over that, and had a bite to eat, we sat up most of the night and talked about it and we decided we'd do it. She had worked in

Paris for a year before the war. Her father, a bolt-and-nut manufacturer in Unionville, Connecticut, a Pure Yankee, had her trained as a pianist, good Yankee insurance against the future. She had discovered in Paris that she had what she did have, one of the loveliest lyric soprano voices, so cheating on her father, she let the piano go and went to work as a singer. To get ahead of myself, during the time we were in Paris she was working with Croiza, who was the great soprano of her day. She was also working with Povla Frijsh, who was a magnificent musician with a very unpleasant voice which could mesmerize you. She was a great concert singer largely because even though her voice was difficult to take, the musical consequences were marvelous; and Ada had gotten to know Nadia Boulanger[15] on her first trip. Ada was never personally ambitious but she did want very badly to go on singing and it didn't take us very long during that night to come to a conclusion. We just made up our minds we were going to do it. I don't think I got more than two hours sleep. The next morning I went to the office. What happened then is like a badly written play: I mean it was so neat that it's badly written. I had gotten to the office early, and walked right down the corridor to Mr. Choate's office. His secretary, Miss Johnson, was sitting outside. I was astonished to hear her say, "Well, how did you know I wanted you? I was just picking up the telephone." And I said, "May I see Mr. Choate?" She said, "Go in; they are expecting you." That alarmed me, and I opened the door and there was the whole firm standing around the wall. And Mr. Choate, a very tall, gray-haired man, with a girl's skin—when angry or excited, he'd blush—was sitting there, looking happy as a cat. And he said, "Archie, I think I'm going to tell you that we've decided to ask you to join the firm." I thought to myself, either you speak up now or never. I took a deep breath and I said, "Mr. Choate, I came to tell you that I'm giving up the law." His face turned scarlet and he wouldn't speak to me for two months. He never really forgave me. I don't blame him, either. They shouldn't have taken me in there. I had only been there two years. It was much too soon. Well, it was a very dramatic business. We really burned, like Cortés on the beach of Veracruz, every damn ship we had. Mr. Choate wouldn't have hired me as a busboy after that. We just definitely, firmly, and completely did it. And the resolution was pretty grim for a couple of years; in fact, it stayed grim for quite a long period of time.

How would you describe your background or education in poetry before you went to Paris?

That is a very relevant question, indeed. My poetic education was abysmal. It was just about as bad as it could be, except for the fundamental basic fact that

I started with my mother—the great texts, heard in the ear—and that stayed with me. I have to go ahead to answer your question. When we got to Paris and finally got ourselves established, Ada made her connection with Nadia Boulanger again and was sailing under full sails. Nadia was the great teacher of composers at that time and she wanted Ada to work with her composers and sing for her composers. In a short time she was giving the most beautiful little concerts of works by unknowns like Aaron Copland, who was then a student of Nadia's.

While she was doing that, I was working on my education as a poet. I was totally ignorant of the new challenge to the poetic tradition that had been opened largely by Pound and Eliot who, after all, were both Americans. Nobody at Yale knew about Rimbaud. Nobody at Yale read Arthur Waley; nobody I ever met. Nobody knew the names of Tu Fu, Li Po, Po Chu-I.[16] Nobody'd found Emily Dickinson. The only really passable American poet I was reading at that time was Edwin Arlington Robinson, who was a hell of a good poet, but not much use to me. I had to feel my way. I had to find out what I needed to find out, nothing less or harder than that.

So during my first two years in Paris, I wrote very little.

I was working in the *bonne*'s room up in the attic—in a cold-water flat on the fourth floor of a building on boulevard Saint-Michel, up opposite the Accordimine with the Luxembourg out in front. And this room had no heat of any kind, had a skylight that had a half-inch leak in it. Paris winters are brutal. And I sat up there. I had the sense not to sit down and wait for something to happen. I immediately started work on the Italian language to try to read the *Inferno* in Italian and by the end of the year I succeeded in doing that. And that was a very wise thing to do but it didn't advance me any. I did do a certain amount of writing: a few poems which Eliot published in the *Criterion*, and some poems that were published in the *Commerce*.[17] Most of the time I was simply working on this education that you spoke of. In other words, to sum up the answer to your first (the long, long answer to your first) question, the reason we went to Paris was that I had, by making a couple of damn fool assumptions, put myself, and therefore all of us in my family, into an impossible situation, and the only way we could deal with it was to get out and start again and there was only one place to go to start again. First of all, everything in the world of art was going on in Paris in that decade. That's where the young of the world were flooding—into Paris. It was the natural place to go. Second, Ada had worked there. Third, I had seen it. I got two leaves when we were on the front, forty-eight or seventy-two hours, whatever it was, and both times I went to Paris; I had a terribly strong desire to know more about that place. So returning there was the logical thing to do. I never did answer my fundamental underlying question because once I'd seen Paris, I didn't need to. Seeing Paris and seeing the light!

Malcolm Cowley, in his book Exile's Return, *talks about expatriates and one of the reasons they went to Paris. He said it had to do with the intellectual climate or lack of it in this country, specifically New York. Did that reasoning apply to you, too?*

Not a bit and it doesn't apply to anybody! Malcolm I love, a darling man, but he's just crazy. I never met an expatriate in Paris. Henry Miller was in Paris at the time and Henry Miller was undoubtedly an expatriate. He's an expatriate from the world, from the earth and I never met him. Of the people I did know nobody was even remotely concerned with what concerned Malcolm. Now I agree there is every reason to talk about it as of now, but not applying it back then. It's briefly apparent now what those three predictable presidents of ours, Harding, Coolidge, and Hoover, were up to; we know what they did to us. The thirties are the answer to them, but the twenties, as seen from Europe, were largely nonsense. To understand Paris, when we were there, you have to talk about things that Malcolm apparently never saw. Paris was full of the young from Africa, from Eastern Europe, from Asia, the Swedes, the Norwegians, the Finns, the Latinos, every kind of Latino. They poured into Paris after the war. I think it is possible to say (it may not be possible to prove) that they felt a kind of vacuum. The youth of Europe had been slaughtered. The thing I used to notice in Paris, when I got there earlier, was the total absence of the young, even young women, because young women didn't look young. They looked old. They were dressed in black and their faces were unsmiling. There were old men; there were sick-looking, middle-aged men; there were boys; there were no young men. There were an awful lot of people and a great deal of talk about disease and so forth; but the great slaughter was on the battlefield in that worst of all wars and the greater part of those killed were young men. It did create a kind of vacuum, so the young flooded into Europe. We were all there. If you read that, to me, thoroughly bad book, Hemingway's *Moveable Feast*,[18] which I'm sure he never would have published if he'd thought about it, you get Ernest's memories (at sixty, sixty-two; he finished it when he was sixty-two years old) of what Paris felt like to him. But when he and Hadley[19] were there in the very beginning he thought about the feel of Paris, the young in Paris. He was young in Paris. In fact, there is an epigraph on the title page which says: "If you were lucky to be young in Paris, no matter where you go in the world, it's with you." Well, I think Malcolm is just completely cockeyed and the entire educational community in the country has bought that! Wherever I go, and I used to go around quite a lot, I'm asked questions about it. "Oh, you're one of those expatriates" and every time I hear that I could wring Malcolm's neck!

The Sacco-Vanzetti trial occurred just prior to your actually joining the law firm in Boston. How did you respond to that trial and the series of appeals and the ultimate execution?

The Sacco-Vanzetti case began to affect people like Katherine Anne Porter but particularly Dos Passos much later.[20] We left Boston in 1923. At that time, there was next to no concern about it. The liberal concern about it hadn't even begun to kick up.

You were in Europe at the time of all the appeals, demonstrations, and the tremendous controversy here in the United States at the time of the execution. How in touch were Americans in Paris with what was happening in this country?

In my case very, very little. I knew nothing about it. I didn't even know of the execution. I was very much out of touch with things at home. My connection with it was later on. My friend Felix Frankfurter[21] was very much involved. In fact, the best treatment in print of the Sacco-Vanzetti situation, from the lawyer's point of view, is Felix's. Felix was not very popular with the State Street lawyers. Neither was Brandeis[22]—there was a great deal of anti-Brandeis feeling. My whole connection with it was after I got back. I did some writing about it myself, but that was in connection with work with Felix and about Felix. I don't remember any knowledge of it at the time even in conversation with Dos Passos, who had been through the early disturbances. The only explanation I can think of is that we really saw very little of other Americans. We saw very little of anybody. We had our friends, but Ada was so busy with her music that I regarded it as a star day when I could see her, really talk to her at all. I was very much in love and once I let myself begin to write, I wrote four books of verse in the last four years of that decade, and that doesn't include *Conquistador*. So the picture of a young man over his head in the froth, that's exactly me!

Do you remember the circumstances of your trip—things like getting the children ready and getting packed?

Oh, God! We sailed from Boston on a boat called the *Lafayette*—I don't know how many tons it was, not many thousand, I'm sure—and landed at Le Havre. And the trip did include a good deal of difficulty, because Kenny was six and Mimi was a year old. We got a wonderful old Irish nurse who agreed to go over with us to get us through this problem you're talking about. As I look back on the whole thing, it just overwhelms me: the blind trustfulness with which I approached all these things! We had no financial security. I had no letter of credit. I had nothing. I just had all these human beings completely dependent on me. There must have been some fun somewhere. When we arrived, fortunately, we had some friends that were extremely kind to us. Billy Emerson, the architect and head of the department of architecture at Tech,[23] married a cousin of mine, my cousin Fran. They were both passionate Francophiles. They were devoted friends of ours. They were kind enough to meet us at the train at the Gare de Lyons. They had found a pension near the Arc de Triomphe, the most unlikely, god-awful spot, where we stayed for two or three weeks. Then they returned to the United States and let us rent a flat that they had near the Champs Elysées. Everybody knew it wasn't going to be big enough, it wasn't going to be right, and the winter was coming on, but at least it was a place where we could shop for ourselves and eat our own food. We blithely sailed ahead and had the great good luck to run into Alice-Lee Myers, who knew everything and everybody in the city of Paris, and knew that there was, on the boulevard Saint-Michel, a cold-water flat, four flights up, without an elevator, which was available if you went quickly, and we went quickly, and it was, and we took it. We lived there for three years with a baby to get up and down and Kenny who was put in school across the Luxembourg, the River Seine, on the other side. If we were faced with these problems now, the mere thought of them would drive us into a nursing home!

How did you solve the problems of paying your bills?

They were solved in exactly the same way as before. I don't know why I shouldn't tell this story because it's part of the records. My father had a Scotsman's respect for the making of books, even the future making of books. He also had been told by Arthur Twining Hadley, the president at Yale, when he went down to my graduation, that I was a "lad of parts." If I was a "lad of parts," he could do something about it! So I said, "Father, you've got to admire my gall if you can't admire anything else. Here you've put me through Yale and the Harvard Law School and I'm now telling you I'm leaving the law, and I'm going to Paris to try to write the kind of poetry that I am not now writing." I made it just as black as I could. I had one powerful ally in the fact that my mother's sister Mary Hillard, founder and headmistress of the

Westover School in Middlebury, Connecticut, had been so outraged (I don't blame her a bit) by my decision to leave the law when I'd just been offered a partnership in Choate, Hall & Stewart, that she wrote me a series of unspeakable letters, insolent letters, if one can speak of insolence in a woman of fifty writing to a young man of thirty. These letters were then shown, not by me but by somebody else (probably by my mother), to Father. And that helped a great deal! The last thing Father wanted was to have his sister-in-law interfering in the life of his son. I discovered this all later on. He said to me, "Well," he said, "I'll do as I've done before. I will renew the allowance I made you in the law school that you used to get married on. Maybe," he said, "four can live as cheaply as one in Paris." And that was just about what it was. It was just money enough to count at the beginning of the month, and there wasn't any money to count the last day of the month.

Besides having the usual expenses of food and the apartment, did you pay somebody to help with the children?

Yes, we had various people. They weren't expensive in France. We had to have a cook. My wife was living a full-time life as a musician! She was busier than anybody else singing in Paris at that time. And we were beneficiaries of the inflation that was murdering the French. You could practically count on the franc to drop two points against the dollar every month. Every month you were just two points better off than the month before. Your income in dollars was constant, bear in mind. But the number of francs we had available went gradually up, gradually up, gradually up. We never could take it easy but we could eat all right.

Did you have a natural taste for French cooking?

Oh, of course. It is the best cooking in the world!

Did you know that before you went or did you discover it afterward?

I knew it from the two times I got into Paris during the war. And after we got settled, we dropped into the usual pattern of cafés. On the boulevard Saint-Germain there was and still is a very good café called the Deux Magots and right across from the Deux Magots there was an Alsatian beer-drinking place called Lipp's, where you could order a demi-blonde and a liter of light beer, and sit back of it for a couple of hours. Nobody ever threw you out or said, "If you're going to stay here, you'd better order another." That's not the way the

French do things. Ada hates beer, but I like it and Lipp's was a wonderful place for me, and she and I both used the Deux Magots. But there were a couple of restaurants right back of the Deux Magots which were extremely good. The restaurant we used to go to regularly, once a week, was called the Petite Riche, which meant just what the phrase sounds like. There's a Petite Riche in every small town in France. It is always a bourgeois restaurant where the butter and the veal are excellent and the bread is delicious and you're taking your chances on anything else. The wines are very ordinary wines, but it is always an extremely good place to eat lunch. We did a good deal of theatergoing. The Vieux Columbier had opened and was extremely exciting. And neither of us liked opera to begin with but Ada was singing Mélisande[24] at the Comédie-Française and that changed our views, of course.

During this time you also published some poems in some of the American magazines. How did you make connections with these magazines?

I really don't remember.[25] I had some poems that I liked very well and I sent them over to Tom Eliot, who was not at that time a friend of mine at all. In fact, I think I'd never met him, but he took them to the *Criterion* and that was a great help. Marguerite Caetani started *Commerce,* and she liked all the things I sent her. I published some things in the *Nouvelle Revue Française.* I don't remember publishing anything at home, but Houghton Mifflin was standing by gallantly. Harry Crosby and Caresse Crosby with their Black Sun Press, as you know, brought out special editions of *New Found Land* and also *Einstein.*[26]

What schooling arrangements did you make for your children?

Mimi was too young to do any schooling at all. Kenny went to an American school on the rue de Seine, a tiny little school. It was sort of a quid pro quo thing. The school was extremely inexpensive and there were ways of paying, not in money. Ken then later on had to go to a local Paris school. It turned out that he had infantile paralysis while I was in France during the war. Nobody knew it until he began to show signs when he got to be three or four years old. Paris was not very good for him. So we sent him to the Chalet Marie José, a boarding school in Gstaad, Switzerland, and that had to be financed separately. The whole experience for Ken was a marvelous one. He still relishes talking about it. He speaks French so there is no perceptible difference any ear can catch between Ken's French and French French. He's completely bilingual. Ernest Hemingway was terribly fond of him and he'd go up with us to

Gstaad. We'd go up there skiing—to see Ken. Ernest would get Ken out of school and take him to the slaughterhouse to watch a cow being slaughtered. It made an undying impression on Ken.

You obviously had to learn French to live in a French city, and you were studying Italian to read Dante. How did you handle language in your home?

I tried to do something specific about that. I wanted to speak French better than I was speaking it. I'm really not a linguist although I get around all right, read French, even write it to some extent. Talking it is a considerable problem for me; so I agreed to trade lessons with a professor at the Collège de France. He would come out and have dinner with me. One dinner we would talk French and the next we would talk English. It didn't do me any good. It did him a lot of good! He became an excellent speaker of English.[27] My French is something that has to be heard! Ada, of course, had to become proficient in French and German. She's a very quick ear. Her triumphs were infinite. It's extraordinary. And it was a case of exactly the right voice at the right time in the right place. Poulenc, and Stravinsky even more so, were writing songs that required perfect musicianship, perfect ear, perfect placement of the note: notes used as they would be used on a flute, on a wind instrument, but with the quality only a human voice has. And that is exactly the kind of voice she had—a heart-breakingly beautiful voice. I think I'm now the only living witness of it but there were plenty around then who knew what she was. She had what the French call "une voix blanche" but it's not what "une voix blanche" means literally. It's not really a "white" voice. Her voice was much more like silver. It had a very real tone—but never a quaver, always a pure sound. I remember once being outside this house in what's now a garden. It used to be just a little lawn. I had a researcher (I was working for *Fortune*) with me and we were working on a story. Ada was in here and she was singing "An die Musik."[28] Our voices dropped and then stopped and we looked at each other with tears running down our faces.

Can you think back and talk about a day in the life of the budding poet?

It's very easy. It's the same schedule I've kept all my life. I started very early in the morning, as early as possible. I had to walk Kenny to school, which made it a little later than it would have been otherwise. Of course while I was making up my lost homework, repairing my ruined education, I would work all day long, but when I began working for myself I found I could only keep that up for two or three hours at the most. And after, I would usually get out and do whatever chores were necessary. Eat lunch. I usually never met Ada for lunch—she was always off somewhere. I tried to meet her later in the afternoon, but one day a week Ada and I would lunch at a restaurant and occasionally friends would join us. Very, very rarely there would be dinner parties. We would sometimes have people in for dinner.

During those years in Paris, did you live always on the boulevard Saint-Michel?

We moved into an apartment that the Comte Etienne de Beaumont[19] had fixed up for Picasso, a studio apartment, and Picasso wouldn't use it. He didn't like the light. And we were able to rent that because Picasso didn't want it. Nobody would take it, so we took it and we lived there for quite a while. Big room, everything else about it crowded, but on the rue du Bac, which is a wonderful street right off the boulevard Saint-Germain.

During this time were you communicating with other poets?

I never really liked that. With the exception of Mark Van Doren, I never have done it. I avoid writers like the plague. I found that most writers reciprocate. There always are, in cities like Paris or New York, groups of writers with common interests who see a lot of each other. I didn't know them. I saw a lot of John Peale Bishop, who was a very gifted poet, but we had a sort of unbreakable rule—we never talked about writing.

Ernest and I only talked about writing twice and once was at the bullfight in Pamplona where we got talking about Joyce. I was complaining to Ernest that he just ought to relax a little bit and give Joyce credit, and then criticize whatever he wanted to but at least give him fundamental basic credit. I think I even made the mistake of suggesting that maybe there were some aspects of Joyce's work that Ernest ought to think about, and indeed there were. One thing led to another and we ended not speaking to each other for about two days. We were down there alone and sleeping in the same room so it got to be a little awkward.

He thought Joyce was a nasty man?

I think I saw a great deal more of Joyce than Ernest, and I never saw the slightest sign of what Ernest would mean by that even though Joyce was dyspeptic looking, and he acted like it on occasion. Anyway, the bullfight was one occasion. Another was, I was new to skiing. Ernest had been skiing for quite a while. He and Hadley went up to the Vorarlberg and spent winters up there. He went at it in a very businesslike way, attending skiing class. He became very good. He was never a graceful skier but he was a powerful skier, and he was safe anywhere. Well, Ernest went up to Gstaad with us one winter several times. Skiing back of Gstaad is tame from his point of view, but it was fabulous from mine, and I got very much excited about it. A couple of pages of prose came out of that, and I said, "Ernest, do you want to take a look at this?" And he said, "No" and I said, "All right. Even if you don't, take a look at it!" And so he took it and a couple of days later he handed it back to me, sort of back of his hand, and he said, "Never write about anything you don't know all about." That was the only piece of literary advice I ever got from Ernest and very sound.

Did you have contact with any writers, editors, or critics in this country?

Well, Bob Linscott, who had been my editor at Houghton Mifflin—it sounds very pretentious because I didn't rate an editor, but he had been one—had never been abroad. I don't know if you know who Linscott is—he looked like Lincoln. He came from a Yankee family, north of Boston, very poor indeed. Bob went to work as a stock boy for Houghton Mifflin when he should have been in high school. He used his lunch hour to walk to the public library, which was just as far away from 2 Park Street then as it is now. And he would spend his lunch hour not eating lunch but reading. By the time I got to know him (he was about five years older than I) he was one of the best-educated men I ever met, educated in the sense not only that he'd read the texts, but he'd made his own particular kind of peace with them. They were part of his life. He had never seen Europe. He wanted desperately to see Europe. I had a windfall of some kind and I cannot think what it was. It was something that suddenly produced enough money to get him across the Atlantic and keep him for a couple of weeks. That was a marvelous experience—seeing the city again through those eyes.[30] But no, I think the answer is no. I didn't have very many literary friends then or later. Looking back from the end of a life I have to qualify that with some pretty large qualifications. St.-John Perse (Alexis Léger) was a dear friend of mine, closest thing to a brother not a brother as you could have. Carl Sandburg was a very dear friend. Robert Frost and I got along all right—after the first thirty or forty years! And Mark, of course, my darling friend Mark Van Doren.

Did you arrive in Paris with a specific plan for becoming a poet or did things just happen?

We looked forward but didn't know what we were looking forward to. There wasn't any plan. Why Paris? To get away from Cambridge, because of the situation I'd created there, not because of anything in Cambridge that I didn't like. The situation I created for myself was something I couldn't live with. And so our purpose was to put an end to that, to get to Paris, to begin to occupy ourselves with what we had to occupy ourselves with—what we were committed to, God knows why, but were. It worked perfectly for Ada from the very beginning. It took me, I think I can say without exaggeration, really very close to two years to break the log jam of my poetic miseducation. But then this was the time to do that and the place to do it.

You've talked about the connections between your childhood and high-school experiences and Paris. Can you describe the bridge between Tower of Ivory *and* Streets in the Moon?

No, I don't know that I can see it from the outside to that extent. I was very much aware (I don't like to say this because it sounds ungrateful) when *Tower of Ivory* appeared with Lawrence Mason's title and his notes and so forth that it was a book I was going to have to live down. It was very generous of him to do it, but I knew that wasn't the book I wanted to write. I knew that *Happy Marriage*, although *Happy Marriage* was already beginning to be something, wasn't what I wanted to do. I knew that *Streets in the Moon* was, and above all *New Found Land*. I felt that that spoke; but when you're in the middle of a high dive from a 150-foot cliff, you aren't really aware of yourself falling through the air.

Your "education" involved, as you said, the study of Dante. It must have involved some kind of experimentation with verse because almost every critic of Streets in the Moon *comments on your mastery of the various forms and techniques that are present in the book.*

You don't study verse forms as verse forms. That is, a critic very well might, but if you're going to use them, you're trying to find the rhythms that are natural to your speaking. This means knowing the rhythms that have worked for other people. One of the remarkable things about Arthur Waley is that he imposed on Chinese poetry his, Arthur Waley's, sense of rhythm in English, and it works. I have a very good idea what Tu Fu sounds like in Chinese because I used to open my course at Harvard with two weeks of that done by Chinese professors in the Far Eastern Department at Harvard. But although I know what Tu Fu would sound like in Chinese if I were Chinese, to me he sounds like Arthur Waley in English because Arthur Waley's rhythms are appropriate to Tu Fu's concerns and Tu Fu's emotions. So you're always looking for the successful use of the English language by anybody else, not because you want to imitate it but because you want to know why it is successful for him. That teaches you something about what would be successful for you. So that I think the answer to your question about *Streets in the Moon* is that by the time I gave myself permission to start work again, I knew so much more about the possibilities of rhythms in English than I'd known before and I knew them so much more, not by reading English only but by reading Dante, whose use of Italian even an ignoramus can grasp to some extent, and the triumphant successes of Waley as a translator out of Chinese. I never thought about this before, but I think what I just said is probably true.

Could you describe the specific steps that led from apprenticeship to mastery of the sonnet, for instance—as in "The End of the World"?

I don't know if there is anything I can say about that. It really presents itself in a somewhat different way. I had been writing for quite a considerable period of time. Actually I was writing all the way through Yale, constantly writing. To a certain extent I started before I went to Yale, largely as the result of the enormous Mr. Stevens at Hotchkiss. This means that from 1909, let's say, until 1923 when I went to Paris, which is fourteen years, a fairly long period of time, I had been working consistently and following a pretty definite line. I did have, I think I can say, a pretty good ear, a sense of rhythm and so forth, so that rhythmically the early stuff I did was not bad. It didn't offend. What was wrong with it was its lack of personality—of uniqueness for me. A lot of those poems could have been written by almost anybody. The only really good one is the class poem at Yale in June of 1915 but anybody who looked at it would have a pretty good idea of what I'd been reading. (That's true of any youngster, but it was particularly true of me.) So I was engaged in learning how to write my own verse but in trying to find, as the saying goes (I'm afraid it originated with me too, years ago, and I apologize), "my own voice." In other words, what I was trying to do in those endless days in the *bonne*'s room at the top of 85 boulevard Saint-Michel was to stop writing the kind of thing I had been writing and had been unsatisfied with and try to teach myself how to write what would be native to me and expressive to me. I used to think after I got to know Ernest in the middle twenties that his problem and mine were not unlike although you could state them in very different terms and the end result would be very different—he was trying to learn how to write a really true sentence, a sentence stripped down to its truth. I was trying to find a sentence rhythmically adaptable to the purposes of the poem, which would be my sentence, not Edwin Arlington Robinson's or Mr. Bridges's[31] or any of the other people I was then reading. So I think it's not surprising that once I began to find ways of my own I found that I was fairly at home in them. First of all, what I was finding was myself, and, second, what I was finding was my own way of doing something new. I think it would have been really remarkable if in the space of two or three years I hadn't been able to come up with something like "The End of the World." And there are others which are even more to the point: most of the poems of *New Found Land* are poems which I welcomed very warmly when they appeared and which I still love: I have no trouble with them. They don't embarrass me a bit. Some things I wrote later do, but not those.

How does a poem like "The End of the World," or any poem of yours, actually get written? What do you begin with, the idea, or a line or . . . ?

I have some theories about that but I can't vouch for their truth. I used to think (and I say "used to" because I'm not sure of that kind of statement anymore) that what you began with really was a sort of pattern of rhythm in your head which had no relation to words at all. The rhythmic patterns would form in your mind, if your mind were in the right stage for receiving, and they would not dictate their own words but they would leave the gaps open until you filled them. And what you tried very hard to do was to keep the rhythm going. Anybody, I think, with any gift for composition in verse who would read Gerard Manley Hopkins over a period of time, say an hour or two, would inevitably establish that sprung rhythm pattern[32] of his in the head and with little or no urging go on to write it—but you'd be writing, in that case, as Gerard Manley Hopkins, and what you hope for is a rhythm of your own—a rhythmic form of your own and finally a rhythmic voice (I've come to hate that word) of your own. I'm not at all sure now that that is true. I think you have to put it in much more general terms, terms that I used to use in my lectures at Harvard. That is to say, that the beginning of any work of art is probably something very strongly approaching a conviction—a conviction without reason or proof—that there is a work of art available to be made right near you, right in front of you, before you somewhere. And the best metaphor for that is the story told of Michelangelo, I think, that looking at a given piece of marble, he saw at once that there was a figure there. He could see the general conception of it in a particular piece of marble. It had a certain quality. I think this is probably true although I never sculpted anything in my life. What is true in the art of poetry as distinguished from the writing of verse is that, faced with an amorphous emotional situation, an emotional situation which may be pleasant or unpleasant, exhilarating or depressing, there is, in that emotional situation, an articulation which is probably a poem. The problem then becomes one of working it until you begin to see what it is.

Which raises another very closely related question, a question about the working over of poetry, the question of the spontaneous poem. There are always people coming up with the statement that they wrote such and such a poem or such and such poems, usually quite a number of them, right off, never changed a word. The minute you hear that you know the man is (a) lying and doesn't know what he is doing and (b) that he's probably no poet at all, because that just doesn't happen. The poem called "You, Andrew Marvell"[33] I wrote practically without any change, in the course of a day, which means in the course of part of a day, probably two or three hours, and really never did touch it to any particular extent afterward. But I know the explanation of that. It is the only such experience I ever had and it has nothing to do with whether the poem is good or not. What it does have to do with is the fact that that poem is one single sentence (Allen Tate[34] is the only man who ever noticed it; he notices quite a lot and I'm glad); and since it is one sentence, from the writing point of view as distinguished from the reading point of view, it is very easy to continue on with it.

You, Andrew Marvell

And here face down beneath the sun
And here upon earth's noonward height
To feel the always coming on
The always rising of the night:

To feel creep up the curving east
The earthy chill of dusk and slow
Upon those under lands the vast
And ever climbing shadow grow

And strange at Ecbatan the trees
Take leaf by leaf the evening strange
The flooding dark about their knees
The mountains over Persia change

And now at Kermanshah the gate
Dark empty and the withered grass
And through the twilight now the late
Few travelers in the westward pass

And Baghdad darken and the bridge
Across the silent river gone
And through Arabia the edge
Of evening widen and steal on

And deepen on Palmyra's street
The wheel rut in the ruined stone
And Lebanon fade out and Crete
High through the clouds and overblown

And over Sicily the air
Still flashing with the landward gulls
And loom and slowly disappear
The sails above the shadowy hulls

And Spain go under and the shore
Of Africa the gilded sand
And evening vanish and no more
The low pale light across that land

Nor now the long light on the sea:

And here face downward in the sun
To feel how swift how secretly
The shadow of the night comes on . . .

The physical images which are involved in the beginning of it, which set the tone for all the rest, were very fresh in my mind because I'd just come back from Persia, come over the Pitak Pass, which is the way you go in from Baghdad, etc. The whole thing was extremely fresh in my mind and the emotional experience, which was my father's illness, was also very clear in my mind. So all the material was there. It started as a long sentence. It couldn't go wrong or if it had gone wrong it would have gone totally wrong and there never would have been anything. There was nothing to rework there. I really don't think many words were even changed. That is, to me, a unique experience and as I say I don't think it's anything to boast about. Quite the contrary, because one finds in writing that it's the meticulous labor of reworking which produces everything that's good. Oh, there are a few things, what the French call *données*, that are put in your hand by god knows who, but very, very few. Hemingway, in the unhappily named *Moveable Feast*, talks about Gertrude Stein's unwillingness to work on anything she'd done. The reason she wrote these enormous books was that she never stopped to rewrite and that's the trouble with them still. It's the labor of rewriting—and rewriting isn't really the right word for it; it's sort of "again writing," not rewriting—that signifies. Of course, you can spend much too much time and the poem always shows it. That's true of a longish poem of mine called *Einstein*. I never really liked it. I never got it the way I wanted it and I kept on working at it long after I should have stopped. You can feel that now. It sets my teeth on edge. I just can't read it.

Could we take a poem like "The End of the World," and approach it as a practical example of what you are saying? You have a somewhat nebulous idea associated with either the end of the world or emptiness, and you're striving to find the means of articulating it. In this poem you come up with images and you also come up with a form—the sonnet. In the process of creation, does all this happen spontaneously or is it more deliberate than that?

It's hard to say what that phrase "happen" means. But, I just happen to remember quite a lot about the raw materials which produced "The End of the World." It was the summer of '24. We had been in Paris for a year. We had been extremely busy and we knew next to nobody and didn't particularly want to. Instead of making plans for that summer—as most people we later learned did during the worst months of the Paris winter (terrible months! You had to have something to keep your mind off what was going on in the streets)—we had no plans. We weren't going to go anywhere with anybody. Then somebody (none of our friends because none of our friends ever showed up there) told us about Granville in Normandy. Granville is a town on Palisades, facing out toward the Channel Islands. You can't see them. They're just there. Granville was a town of no character, no distinction. But I went down, had a look at it and liked it, and found a house that we could rent for next to nothing. Beautiful location. It was on top of a cliff and had a beach with very shallow tides where our tiny daughter could play. So we took it and finally moved down. We were as isolated as ever, even more isolated.

At which point I'll introduce a parenthesis: Ada was, of course, practicing all the time. In Granville we got hold of a piano and she was practicing. And she was working on a concert of songs of Satie[35] she was going to do, Satie being then very new although quite an old man. Back of us a little farther up was a large house, to which the little house we rented belonged, which used the same path to get down to the beach. And one morning a nineteen-year-old boy with great wide, amazed eyes showed up at the door, nobody I'd ever seen before. He said (he had very bad English), "Who's singing?" And I said, "My rife," and he said, "It is Satie" and I said "Yes." He said, "But nobody sings

Satie," and I said, "She does." And he began to cry, tears running down his face. This was Christian Dior. He was a composer as a boy, and this was his family's place. He had always hated coming to Granville. It was the most boring place he knew and now suddenly it was heaven because what he loved was music, particularly modern music, contemporary music, which I must say was very lovable music. And we got to know him very well, so well that when many, many years later we returned to Paris, we were called upon by Monsieur Christian Dior, who had put on quite a bit of weight, but was just as charming as ever. When Ada got to him, he was having a new fashion show. All the world was there, the wife of the American ambassador, all sorts of people. There was a chair right in the middle. That was "pour Madame MacLeish." She could go and sit there when she pleased. She would always refuse to buy things. She just told him she couldn't agree to live that way. He said, "You cannot talk to me like that," so she did have some things.

But to get back to the apparatus from which "The End of the World" came:

The End of the World

Quite unexpectedly as Vasserot
The armless ambidextrian was lighting
A match between his great and second toe
And Ralph the lion was engaged in biting
The neck of Madame Sossman while the drum
Pointed, and Teeny was about to cough
In waltz-time swinging Jocko by the thumb—
Quite unexpectedly the top blew off:

And there, there overhead, there, there, hung over
Those thousands of white faces, those dazed eyes,
There in the starless dark the poise, the hover,
There with vast wings across the canceled skies,
There in the sudden blackness the black pall
Of nothing, nothing, nothing—nothing at all.

First of all, Granville was an almost unspoiled town which had, at a lower level beside the sea, a sort of open campus where visiting circuses could move in. Circuses of the European variety, that is mobile, Gypsy circuses. They all had one tent, a very few animals, a few clowns, a few acrobats, and that was it. But the circuses were absolutely fascinating. They were lighted by torches, which gave a keen sense of the nearness of death because just one touch of the torch on the canvas roof and we were gone. But the lighting produced extraordinary effects. I began on this poem after one of the traveling circuses had been in town, after we had gone down and taken the children. That's one thing, the circus is a reality. The circus wasn't a metaphoric concoction. It had been there. Second thing about those circuses was the location, this flat open ground beside the sea. Normandy, even in the summer, is always menacing. The sea is never quiet. Gales will come up. The channel is just what people say it is; awful, awful to live on. There was always a very considerable degree of danger and the ropes and the guys and stakes with which the tents were set up kept you constantly in mind of the fact that they could easily take off. That's one thing that is very clear in my mind. So the action in the first eight lines of the poem, although not taken from any particular circus, was common fare. There was always an elephant; there was usually a lion, a mangy lion; there was always a large buxom lady who had seen better days, but who had been quite a beauty once, and clowns, and so forth. Although the particular things, like Madame Sossman, had some invention, nevertheless they all were related to what I saw there. The rhythm of it (it is a very unsonnetlike rhythm, of course) comes from the phrase with which it begins: "Quite unexpectedly." Where that came from I don't know but it got working in my head: "quite unexpectedly," "quite unexpectedly"—then the repetition, "quite unexpectedly the top blew off." That was another element: the final, unrealized but imagined image of what would happen if the top did blow off, what you would see overhead. These are all total irrelevancies. They have nothing to do with the poem as achieved, but they are specific instances. That is almost the only poem I ever wrote in which I can remember quite clearly where the parts came from and trace them back. Once I could trace them better than I can now. One other thing to say about that is that the end of it is a good example of the closeness to each other of triumph and total disaster in poetry. They're a hair's breadth apart. The end of the poem, "nothing, nothing, nothing—nothing at all," is a terrible line—very close to being disastrous except for the fact that it works. And this I can't explain. It's an awful line. The caesura's in the wrong place, the pause is in the wrong place. It also reverses the rhythm: "quite unexpectedly—" ta da da, ta da da." That trips along a jolly way. This reverses it, throws it back on itself. In the sonnet it works, but out of the sonnet, I wouldn't give it house room.

Now as far as that poem is concerned, you have the images, you've got the raw material. Just to take it a step further, how many times did you have to rework that one before you were satisfied?

I don't know, I don't remember. It was a long time ago. I would guess not too long, not too often. But I have a sort of running rule with me always to stay with a short poem until I feel quite sure that it is going to turn into a poem. That's usually a matter of some days or a week. Then I put it in a drawer and forget about it and then go back to it at the end of about a month, go back to it without planning to go back to it. You know every now and then you look through your drawers and there it is. What you do to it then is definitive. You can spoil it then, or you can really fix it.

Did you ever use your wife as an audience for your work?

No, not very much. Really not at all because I have theories about this. I think one of the reasons we have the kind of marriage we have is that we have tastes which, though far from opposite—I love music, and I was particularly mad about her singing—are very different. She has a wonderful, literal-minded, womanly approach to the experience of life. Literal-mindedness is very, very close to literality, to what is truly true. And women are really close to what is truly true most of the time. I hate to be pinned down that way, although I'm also literal-minded in my own terms. The result is that although I loved her singing, whenever I tried to talk about why it is good she would begin laughing, almost in hysterics. She told me I said some of the funniest things she had ever heard in her life, and, she said, without intending to. Which is quite fair and it worked to some extent the other way around. She has very good taste in poetry but she's a musician. Musicians don't like poems; that's the stuff that gets in the way of music.

Why did you go to Persia in 1926?

The trip was the consequence of my friendship with Dean Acheson.[36] Dean was then practicing law in Washington. He was a labor lawyer, believe it or not. This is Brandeis influence. And he was beginning his association with Mr. Covington, Mr. Burling, and Mr. Rublee which resulted in a law firm by that name. He was getting to know people in Washington. Neither he nor Alice came from Washington; they went there because of Dean's interest in the Supreme Court and his relationship with some of the people on the court. And he ran into a man who was a maternal uncle of Mr. Roosevelt's, a Col. Frederic Delano, the president of the Wabash Railroad—a big, nice, pleasant sort of shambling man—meaning he sort of shuffled along. He had been appointed to the chairmanship of a League of Nations commission made up of one French and one Italian member who were to go to Persia, as it was then called, to look into a position taken by the Persian government that it could not accept a narcotics convention as part of the League of Nations because its means of transportation were almost nonexistent, and the only way the country could survive financially was to find something which was very valuable in very small bulk, and you can guess what that was. It was poppies. That is, poppies as morphine, opium. And the League of Nations in its wisdom decided not to let this pass, so they accepted the invitation of the Persian government to send out a commission.[37] Mr. Delano was looking for somebody to go as his secretary who could speak French because both his colleagues spoke French but no English. Dean suggested me, knowing that I was in Paris, and this invitation came and it just happened to fit in. I was at the end of about three years of work and I wanted to get another perspective and I had also made the discovery, which I suppose everybody makes, that although travel doesn't really teach you anything, it can so radically change your point of view that you begin to see things you haven't seen before, including things in your own mirror. So Dean asked me if I would go; I talked to Ada about it, and I said of course I wouldn't dream of it, and she said, "Why not? I'm going to be working this spring." She had a lot of concerts going and she was going to be extremely busy. We found somebody who was really very good to take care of the baby; Kenny was in Gstaad, and so I accepted. The commission consisted of those three and a man named Knight who was an American agriculture specialist who had a lot of experience out of the country, as well as a British permanent secretary of the commission and a couple of clerical hands. As a trip, as a journey, it was simply remarkable. We assembled in Geneva, met the various officials of the League of Nations, got our sailing orders, took the Orient Express, getting side connections, then finally ended up at Trieste. At Trieste we took a ship down the Adriatic and across the Mediterranean to Alexandria and then went by rail up to Cairo—if you can imagine a more devious way of getting anywhere! A couple of days in Cairo (which was a fabulous place at that time, totally unlike what it is now) and we took a railroad that crossed the Suez Canal, skirted the coast of what is now Israel and went to Beirut in Lebanon. There (by this time I was more or less the manager of this traveling junket) we brought down some Nairne transport automobiles—old Cadillacs. We crossed the desert from Beirut through two or three of the most marvelous ancient, never-before-by-me-seen, Greek colonial cities, crossed the two rivers and ended up in Baghdad in a large English hotel with slow-moving fans on the ceiling. The only risk in crossing the desert was that there are no roads. There can't be any roads. It's hard-packed sand but the sand is always shifting. Two cars try to avoid each other, but they inevitably attract. There is one famous case in which two hit head-on and killed everybody—a fantastic piece of psychological warfare. From Baghdad we went to Hamadan—which was the old Ecbatan and finally to

Tehran, the capital. We lived there in the "andasun," that is the harem room of one of the Bakhtiyari chiefs, south of Persia. And then we took trips down to Esfahan and Shiraz and Büshehr on the gulf, up the gulf to a new oil establishment. We took a trip to Persepolis as a possible future tourist attraction, if Persia was ever going to have one of those. We went up to the Caspian and the territory of Alalan. We went east to Kuhsam, which is the very edge of Afghanistan. I saw more of Persia than any Persian I've ever met, and I met quite a few Persians. What we discovered was that the Persians were absolutely right. There not only weren't any roads from Tehran west to Baghdad through the passage, what there were elsewhere were just as bad as the Persians ever said they were. For example, to get from Büshehr, which is on the Persian Gulf, you have to come up a series of hairpin turns, which are famous in the world as the most dangerous place you can take an automobile. They were one car wide. You were hanging on a cliff. If a tire went, you were gone. When you come around a corner, you look ahead. When the other fellow comes around the corner, he looks ahead. There's an understanding that the car going up has the right of way. So if the other fellow is coming down and you're going up, and you see each other, he backs (it must be a risky thing; we never had to do it) onto the corner, onto the curb, and hangs on there while you go by. Well, when we were finished, we reversed our process, got back to Beirut eventually and went to Marseilles. Ada turned up there with the Murphys, danced on the wharf as the ship came in, and then she went up to Geneva with me. And at that point, here is a very curious piece of information: I had an agreement with the colonel that if I would put in a couple of weeks in Geneva, helping to get the report into shape, he would let me go. I told him I had obligations. This was all agreed to. So Ada came and things went along and finally on the last day (we were going off the next morning) the colonel came in and said, "I just simply cannot, . . . I'm no penman, . . . I cannot write my part of this report, which is supposed to be a recommendation for a railroad" (we'd made our recommendations about highways and so forth, but we were also supposed to recommend a railroad) and the colonel said, "I just can't do it, Archie. Can you help me?" and I said, "Of course I can. How long of a piece are you supposed to write?" He told me how long, and I said to him, "I will recommend a line. Of course it will be all wrong. It will be nonsense; but you just follow my sentences and put in the right words." He was just overcome with gratitude and he went out. The next morning we went off. That was the last I heard of it until the report of the commission was published by the League of Nations. And I discovered that what I had written as a draft was in there verbatim. Nothing had been changed. It recommended a railroad line from Tehran down south of Hamadan to the gorge of the Karun

River. We had gone up the Karun River and it was quite evident to any eye that on one side or the other—I've forgotten which now—there was quite a good deal of a sort of ledge, parallel to the river, and it looked to me as though (I know nothing about railroad building) you could build a spectacular line right along the edge of the river, and it would come out just where you wanted it to come out—at the Anglo-Persian Oil Company wells. Well, there it was. That's only half the story! The Persians later built it! I've been told this by friends of mine who have been in Persia, who know that railroad and have been down it, and their description of it sounds to me just like the one I read off the map. Anyway, I was away from home for a long time. I almost went out of my mind. I didn't try to work on poetry at all, but I came back loaded for bear, of course.

What kind of social life did you have in Paris?

During '23 and '24 we saw next to nobody. We were very, very busy. We were also interested in the city and getting around and looking at it. Our first relationship was with Hemingway, who became for a period of three, four, or five years a very, very close friend; he was practically a member of the family! There was always a place for him to sleep—between wives: after Hadley left him and before Pauline would marry him! And we were very fond of each other. After we got back from Granville, we met the Murphys, who had been avoiding us just as we had been avoiding them—we knew about them; they knew about us. Gerald Murphy was known during that period largely through his appearance, à la Proust, in Scott Fitzgerald's *Tender Is the Night* where the Murphys are the prototypes for Dick Diver and his wife.[38] Murphy turns out now to have been probably the most interesting of American painters in Paris. Picasso thought he was. Those ten paintings are pretty good proof of it![39]

What was wrong was that Gerald was also a "Bones" man at Yale and he was just instinctively leery of "Bones" men. I had exactly the same feeling about Gerald but for opposite reasons because I'd seen him at Cambridge and I'd thought, "He isn't the real thing—he just doesn't look right to me!" So we avoided them. They were great party people. They had given one of the most fabulous parties of all time—barge on the Seine which had cost them next to nothing to rent, paper toys for ornaments! They laid on food in whatever way you do under those circumstances—not very expensive in Paris. Everybody who was anybody went. It was just the sort of thing that Ada and I both instinctively hated. It had happened before we got there, but we wouldn't have gone even if we had been asked. And then we met them and almost immediately we became the most intimate friends. We really knew them pretty much in French terms. We saw them all the time when we were seeing people, which wasn't very often because Gerald was then beginning to paint and Sara had her two sons who later died and a daughter who is still alive; and they lived in St. Cloud, in Gounod's house.

Why did you say that you knew the Murphys "in French terms"?

We had very few common connections in this country; our common connections were all in terms of Paris and parts of France. Gerald and I took a number of bicycle trips. We put our bicycles in the express car of a train, headed out to the Côte d'Azur, and spent a week or ten days on the road there—sampling vintages and generally enriching our understanding of French life. And the Murphys also built themselves a villa, which they called the Villa America, on the Cap d'Antibes, and Ada and I rented houses down there in the summer. Now of course it is just jammed with people, but at that time the summer on the Mediterranean was regarded as unhealthy and no one would go down there so we could rent almost anything for nothing in the summer months. Gerald was a remarkable companion and very knowledgeable, not scholarly, but very knowledgeable. He knew Natalia Goncharova very well, the Russian painter who did scenery. And he knew all about the operations of the Ballet Russe. Gerald did a ballet of his own, early, called "Within the Quota," which was a very, very large and cumbersome but very funny ballet about immigration to the United States from the French point of view.

Could you talk about some of your other friends?

We knew Dick and Alice-Lee Myers, University of Chicago graduates, both of them. Dick was a composer with a light but charming gift, who supported himself by working for the American Express. He never changed. He was always the same. He was always producing or about to produce a bit of music. It never turned out to amount to very much. It was just charming. Alice-Lee was full of good work. She knew every Russian admiral working as a taxi driver in Paris and saw that something was done for those who were in greatest need.

Dos Passos and his Katy became very good friends of ours. Cummings[40] was also. I saw a good deal of him while he was in Paris, which wasn't often—even though I had never met him in connection with Harvard—I was in the law school his last year in Harvard College. And outside of these few people who were close friends of ours, who would have been friends anywhere at any time, there were very few in Paris whom we knew well and saw much of in a way that could only have happened in that city at that time. Joyce was one. Sylvia Beach,[41] whom we saw a little of but not very much, was another; but much more than Sylvia, Sylvia's friend Adrienne Monnier, who had the bookshop across the street, "Amis des Livres." And then, Fernand Léger, the painter; Picasso, and André Masson. . . .

Didn't you also know Eliot and Pound?

I met Pound only twice in my life, once in St. Elizabeths Hospital and once up in Cambridge. Tom Eliot I knew quite well when I became Boylston Professor because I got him to come over on several occasions. Ernest also knew Joyce, but Ernest was very human and Joyce was just becoming a great writer, and Ernest wanted very much to be a great, great, great writer and at that moment wasn't, and may not be now. There's no question about Joyce, I should think. I never saw them together much except that we got them together on various occasions. We were very fond of Joyce. And because of Ada, we saw him in nonliterary terms. We reached the point eventually where we had a sort of ritual on a year's basis—we'd meet them about twice a year and they would meet us twice a year. They would invite us and we would invite them, and we always gave Joyce a case of a new kind of white Alsatian wine every Christmas. So did everybody else. That was expected. He must have started the year with some dozen cases of white Alsatian wine. Marvelous man! Difficult, impossible, and marvelous!

In Mary Hemingway's How It Was[42] *she tells about an incident in Paris. Ernest Hemingway was standing in front of a mirror in the bathroom and the skylight collapsed and gashed his head and she called you, and you called a friend named Dr. Carl Weiss. Is that the same Dr. Carl Weiss who later assassinated Huey Long?*

Some of it is true and some of it isn't. Ernest called me up about two o'clock in the morning and he said, "I've done the god-damnedest thing that I've ever done in my life. I'm perfectly cold sober. I was invited to use the can in this house and I went in and pulled the chain and it happened to be the chain that held the skylight up and the skylight clashed shut and a piece of glass sliced me across the forehead," and indeed it had. He said, "I really need somebody to take care of me." I immediately called up Alice-Lee Myers because she knew everybody in Paris and I assumed she'd know the American hospital very well. I asked her to get a taxi somewhere and come pick me up, and we would go and pick up Ernest. It couldn't have been ten minutes before she was there. We went to where Ernest was. We found him standing on the sidewalk with a great towel around his head. We got him into the cab. Alice had already called the American hospital and said we were coming, so we were met by a young doctor, a young intern, I thought, maybe not. So they took Ernest into the next room and, without anesthetic of any kind, stitched up this huge gash. When we picked Ernest up, he was giddy; he was chattering away like a hysterical child. I thought it was blood loss. He, of course, uttered not one squeak while the needling was going on. He and the doctor became very friendly and cheerful. We then took Ernest home and I took Alice-Lee home and I think about four o'clock in the morning I got to bed. Ernest was all right. The thing healed. It was not the most beautiful job you ever saw. In fact, it changed his entire face from that time on. The stitches were very visible. I don't remember anything about the doctor except that he was young.

What about other people that you knew there later on?

One person I saw increasingly more of as the years went by was John Peale Bishop, a very gifted young poet—a Princeton man, very scholarly, with an extremely socially minded wife. John was a good friend; at least I always thought he was. I was told by people who had gone through his papers at Princeton these feelings weren't altogether reciprocated. I don't know what the reference is to because I always thought that John and I got along very well. When I became Librarian of Congress, I set up the consultantship in poetry so that it became an annual thing. I started out with Allen Tate and then John next.[43] John was marvelous that year, and he died shortly after from a bad heart. I also saw a little of Red Lewis, Sinclair Lewis; that was a difficult man to have around because he never stayed sober long enough to really complete a conversation. André Masson became a very good friend and still is, although I never see him anymore. Fernand Léger, the painter, was a great friend of the Murphys' and became a greater friend of ours. I actually stayed at his house for quite a while. Picasso—everybody knew Picasso; nobody knew Picasso. He was a very agreeable man but you got no part of him. He was busy with something else, but we saw quite a bit of him. And the Crosbys. Caresse was a pain in the neck but she was touching. There was a lot of silly affectation about them which I can sample with one story. We went to have a meal with them, which worked out quite well. They were very helpful and very kind to me in their editions of the *Einstein* and *New Found Land*—just beautiful pieces of craft. We then asked them if they would come and have lunch with us and we got a note from Caresse, saying "but you know, my dears, we always eat lunch in bed" and all we could think about was the crumbs!

Some of your friends were wealthy. Was there any problem for you with them because of your own financial situation?

Was there! Three thousand dollars a year with two of us and two children and the continual necessity of a governess of some kind and then a school for Kenny. It was not easy. In fact, it was almost impossible. And aside from that I had sold nothing. I mean what I did sell, I got nothing for, to speak of.

The Murphys had quite a lot of money?

No. Scott Fitzgerald liked to create the impression that all the people he liked were very rich but the Murphys weren't rich. They had a fair amount of money but they believed in using it. They would never be young again and they proposed to live well. But they knew how to live without throwing money around. For example, one of the best luncheons I ever ate in my life was eaten under a linden tree outside their little villa on d'Antibes. It was served on a blue china dish on which were some perfectly boiled new potatoes and some butter. Then there was a white wine, probably something like muscadet—at that time very cheap. And bread and butter, and that was all. It was just an unforgettable lunch. All the potatoes you could eat, excellent wine, bread and butter. And Sara could also lay it on if she wanted to, but she didn't very much.

The Crosbys were wealthy.

Well, yes and no. Caresse had nothing; Harry's mother was a sister of J. P. Morgan. (Incidentally, she was a marvelous woman. I went through that whole night with her.[44] I've never seen anybody behave any better in my whole life.) This meant there was a lot of money around but Harry had extremely expensive tastes. There were two men in Paris in that time, two great swells belonging to Edith Wharton's generation, one called Walter Berry[45] and the other called Barry Wall. One or the other was Harry's uncle, in another direction; Walter Berry I guess it was. And when he died, he left Harry a mink-lined overcoat. Harry was about my height, very slender, a beautiful boy. But the donor of the coat had been quite a bit taller, so the coat came down about to his ankles, mink lining and all. He wore it all the time, without alterations.

Martha Hillard MacLeish reading to her children,
Glencoe, Illinois, c. 1898. *Left to right:* Ishbel,
Archibald, Kenneth, and Norman (standing).

Andrew MacLeish with his four sons, 1907. *Left to right:* Bruce, Archibald, Norman, and Kenneth (seated).

Ada and Archie, c. 1916.

Archie and Ada, c. 1918.

Archie and Ada with Sara and Gerald Murphy,
Vienna, 1926.

The Commission of Inquiry on Opium Production
in Persia, 1926. MacLeish is on the far right.

MacLeish with his daughter, Mary Hillard (Mimi),
1927.

Harry also had a lot of crazy theories, one of which was he would never touch paper money. He carried only French gold pieces down to little tiny slivers of gold. Harry paid for everything in gold, was famous in and around the Right Bank (the hotel area) as a man from whom you would expect a gold tip. They lived quite well but not well at all—quite pretentiously; but they put a lot of money into their printing press. Actually, the Crosbys were not that rich. If you look at a contemporary Texan or Californian, you wouldn't even say that they were well-to-do.

In Black Sun *a letter from Harry Crosby to his mother says that he let you and Ada and your family stay in his apartment while he and his wife took a trip. Because you were having (quote) "a very hard time getting by" and you "deserved better than that."*

Wasn't that nice of him? But it never happened! Pierpont Morgan Hamilton, a son of Sandy (Alexander), and his wife, Marise, had a terrible fight and decided on immediate divorce and flew off in several directions.[46] We were at that time moving out of an apartment that we just couldn't hold on to and Pierpont (Peter he was called) came around and said, "Look. I'm going off on a train in an hour. That apartment of ours on the avenue du Bois de Boulogne is completely stocked. There's a beautiful butler. It has everything in the world in it. Please move in, at least until you find an apartment. I'm sure this is all going to blow over. We'll be back in the spring." Well, it didn't blow over. They didn't come back in the spring. Everything *was* paid for. We paid no rent; we didn't pay the butler, but we paid the rest of the servants and we paid for the food that the butler ordered and within a month and a half we invented a trip to Germany to get out.

Could we talk about your publishing while you were in Europe? Had you made previous arrangements with a publisher or did you reestablish your contacts with Houghton Mifflin?

I had those contacts all the time. The Black Sun Press published these special editions by permission of Houghton Mifflin. Houghton Mifflin have been my only publishers all my life, except for the brief period in the thirties when I was working for *Fortune* and living in New York and had decided, as all writers about that age do decide, that their publishers are hornswoggling them and if they only changed publishers things would be better. So I went to Duell, Sloan and Pearce, a concern that has now vanished, members of which were good friends of mine, and also Random House, and I published the *Frescoes* through the John Day house, and I can't remember what else. I began to see the light very quickly and I went back to Houghton Mifflin.

What were the communications between you and your family while you were in Paris?

Well, they were perfectly normal. We corresponded. By that time I'd been away from home for four years at Hotchkiss, four years at Yale, three years in the Harvard Law School, two years in the war—you add all that up and that's how long it was! Since I was fourteen! I had a very close relationship with my mother and a very affectionate relationship with my father, a very grateful relationship. My father died while we were still in Paris; he died in 1928. We came back shortly after that.

Were there any visits from your family?

My wife's mother and father[47] came over here—a wonderfully comic thing! We were still living in the boulevard Saint-Michel up opposite the Luxembourg and we were great admirers of a restaurant and hotel near the Luxembourg on the north side called Drouot's—a very famous restaurant and hotel. We pulled every string we could, which wasn't many, and got rooms for them and installed them. And my father-in-law, who had been very little outside of this country (he was a Connecticut Yankee—he was *the* Connecticut Yankee; "Uncle Billy" to everybody in Connecticut), didn't take to Drouot's. The first morning he got up, went down to the restaurant, and, of course, found it closed. It wouldn't open until around noon. He couldn't get breakfast! He was informed in sign language (he spoke no French) that if he went back up to his room, they'd bring him breakfast. Well, nothing wrong with him—he wasn't sick! Why should he go up to his room? So, we heard about this very shortly and went around and talked to the management and were very apologetic about suggesting that perhaps Mr. and Mrs. Hitchcock ought to move. We found the manager was just delighted! That was the best news he'd had! Not that the Hitchcocks weren't delightful people, they were; but they were an awful lot of trouble if you were running a French hotel!

Was your father inquisitive about your progress as a poet?

No, not inquisitive but very much interested. My father's formal education stopped at the age of twelve, after a year in the Glasgow high school and then he just pulled out, went to London—the London of Dickens's *Christmas*

Carol—slept under the counter in the store. He stayed in London for six years, earning his keep, finally earning his fare to cross the Atlantic at the age of eighteen, going to Chicago. He had the kind of interest in books and the making of books which seems to be in the Scottish genes—every Scotsman has it, one way or another. And my father, during the period of his youth in Scotland, in London, and in Chicago, just set about educating himself. By the time I came along (I wasn't born until he was past middle age), he was a remarkably well-read man—the only man I've ever met in my life who had read the Code of Hammurabi,[48] which is one of the basic books in jurisprudence. His reading was like that, very widely spread! So far as poetry was concerned, he was a great admirer of "Robbie" Burns, which means more to a Scotsman than it sounds. Burns was a really tremendous poet—a much greater poet than he's supposed to be! And my father's outside reading was what you'd expect (he was born in 1838—the year of Queen Victoria's coronation)—Wordsworth, Keats, but not a great deal, Tennyson, but mostly "Robbie." He was interested in what I was doing and impressed. Actual books! He could look at them! There they were! But he was not at all inquisitive. He didn't make problems. He lived up to his side of the agreement and we lived up to our side. We got no help from my wife's family whatever! But we hadn't expected any—we never asked for it.

Did your immediate family visit you in Paris?

My father was in Paris on several occasions, but I can't remember his being there while we were there and I'm almost certain he wasn't. But I made trips back home when he was very ill in '26. I'd been in Persia and immediately went out when I got back. The poem of mine, "You, Andrew Marvell," is based on that journey from Tehran right straight back to Glencoe, Illinois. Mother was a marvelous writer of letters, but my wife was the correspondent! I never was much of a letter writer! In other words, the answer to your question is that it was a very amicable relationship.

Did the opposition of some of your family continue during your stay in Paris?

My wife's immediate success as a singer silenced the howling dogs. They had barked a lot when we left, but that was the end of it.[49]

Your reputation as a poet grew, it seems, almost in direct relationship to your experience and your power. . . .

Happy Marriage didn't make much of a stir. People at Houghton Mifflin liked it. That was the book that was published the year we went, and the *Pot of Earth* didn't make much of a stir either—at first; it later came alive. The reputation really began with *The Hamlet of A. MacLeish* and then began to operate with *New Found Land* and *Streets in the Moon*. By the time we came back, near the end of the twenties, my father began to read reviews that gave him a good deal of satisfaction, although there were some reviews I'd just as soon he hadn't read.

As your reputation grew, did your relationships change at all with the people you knew in Paris?

No, I don't think so. I never knew the large population which Hemingway describes so luridly both in '22 when he first came to Paris and in '24 when he came back. In '24 he was hard on the people at the Dôme and the Rotonde.[50] But I never knew those people. I didn't even know his friends among them or friends who knew that world. By "that world" I mean people who were mostly fakers and phonies. They pretended to an interest in the arts but they never produced anything. But they adopted the "vie de bonshommes" and the uniform and everything else. It's a familiar phenomenon and very unpleasant. And it's particularly unpleasant in a city such as Paris was at that time. But it was not too bad for me; I'd neither the time nor the money to play around or do much drinking and that was a drinking society! But the people I did see (this either indicates a remarkable prescience on my part or a remarkable luck!) were all people who turned out, or in one case actually were at the time, really very seriously good artists and writers. That is, the people that we saw most of like Hemingway and the Murphys. Sylvia Beach and Adrienne Monnier. And Ada had all sorts of friends—musical friends. She was singing "Mélisande" at the Opéra Comique, quite a place for a young American woman to be singing under any circumstances, and she knew lots of people—French—and American, like Aaron Copland, who was working with Nadia, and Virgil Thomson and Roger Sessions. They were the three best composers of their generation. But we had, as I said, either remarkable prescience or remarkable luck! These friends that we had and that we saw (I'd have to add John Peale Bishop, and there was also Scott, more than just ordinarily gifted) were all people who were actually working, really producing. But I was not in the least involved in the literary world. I had some poems in the *Transatlantic Review* and I knew a little the people who were running that but not much and didn't want to. So (this again is a long answer to a simple question) I don't think my relations to our real friends changed in the least with the establishment of a position. One qualification perhaps: there was an American woman married to a member of the famous and incredibly old Italian family, Marguerite Caetani, born Marguerite Chapin, and Marguerite had started a review, *Botteghe Oscure,* which she published in Rome.[51] And I got to know her through French critics, like Valéry Larbaud, who had nice things to say about things of mine; so perhaps that was one case where having a little position helped. Her husband, Alfredo, later became a duke of some famous hill town, south of Rome—a very great swell, indeed! He owned the Glacis Caetani in Rome and we used to stay there. They'd invite us in. We'd see a little bit of Rome that way—the Roman aristocracy. But that's all sort of marginally—we're talking about Paris and work in Paris.

Did you find it at all difficult that your wife was successful almost immediately and that you had to work so hard to achieve that kind of success yourself?

No! Heavens! It was a godsend! We never would have been able to stave off the wolves if it weren't for that!

In Black Sun, *Wolff talks about a tour that Crosby took with you and Ernest Hemingway in Switzerland.*

Wolff is mixed up. Crosby and Ernest and I did do quite a bit of traveling. Ernest was very fond of him, and you couldn't help being fond of him. He was frightening because it was perfectly apparent that he didn't exist—he didn't live in the real world at all. But if you could forget that, he was a charming person. He was related to everybody. And he would tag along—he really did that! It was sometimes hard to get rid of him! If he remembers a tour, he remembers a dream. We saw them somewhat. They were, of course, both he and Caresse, a very great help to me because of those Black Sun publications of books of mine, which were beautiful books. That helped a great, great deal; just the physical books, I mean; it helped me; I would look at them and see them.

As you were there, other reputations grew besides your own, reputations of people that you knew. Did you have any response to growing reputations of people that you saw? For instance, did you think that some of it was deserved and some of it was not deserved?

Well, the great instance of this, so far as Ernest is concerned (that's all in a poem of mine called "Years of the Dog") was Joyce.

Years of the Dog

Before, though, Paris was wonderful. Wanderers
Talking in all tongues from every country.
Fame was what they wanted in that town.
Fame could be found there too—flushed like quail in the
Cool dawn—struck among statues
Naked in hawthorn in the silver light.
James Joyce found it. Dublin bore him.
Could have sung with McCormack! Could he? He could.
Did he? He didn't. He walked by the winding Seine.
And what did he eat? He ate orts: oddities:
Oh he was poor: obscure: no one had heard of him:
Rolled on the floor on the floor with the pain in his eyes.
And found fame? He did. Ulysses: Yule Book:
Published to every people even in Erse.
(Molly Molly why did you say so Molly!)
Or the lad in the Rue de Notre Dame des Champs
At the carpenter's loft on the left-hand side going down—
The lad with the supple look like a sleepy panther—
And what became of him? Fame became of him.
Veteran out of the wars before he was twenty:
Famous at twenty-five: thirty a master—
Whittled a style for his time from a walnut stick
In a carpenter's loft in a street of that April city.

Where do they hang out now, the young ones, the wanderers,
Following fame by the rumor of praise in a town?
Where is fame in the world now? Where are the lovers of
Beauty of beauty that she moves among?

Joyce had become really a personal friend. As I said previously, we fell into the habit of any number of certain things we did together. We had a dinner, always with the same people, about Christmas time. This couldn't have happened more than four or five years, but by that time it'd become a tradition! And he was, of course, very much interested in my wife's voice. He loved it! He had a beautiful, I call it a choir boy's, tenor voice—an Irish tenor like McCormack.[52] His wife, when she was particularly fed up with him, used to look at him and say, "James Joyce, the writer! And he could've sung up that storm with McCormack!" Then she'd shut up! He would just look a little sad! Anyway, that was the great case of growing reputation and this caused me no problem at all because I was tremendously taken by *Ulysses* and did what little I could to get it published, which turned out not to be so little at all. I don't mean that I played an important role, but what little I did have to do worked. Also, in so far as what used to be called "work-in-progress," Joyce very, very early on, read us *Finnegan's Wake* one evening. . . . Adrienne Monnier invited Ada and me and Joyce but not his wife, or his wife wouldn't come or something—so it was Adrienne and Sylvia, Ada and I, and Joyce— plus somebody else whose face I can't see. After capon and a bottle of chilled white wine he read to us. I didn't feel that I needed to read *Finnegan's Wake* through after that. I just was completely sold. Then there was Louis Brom- field, who's practically dropped out of consciousness now, a novelist with an attitude toward his own work that put everybody off. As Louis went from triumph to triumph I can remember feeling that the world wasn't really very well organized! But the world took care of that!

Could you tell us specifically how you helped Joyce get Ulysses *published?*

I don't want to leave you under the impression that I was in any sense a princi- pal mover. I wasn't. It was Sylvia Beach who was the constant champion. Kept flailing around! But the problem was simply money—pure money problems. And in order to start the glacier moving, which was eventually done, one had to get the kind of statement from the kind of critic which would be accepted by the kind of man who had the kind of money that would get this book pub- lished. And so a lot of us were able to do a little because we happened to know somebody.

Fitzgerald was pretty well established, too.

Well, he was established but not really! Fitzgerald's reputation now is a lot higher than it was then. There's no question that he was a very successful short-story writer who was making more money than anybody in Paris ever dreamed of a writer's making. And then the dollar, the valid coin, meant something. I don't think Scott got from the *Saturday Evening Post* more than perhaps $100 or $150 for a story, but $100 in 1925 currency was a very, very large sum of money. But in a sense, people watched Hemingway and watched what Hemingway was doing and cared deeply about it, as I did, and weren't too much impressed by Scott. They liked him very much when he wasn't tight—but when his eyes took on that Irish blur, no! But anyway, Scott doesn't exist when you're talking at the level of Picasso and Stravinsky. Those were the great foundations; that is, there were major world artists, total history world artists, to the number of at least three or four, in Paris during those middle twenties. You could see them; you could, for example, go and hear Stravinsky rehearse and conduct the *Sacre*.

Earlier you made a comment that even though Ernest Hemingway didn't like James Joyce, you made the suggestion to him that perhaps he could learn something from Joyce after all.

Oh, yes. I already told you about that quarrel we had in Pamplona. We got talking about Joyce, and Ernest had competitive feelings toward Joyce. Ernest was born in 1899 and was just one year older than the year all this time in Paris; that is, he was twenty-five in the year '24 and so forth, and Joyce was late thirties, going on forty—about fifteen years between them. A comparable relationship was mine with St.-John Perse (Alexis Léger), whom I never knew in Paris but later got to know quite well. It never would have occurred to me to feel any professional anguish about Perse. He was just too great a poet! And also, I wasn't in competition with him. One of the great things—I'd just like to use a parenthesis—one of the really great satisfactions of that period in Paris was that personal competition practically didn't exist. It was like golfers playing bogey or par, and what you were doing—what almost everybody was doing or trying to do in those years—was to compete against the art itself: to change the possibilities of the art, to increase them. Here was Picasso setting the model for everybody by changing the forms. And Joyce did too, and this (Joyce's acceptance as a great writer), as we'd say now, "bugged" Hemingway. He didn't think *Ulysses* was so great as all that and so forth. Well, this is natural enough, if you think about it. What Hemingway was engaged in doing was trying to perfect a condensation, a paring away and a condensation of what remained, of the English language to produce the prose style that he finally produced. Joyce was moving in exactly the opposite direction in *Finnegan's Wake*. But I finally said I thought Joyce could be of some use to him and thus brought the deluge down. I replied that he wasn't reading Joyce as open-mindedly as he should, which was true. But nobody likes to be told that.

You had a later argument with Hemingway which really broke up your friendship in 1933 or 1934. In your dialogue with Mark Van Doren,[53] you said almost every friendship with Hemingway had ultimately ended that way— in some kind of violent quarrel. What was the cause of the breakup?

Ernest himself is the authority for the statement that every real friendship he'd ever had had been destroyed by himself. In one of the letters that I have from him, a long, eighteen-page letter that is in the Library of Congress—a letter which has a fifty-year seal on it—he starts off with the statement in familiar Hemingway vocabulary that he was a "shit" and had been a "shit" to all his friends. And either in that letter or another one he said to me that he had destroyed every real friendship he'd ever had. And it's true that people he was associated with at the end of his life were people who didn't know him and whom he didn't know or really much care about. It's quite sad! I'm not referring to his wife Mary. She was an angel and deserves all the credit that can be given. Now the actual cause of this quarrel—like all really serious quarrels, it had no cause. We'd been out at Dry Tortugas. Ernest and Charlie Thompson of Key West, who was a good friend of his in those days, and Pauline's Uncle Gus and Hank Strater, the painter. So it was Ernest, Hank Strater, Uncle Gus, Charlie, and Bra,[54] who was Ernest's guide, philosopher, and friend during the whole time, a Key West fisherman, and I. And we went out to Dry Tortugas, which in those days (I believe it's now overrun by tourists) was totally uninhabited. We got caught in a norther. A norther in that climate and at that season of the year (this was January or February, I think) is a nerve-wracking thing. It's a very cold, rasping, dry wind that has nothing to do with the Gulf Stream and should never be allowed down there! But it gets down there and it raises hob when it does. And we just got on each other's nerves! In fact, there was quite a lot of nerve-getting-on. Hank Strater and Ernest came awful close to fisticuffs. I'm glad it didn't because I'm afraid Hank would have been killed! Hank was a big strong boy, but not that big! When we got back from Dry Tortugas I went back to Ernest's house with him. The rest of them scattered somewhere; even Uncle Gus wasn't with us. We had a meal together and we just started to fight. It wasn't possible to recover ground.

You didn't totally terminate communication, did you?

No. I saw him on several occasions afterward. We were always very polite to each other but the old warmth was gone. I got him to come up to a Carnegie Hall meeting sponsored largely by the American Communist Party, which I agreed to chair on the understanding that I would say what I thought about my relation with the Communists, which I did. (That didn't save me from Joe

McCarthy later!) And Ernest came up for that. It was terribly good of him. And I saw him from time to time. We saw him in Cuba in the early or middle fifties and then we began corresponding again, he and I. We corresponded quite frequently. But in order to understand this quality in Ernest which, as he says, destroyed his friendships, you have to be familiar with a bitterness of tongue which would break through all inhibitions on his part and do enormous damage! He had an ornery instinct for the thing that would really hurt. For example, when he and Dos Passos were motoring near Billings, he broke his arm. He had to go into a hospital. Pauline was sent for. She found that she couldn't deal with him! Nothing serious, just a broken arm, but she couldn't keep him quiet. The nurses spoiled him. So things were going wrong and she telegrammed me (I was working for *Fortune*), and asked if I could come up. I really couldn't afford to, either in time or money. I was working hard on a story and getting out there—this was very early in civilian aviation—meant taking something called Northwest Airline, which flew aerial perambulators, flying at heights that were just terrifying! Fifty and a hundred feet! They had no instruments to go on. Well, I got out there. I had to borrow money to go. It took me two days to get there from New York. I spent a night in Minneapolis. I arrived and found Ernest surrounded by adoring nurses and looking rosy and fine with a magnificent, glossy, black beard. And he looked at me with a savage look; and the savageness, I learned later, wasn't for me. It was for Pauline, who'd sent for me. He didn't like that! And he said, "So! You've come out to see me die, have you?" There couldn't have been a more brutal remark! And he knew it! This was a quality he had. It affected his relationship with his family and everybody else. I suppose a psychiatrist would suggest what aspect of a personality would produce this kind of behavior.

Hemingway was close friends with Pound, wasn't he?

No! Not as I would use the phrase and not as Ernest would use it in conversation, although I think he has remarked somewhere in *The Moveable Feast* that Pound was a good friend. Pound wasn't really a very good friend. He was a great admirer of Ernest and that's always nice, particularly when you have a considerable reputation as a critic, which Pound had. (I think undeservedly. His little finds—Ernest was not his find exactly; but Paris was full of little finds of Pound's—they usually died within two weeks.) In other words, I don't think that Ernest and Pound ever took a trip together, ever did more than pass a meal together. There's a great deal of talk about what good friends they were but I never saw them together! Ernest went back to Toronto in '22, '23, to work for the *Star* as a reporter and try to get a little money put by. Took

Hadley and Bumby back with him; returned again in '24. And it was in '24, I think, that Pound went to Rapallo. That's easy to check up but anyway Pound was not in Paris. Or anyway if he was, I never heard of it or saw him. He, incidentally, had been up to his neck in these fakes and phonies at the Dôme and the Rotonde. He had the worst taste in people. He was always taking up some young, weird, totally ungifted poet and pushing him like hell and publishing his dreadful work. He'd do this over, and over, and over, and over again! I don't remember any of the people, but by the time I met Ernest, which was the summer of '24, Pound was gone and Ernest never mentioned Pound to me. Never talked about him! I think that the story of Ernest's close friendship for Pound is just a fable that somebody dreamed up at some point and it's gotten into the canon and now it's accepted! Really, there was a period, I'd say five or six years, in Paris and back home when I knew Ernest as well as I've ever known anybody. We didn't talk letters ever; but we talked people a great deal. And he never mentioned Pound. That I can remember!

During the forties, when you were in government, and Pound was doing his fascist radio talks, he made a statement—he made more than one—but one specific statement very critical of you. He said that you were the man who handed out $4 billion to Jews on the London gold exchange firms. And yet, later, when Pound was awarded the Bollingen Prize and then when he was ultimately released from a mental institution, you were very, very active in working toward both of those accomplishments.[55] How could you be so objective about him after that kind of public attack!

First of all, I had great admiration for the early cantos, the first ten. And I owed Pound a great deal for his translations of Chinese. The early cantos had an incommunicable sort of thing, not the sort of thing that could be communicated from a to b, b to c, c to d, and so forth down the line. Nor can it be communicated to a million people standing around a, but to somebody, x, let's say, who is on the right wave length. I'm referring to the rhythmic construction of Pound's verse, not in later cantos, although there's a touch of it in the *Pisan Cantos*. I never tried to imitate it. Nobody could imitate it! And I wouldn't have wanted to! But it moved me, excited me. I have frequently said in lectures at Harvard and wouldn't hesitate to say again that Pound never wrote one single good poem! But there is hardly a poem that hasn't got something in it that is very exciting indeed. Well, that's one aspect of it. The second is that the incarceration of Pound in St. Elizabeths Hospital (which I proved myself by going to see him) and the way his trial was handled seemed to me just

incredible! I had done everything I could to try to get him a decent lawyer. At
that time, he wouldn't even communicate with me, wouldn't talk to me. The
trial had nothing to do with justice and nothing to do with decent understanding. And afterward I did what I did to get Pound out, and (although I've never
talked about this and I've never written about it and I never will, but I don't
mind saying now) I did, I think, more than anybody else. In fact, I did get him
out! It was frequently said, and it's true! I got Ernest, who was helpful; Tom
Eliot, who was somewhat helpful; Robert Frost, who was enormously helpful
but enormously unwilling to help. I got them all to move. I got Robert to come
down. I got him to see the attorney general and so forth. And we got Pound
out! Well, let me get rid of one other thing: the Bollingen Prize. I had nothing
whatever to do with that. The operation which ended in the Bollingen Prize
was set up by my successor, Luther Evans, as Librarian of Congress. I knew
nothing about Pound's nomination. I would have been strongly against it if it
had ever been put up to me. I did, however, do everything I could afterward to
try to clear Pound of any involvement in that procedure. That wasn't his idea.
It was something that Allen Tate and some others thought would be a bright
idea. It wasn't a bright idea. Well, now, to go back to the thing you referred to,
Pound's remarks about me. Mr. Roosevelt had made me the head of the Office
of Facts and Figures (OFF), the predecessor of the Office of War Information.
This was in the fall of '41. And we got ourselves set up just about at the time
when Pound was starting these radio blasts on Rome Radio. And I, being
director of OFF, was to see everything that had a possible bearing on the kind
of intelligence which OFF would be concerned with. This was everything
except strictly military intelligence. I saw all those speeches and, believe me,
they're a lot worse than you think they were! There are things in there that are
just unforgivable! The reason that they didn't bother me was that the whole
tone of the thing was established by Pound's attitude toward Mr. Roosevelt,
who is referred to as "Roseveld" and any distortion of his name which would
turn him into a Jew. He was constantly called a Jew. Dreadful things were said
about him. Well, it was an honor to be in the same box! And, at that time it
was perfectly clear to me that Pound wasn't talking to actual human beings.
I never thought he was out of his mind, but I did think (what I had thought in
the beginning and still think) that he was a very silly man who had some
remarkable gifts, which largely appear in terms of his handling of English
rhythms. And because of these gifts, these ingrained, deeply embedded qualities, he was the most influential man writing not only in English but in any
European language over a long period of time. And although he was not a great
poet, he had a very great influence on poetry and was the reason why some

great poetry was written by, let's say, Yeats (he had some influence on Yeats). And he did a good deal for Tom Eliot by blue-pencilling *Waste Land*. So that his treatment of me has nothing to do with what I did about him. They're on different levels and in different places. I think I ought to add to this, having gotten into this as far as I have, that when Ezra got back to Italy (which again was something that took a lot of doing because once out of St. Elizabeths, there were people in government who were going to make damn sure he never got out of the country!) he began learning from his daughter, Mary, things that he had never known about what had happened; and some three or four years before he died, I got a letter from him, the most disturbing letter I've ever gotten because it was a letter of apology. Ezra Pound was the kind of man who should never apologize! He should just make the same admission for himself that Ernest made for himself, but with a lot more reason.

Why did you decide to return to America in 1928?

We knew by that time that we were going to have to. About a year earlier, we had an elaborate scheme to borrow money, buy a house, and we were going to live the rest of our lives in Paris. In fact, we'd got along fairly far in negotiation. But I told Ada we'd made a terrible mistake and that's when the pendulum went way over and we took a real look at ourselves and decided that we wanted to get back. Ada wanted very much to sing in this country, and we wanted our children to be Americans, but the principal reason was that our third son, Bill,[56] was on the way and we just couldn't see trying to deal with a family of three children and two different careers in a foreign country with no more means than we'd ever had. There was every reason for coming home. And then my father died in '28 and I came back to America and then went back to Paris. Except for this playing with the thought of buying a house, we had never thought about ourselves as in Paris for any reason except to make good our commitment to our several arts—to get those moving, to become sure of ourselves, and then return. To go back to the "expatriate" business, not only did I never meet an expatriate in Paris, I never met an American who wasn't, in Paris, busy with American plans and purposes and material. Dos was writing *Manhattan Transfer*; Ernest was writing short stories about the state of Michigan; Scott was writing—well, Scott didn't do any writing that I heard of! Cummings was completely concerned with that wonderful Cloud-cuckooland that he lived in (and I don't say that in the spirit of derogation, either, because it's a wonderful land. I'd like to know the way to get in there!).

John Peale Bishop was profoundly concerned with his home state of West Virginia. Gerald, who had every reason to love his life in France, was very eager to get back and was concerned with American things. The subjects of all those paintings of his are basically American.

If your wife was interested in pursuing a career, how did she feel about returning to this country and settling in Conway? That must have been difficult for her.

No. We built this room for her as a music room. You see, it has marvelous acoustics! Just by chance, because no architect knows anything about acoustics. She had two pianos, that one and another one. They were on both sides of the room. She was always working here. She was doing concerts in New York. By this time, Aaron Copland had also come back and Virgil Thomson and Roger Sessions, so she had two or three very busy years. And then she simply decided that her children were growing older, that she had to make a choice. She never made a thing of it. She didn't present it as a great problem of life or death as plenty of her friends did, trying to put her in a position of being the sacrificing wife who gave up her own career for her husband's. Ada would never buy that. She said she was doing exactly what she wanted to do, what she most wanted to do, and for quite a long period of time what she would do. While we were in Washington, she and Ralph Kirkpatrick, who was a harpsichord genius then at Yale, did a memorable concert at Williamsburg, which nobody who heard it ever forgot. But she just decided to stop and did stop. No bitterness about it! I can't begin to express my admiration for her.

Your children probably didn't remember America at all.

Well, our daughter, Mimi, had only French as a language. She communicated slightly and condescendingly in a few words in English with people who didn't have French. But French was her language. And she was madly in love with Ernest. She was four years old and she wouldn't allow Ernest to speak to her in any language but French, which Ernest spoke like a butcher. My French isn't very good, but Ernest's was something to listen to. But he could make himself understood on any subject. Ken, who was born in 1917 (Mimi was born in 1922) and so was around twelve or thirteen when we came back, has always retained his French. His French is French French! He passes for a Frenchman. Ken is totally an international type. He's at home anywhere, or was before his illness. Mimi immediately lost all her French! The children in the public school began to laugh at her and that was all she needed. She just put French out of her mind and now she can't tell the difference between *oui* and *non*!

How did they feel about coming home? Did they resist coming to America?

We brought them back in '27 while we were looking for houses and found this house. Then we stayed in Ashfield, up the road. They had seen the country and they were very eager to come back here. Ada's always felt that we played a dirty trick on them by bringing them here to Conway where they had no children friends, but they did have children friends! All three of them! Bill was born here, grew up here; but Ken, Mimi, and Bill, all three of them, loved this place. Tremendously! One of the great tragedies to Ken is that he can't live here. We've never been through an entire year here. But many, many years we were only away for a few weeks or so. We'd come as early as we could get here in the spring and leave as late as possible in the winter. Of course, when I was teaching at Harvard it was different and when I was in Washington, we just moved out entirely.

What made you decide to settle here? You didn't have a job lined up, did you?

No, I wasn't planning for a job. I didn't foresee the Great Depression. My father had died and it seemed perfectly clear that we'd have enough money to live. But I found out within one year of getting back here that we weren't going to be able to do that. Henry Luce's[57] offer of a job on *Fortune* was the most encouraging thing that happened to me over a long period of time. We needed it.

As you look back over your five years in Paris, were you satisfied with what you'd done with your time?

I don't think that question ever really presented itself. The question with me was whether the five lines or ten lines that would seem to me to be good could be written. And they were written. By the time *New Found Land* came along, there was no question about that in my mind. And of course, you yourself are your own worst critic, always your harshest critic. And I finally was able to take a poem some two or three months after it had been written and read it and know that the glass rang clear. That was all I'd wanted. Then the only problem was where to have peace and quiet and get ahead with it.

Could you describe your trip home? You told us something about your prepa-rations for the trip to Paris. Do you have any recollections about coming back?

I don't remember it at all. Except that we came into Boston. And the great problem was that we'd bought quite a lot of French goods, at one time or another, and particularly at the very end. And with the enormous kindness of the U.S. Customs, I hired a truck and the customs officer came all the way up from Boston! The truck was sealed; we broke the seals; we passed customs out here on the front lawn. I don't know if they do that anymore! In fact, I was astonished that it happened then.

The
1930s

1929	Traveled through Mexico on foot and mule retracing the route of Cortés.
1929–38	Served on the editorial board of *Fortune* magazine.
1929	*Einstein* (poetry). Paris, Black Sun Press.
	John Reed Memorial Prize awarded by *Poetry* magazine.
1930	*New Found Land* (poetry). Houghton Mifflin Co.
1932	*Conquistador* (poetry). Houghton Mifflin Co.
	Before March (chapbook). Alfred A. Knopf.
1933	Pulitzer Prize for *Conquistador*.
	Poems, 1924–1933. Houghton Mifflin Co.
	Frescoes for Mr. Rockefeller's City (poetry). John Day Co.
	Elected to the National Institute of Arts and Letters.
1934	*Union Pacific* (ballet).
1935	*Panic* (verse play). Houghton Mifflin Co.
1936	*Public Speech* (poetry). Rinehart and Co.
1937	*The Fall of the City* (radio verse play). Farrar and Rinehart Inc.
1938	First curator of the Nieman Foundation of Journalism at Harvard.
	Air Raid (radio verse play). Harcourt, Brace and Co.
	Land of the Free (poem and photos). Harcourt, Brace and Co.

In 1929, shortly after your return from Paris, you went on the trail of the conquistadores.

Yes. I'd started work on *Conquistador* in the Bibliothèque Saint Janvier, which is just off the rue de Saint-Michel. I used to drop over there and look around at things. They had very little in English, but one of the things they had was a set of Hakluyt Society publications. And one of those was Bernál Díaz del Castíllo's *True History of the Conquest of New Spain*. I began reading that and was immediately struck by the metaphor in a way that I had not been in reading Prescott.[1] I mean the obvious metaphor of the unknown West, the difficult and dangerous journey into the West, the wonders of that, the scene at the beach below when Cortés burned his ships, cut himself off from Europe, cut himself off from Cuba, made it impossible for anyone to go anywhere else but West with him. All these things subsume and clarify the whole experience of the Americas to the Europeans, including the disastrous ending—the *noche triste*—and the destruction of the city and the miserable, horrible, beastly decay and degradation that set in afterward. What white men have done to the land was made pretty explicit.

And it was that, the metaphoric sense of the thing, which more than anything else carried me away. I read it several times—it's not very long—and then I started to do what I thought was going to be a sort of a metaphoric transposition of it. But it didn't work out that way. It immediately became clear to me that it was going to be long and take its own time. I started work and first it went along like a house afire and then suddenly it just lay down and I couldn't do anything with it. I put it off because we were coming home and everything had to be dropped, and I lost about a year. Then we started to spend that first winter here, and about the middle of January, because the house had no insulation in it whatever, the northwest wind—which is a dominant wind and is stopped by nothing—went right on through the house. Bill was a baby, lying in his crib—about four months old, with his little baby hair blowing in the drafts. And it just got to be too much.

We got my mother to take us in and, having left my family in Glencoe, I went down to Mexico and did succeed in following that path. And the whole thing started again! I finished the poem, even with my shift to *Fortune*, within a year.[2] The trip itself is not all that far (it took a month) but it's very, very uneven. It's up and down, up and down. I didn't start at once because I spent quite a lot of time down on the coast on the beaches trying to figure out more or less where the ships put in. It's pretty easy, I think, to tell. As a matter of fact, the maps provided in the Hakluyt book were all the guidance I had and all the guidance I needed. Those and the automobile map put side by side, just so I could see what had happened. In Huatusco, which is a town down near Veracruz, I hired a young Mexican who was engaged to an American girl and wanted to perfect his English. And he told me that he spoke Indian dialects, which would be useful as we went up through the monte. Turned out that when he became excited, he didn't know one word of Indian! To make things worse, I discovered when I got back up to Tenochtitlán (Mexico City) after about three weeks or a month in the monte, that the American ambassador, who was Dwight Morrow, Anne Lindbergh's father, had been looking for me high and low because there was a civil war going on in the monte, directly between Veracruz and Mexico City, right through the area that I was going to come through, and both sides were wild young men who would peg you down on an ant's nest if they didn't like you. He was terrified and raised hell with me when I got back. He said word was everywhere that I was to report immediately to him, and he was furious and then invited me to lunch, which was when I met Charles Lindbergh.[3]

Anyway, when I was in Mexico, I went down to Guatemala City and saw the manuscript. The first pages of it are so corroded by time, worms, and various other things that the sense you have at the beginning of my poem of the surviving, abbreviated phrases, that is not a literal use of the manuscript, but that's the way the manuscript begins. It gives you an extraordinary experience to pick up these bits and pieces. The single word for "sea" will appear or one word for the wind and so forth—very exciting. Bernál is very much a part of it. He explains why he's writing it in the prologue of the poem. He's full of rage, anger, at the fact that none of his colleagues or friends had received his just due. What the poem does is essentially to cover the same time and more or less the same ground that Bernál Díaz's *True History*, which was written about ten years after the conquest, covers. So I knew exactly what I was going to do. It's an extremely dramatic story although Bernál Díaz doesn't make it sound exciting.

Was the point of view, that Bernál Díaz would be telling the story himself, clear to you as you began your own work?

If you'd look at the *True History*, you would see that it would be impossible to use it without preestablishing Bernál Díaz del Castíllo. It's not a history, really, at all. It's a very personal apology—"apologia."

Could you speak to the actual writing of a poem of this length, substance, and difficulty—the kind of daily work you did, the division into books, that kind of thing?

I don't think I ever did what a reasonably prudent man would do and attempt at the beginning to determine how many books there would be and what each book would contain. Or to put it the other way 'round, what each book would contain and therefore how many there would be. I don't think I did that. If one can pull far enough away from it to look at it as a whole, however, the story does fall very naturally into parts. First of all, there's the departure from Cuba, the crossing of the sea and the arrival off the coast of the peninsula, the movement north to the Isle of the Women, and the first indication of sacrifices, which was a shocking thing to the Spaniards. Then the actual landing (after the first landing only for the purpose of fighting on one occasion) near the site of Veracruz. Then the meeting and the burning of the fleet. This all falls into two parts: the arrival off the coast and the movement up the coast and the mutiny. Then the ambassadors, who come down from Tenochtitlán, and through Tlaxcala, and toward the pueblo and the great massacre there. Then the crossing of the volcanoes, which began in a hole and ends in the first sight they had of the crystal clear air of the city of Tenochtitlán 750 miles away. (No crystal clear air today. You can hardly breathe it.) Then the description of Tenochtitlán, what the city was really like when they got there, which is quite an idyllic thing, and that goes by itself. And so on. It paces itself. And I think that—I'm just guessing now because I don't remember—but I would guess that I sort of did it book by book and saw how far a book would carry it. And, after all, it's a linear story so that you don't have to be worried about leaving anything out. As long as you stay with Bernál, you're all right! Nobody's going to go anywhere that you don't go.

It was a very laborious writing job but a continuously exciting one. I should have done a lot of things that I didn't do. I should have collected every book I could about the Aztecs and, above all, the Mayan civilization, which surrounded them and qualified theirs. I should have done a great deal of reading. I just didn't do it. I got so involved with Bernál I preferred to stay with him. And that deprives the poem of scholarly interest, but I think it gives it more of a shove as a poem.

An American epic is rare. Writing one must have been a brave experiment!

Yes, there aren't many! Every now and then somebody stumbles on *Conquistador*. A contemporary of mine, more or less, out in the Midwest, a teacher, took just that line, wrote me a long letter about it. He said, "This is the only real American epic and it should be saluted as such." "So," I said, "you go ahead and salute it!" Of course, I didn't start to write an epic! As I said a little earlier, I really wanted to use the incidents of the story as the elements to construct a contemporary metaphor of the American situation, which had begun to fascinate me at that time. And it wasn't until I was in it that I discovered what I should have thought of at the start—that the story of the conquest of the new world is really so little known in the United States that the references wouldn't have been meaningful to anybody—that the thing to do is write it out and let the metaphor adhere to it.

The beginning of Conquistador *is almost Virgilian. What led you to use such a classical device in this work?*

This is, of course, a straight theft from the classical epic construction. "Of that world's conquest and the fortunate wars: / Of the great report and expectation of honor: / How in their youth they stretched sail: how fared they / Westward under the wind: by wave wandered." But that is complete at the end of the argument, and the first book moves into the narration and really concerns itself with Díaz at the beginning of this writing and so forth and introduces the characters—that is, the Spanish characters. I don't remember whether there's anything comparable to that argument. The argument was written long afterward, when the whole thing was finished. It seemed desirable to place the undertaking in time present for the reader as he moved in. It's a curious business, that poem. I don't speculate much about by whom and when I'm going to be read, but I do wonder on occasion why that poem has slipped so completely out of sight. I think it's quite good! In fact, I think it's very good! And it would repay reading and it's very relevant. It isn't even read much in Latin America. There is a translation of the first few books. Quite good, too. But I never hear from that, either. It seems to have plummeted.

The work was awarded a Pulitzer Prize. How does a work get nominated for a Pulitzer Prize?

I don't know. I had no conscious interest in Pulitzer prizes. I mean I was surprised at winning. Wonderful, Pulitzer prizes! I was delighted, but I hadn't been thinking about it. Actually Ada and I were in Paris in the spring of '32. I was on a *Fortune* job of some kind and I took her along. And we stayed in a little hotel, Hôtel Jacob on the rue Jacob, which we knew well from the past. I'd forgotten all about things that happen in May, such as Pulitzer prizes, and I remember getting up, no thought of anything, opening the door because I heard something dropping out there, and there was a newspaper and I was on the front page of the Paris edition of the *Herald Tribune*, with a Pulitzer Prize! I can tell you that was quite a day! I'll never forget the ecstasy of that moment.

You hadn't heard you'd even been nominated?

No, you don't know that. I can imagine a publisher who would try to scratch backs by saying, "I've just nominated you for the Pulitzer Prize!" But a decent publisher wouldn't do that because the chances are one in ten thousand that you'll get it. No, that was a marvelous moment!

Did the Pulitzer Prize have any significant effect on your life or career afterward?

An accepted piece of public recognition like that bolsters up your own subjective judgment and it's helpful from that point of view. The Pulitzer Prize in poetry doesn't have the significance of a Pulitzer Prize in fiction because a Pulitzer Prize in fiction means that you'll make a lot more money in the future. In poetry, it doesn't—you're not going to make any money, anyway! The Pulitzer people had a dinner in New York to mark the fiftieth (couldn't have been the fiftieth!) anniversary of the beginning of the Pulitzer prizes, and Thornton Wilder[4] and I were the only people there who got three of those. We were asked to speak and I'd beat my brains against the wall trying to think of what in the world to say.

I decided the only thing to do was to look at it very candidly from my personal point of view. What really had it meant to me? It was pretty clear to me by then (this was only ten years ago) that Pulitzer prizes don't make literature. They do, however, to some degree, encourage it. And I decided that the principal effect was to give you a sort of association with people who'd won it and also with people who hadn't, in a sort of reverse way—that you then stopped wondering if you were really there at all. You could assume that you were somewhere around. And that aspect of it was very good. Obviously the awards are always questionable and one of the favorite activities of history is to reverse all the judgments at any given time as to its own writers; nevertheless, what it does for a man when he's alive and when he's working is to give him a sense of belonging to something, as it were. And that's not bad. It's quite helpful. Also if you're engaged, as I was throughout this entire time, earning your keep by following an altogether different kind of life—the life of a journalist—and working very hard at it, the award of that Pulitzer Prize particularly, and then again the one in '52, which came just about the time I was starting to teach at Harvard, launched on another career—those two sort of identify me as being what I really wanted to be and was. I thought, here was proof that I was not altogether wrong but maybe a poet.

It was just after you'd gotten back from your trip to Mexico and before you finished Conquistador *that you heard from Henry Luce about* Fortune. *How had you known Luce before?*

He was four years after me at Hotchkiss and four years after me at Yale. Four years after me in the "Bones." And therefore I'd never met him. But I was one of those models that young men make for themselves. He didn't know me well enough to know that I was no model at all. But not having ever seen me, he was an admirer of mine. And he called up one day and asked me if I would consider a job as one of the editors of *Fortune*, a new magazine dealing with business. I said, "Thank you very much but you should be informed that the one thing I don't know anything about, except as a lawyer knows about it, is business." And he said, "That is exactly why I want you! And if you'll accept that as true, will you please make up your mind?" I said, "I don't have to make up my mind! I need that job so badly that I'd take it even if you didn't feel that ignorance of business was no obstacle." Then he proposed something extraordinary. I told him that I had to finish *Conquistador* and I was too far along to let it go and I thought it was too good. And Harry said, "I'll tell you what I'll do. You can work for *Fortune* as long in any year as you need to pay your bills and when you've got your bills paid, you can go off and no questions will be asked and you won't be bothered." And the whole nine years I worked for *Fortune*, he stuck by that. I never heard of anybody doing anything like that! I got a salary of about $16,000 a year. It was always, as I say, adjusted so that I could balance my books for the year on the work I'd already done. Then I had the rest of the year for whatever I could do.[5]

Brooks Atkinson, in his recent Pembroke *article,[6] commented that he could never understand why you went to work for* Fortune *because he regarded it then, and he still regards it, as "the enemy."*

He was thinking about *Fortune* as it is now. *Fortune* as it was then was a wholly different thing. Because of the fact that it opened for business in the middle of the Depression, it was not at all a business magazine. For example, housing was a great issue in business, that is, from a business point of view. I wrote a series of articles about housing for *Fortune*, but it was something that we talked about in terms of "Hoovervilles," because that's what the country was then thought to have. Hoovervilles and Bucky Fullers—those were the two poles in my interest in housing. And I've looked at those pieces since and they're really not all that bad. Bucky Fuller tells me he thinks that I should really have been a housing expert!

Could you explain those terms, "Hoovervilles" and "Bucky Fullers"?

With the Depression and the complete collapse, unemployment was as high as 25 percent, 35 percent, in some places 50 percent, of the population at the time. Farm products were selling at prices so low no farmer could afford to live. The whole economy was shot to hell! People began living in shacks and shack towns grew up called Hoovervilles. One of Hoover's great achievements was to order General MacArthur to drive the veterans of the First World War out of a Hooverville outside of Washington, which he did and then set the thing on fire! This was not a pleasant subject but it wasn't anything you'd kid about! Bucky Fuller[7] is the last of the New England idealistic, weird geniuses. He's a descendant of Margaret Fuller. He's the inventor of the Dymaxion House. It looks like a tree house. It has a central core, which has the bathroom inside it, all prefabricated. And the house is in a globelike thing, quite round. You live in the tree top. It's really a perfectly lovely conception! And he had a lot of them built. He invented a marvelous three-wheel car, which will undoubtedly come back at some time.

How much research had to go into those Fortune *essays? What traveling did you do? Did you have a staff of any kind?*

At *Fortune* they had quite a staff of researchers. It's a technique in journalism that has been copied in many other places; it's really rather standard now. Every man had one researcher. I started out with the handsomest girl who ever went through Vassar, married to Jack Jessup, who was one of the principal editors of *Fortune* later on. Then, after a year, I had a girl named Rhoda Booth. She was an extremely quiet girl—very nice looking but unobtrusive. She was an ideal researcher. But the operation as it went was democratic. You had general discussions, board meetings, conversations with the managing editor. I liked to take subjects I knew absolutely nothing about. That's the way to avoid all pressures, I found.

But you would do the traveling yourself?

Oh, yes. For instance, I did a piece called "The Plow That Broke the Plains," something that Pare Lorentz[8] made a fine motion picture about. In fact, he used that article. I went out and lived in Montana through the whole wheat season with farmer Tom Campbell. Learned more about the disadvantages of raising winter wheat in a dry climate than I'd hoped, in the end. It was a marvelous education. I was all over the country, saw parts of it I'd never really seen before that. And I got to see plenty of it! And then it also edged over into politics. I did a piece on Roosevelt, whom I didn't know, and it performed a useful purpose.

Are there any pieces that you wrote that you particularly remember?

I have very little memory of most of them, but there was an issue on Japan, which I went to Japan to do and took with me Thornton Wilder's cousin, Wilder Hobson, who was also a *Fortune* writer. Wilder Hobson did two of the pieces in that issue: "Government in Japan" and "Profits and Competition." I did all the rest of it! It was the biggest writing job that I've ever done. The Japanese issue was one of the high points in *Fortune's* history because the subject was chosen by Luce himself, who had an unerring instinct about the world. The Manchurian incident[9] had already happened. And, although Harry didn't know it (I found it out after getting there), under the bed behind the curtains, the Japanese Fascists were in control of the government. Knowing what Wilder and I found out in Japan, it was perfectly obvious that something like Pearl Harbor had to be in the future. These people had nowhere to go except to war. And it's a very important piece of journalism. Naturally, I can't say that. And I wouldn't get the credit for it, anyway. It was Harry's idea. Harry edited that. Every now and then, he would come back to *Fortune* and edit an issue. He did that one. And in '36 I did my South American issues, and I did a piece in two parts on the great Swedish match king[10] and that disaster. I also did a piece on Boston, which almost lost me all my Boston friends, who were the most numerous friends I had, even though it wasn't an anti-Boston piece at all. I did a piece on the United States Senate, which almost squashed me as Librarian of Congress because I said some very unkind things about the greatest club in the world! I practically lived in Washington for three weeks for that.

Did you have to develop a Fortune *prose style?*

I never tried to write in any style but my own.

Do you feel that writing so much journalistic prose affected your attitudes toward poetry itself? Your style and your techniques? There seems to be a change between the work of the twenties and later pieces.

Well, yes. There's a very great difference between *New Found Land, Streets in the Moon,* and *Public Speech* and between plays like *The Trojan Horse* and *This Music Crept by Me upon the Waters.* And then *J.B.* And the *Songs for Eve* and *The Wild Old Wicked Man* have a slightly changed tone.

One of the main things that concerned you in your career was defining the role of the poet. A number of critics have noted a change in that definition during the thirties: that early in the decade you seem to feel, as indicated in "Invocation to the Social Muse" particularly, that the role of the poet is to speak about eternal human issues and that later in the decade you seem to do an about-face. How do you respond to that?

I don't think it's ever as simple as that. The "Invocation to the Social Muse" is, first of all, not without irony.[11]

Invocation to the Social Muse

Señora, it is true the Greeks are dead.

It is true also that we here are Americans:
That we use the machines: that a sight of the god is unusual:
That more people have more thoughts: that there are

Progress and science and tractors and revolutions and
Marx and the wars more antiseptic and murderous
And music in every home: there is also Hoover.

Does the lady suggest we should write it out in The Word?
Does Madame recall our responsibilities? We are
Whores, Fräulein: poets, Fräulein, are persons of

Known vocation following troops: they must sleep with
Stragglers from either prince and of both views.
The rules permit them to further the business of neither.

It is also strictly forbidden to mix in maneuvers.
Those that infringe are inflated with praise on the plazas—
Their bones are resultantly afterwards found under newspapers.

Preferring life with the sons to death with the fathers,
We also doubt on the record whether the sons
Will still be shouting around with the same huzzas—

For we hope Lady to live to lie with the youngest.
There are only a handful of things a man likes,
Generation to generation, hungry or

Well fed: the earth's one: life's
One: Mister Morgan is not one.

There is nothing worse for our trade than to be in style.

He that goes naked goes further at last than another.
Wrap the bard in a flag or a school and they'll jimmy his
Door down and be thick in his bed—for a month:

(Who recalls the address now of the Imagists?)
But the naked man has always his own nakedness.
People remember forever his live limbs.

They may drive him out of the camps but one will take him.
They may stop his tongue on his teeth with a rope's argument—
He will lie in a house and be warm when they are shaking.

Besides, Tovarishch, how to embrace an army?
How to take to one's chamber a million souls?
How to conceive in the name of a column of marchers?

The things of the poet are done to a man alone
As the things of love are done—or of death when he hears the
Step withdraw on the stair and the clock tick only.

Neither his class nor his kind nor his trade may come near him
There where he lies on his left arm and will die,
Nor his class nor his kind nor his trade when the blood is jeering

And his knee's in the soft of the bed where his love lies.

> I remind you, Barinya, the life of the poet is hard—
> A hardy life with a boot as quick as a fiver:
>
> Is it just to demand of us also to bear arms?

Second, what it deals with is a point of view which demands that the poet, whoever he is, should—must—involve himself directly in the cause of human justice, all the causes in which the downtrodden are always involved, and on that score I don't think I've changed my position very much. If you take that position in a revolutionary time like ours, the poet's writing must be revolutionary, must be propaganda. That I never have believed, and never practiced. On the other hand, there's a very distinguishable problem, which gets confused in the minds of some people who think about it. There are those who, in their assiduous desire to protect poetry from the degradation of propaganda, have insisted that the poet must keep out of what they call the public world. There I disagree with them absolutely. I think that if you take poetry seriously, if you think of it as being what it clearly is historically and always has been, there is no aspect of human life that a man who writes poems or hopes to be a poet can't involve himself in! Nobody knows when, where, and how you're going to learn what you need to know about human beings, about human life, which is your subject. Now those two things in the minds of some expatiators on this subject get all mixed up together. On the second point, I certainly did change my position! I felt very strongly in the years when I was in Paris and trying to teach myself to be what I wanted to be, that I had to devote myself entirely, if I were going to do the impossible thing that was required to be done, to the internal world, the spiritual world, even out to the fringes of the intellectual world. But once back in the United States and face to face with the Great Depression and the horrors of that time, it became perfectly apparent that you couldn't keep your self-respect and hide that way. That is "The Ivory Tower"! That's what *Tower of Ivory* is all about. And although for some years, as I say, in my self-imposed apprenticeship I felt that I ought to remain in my tower, I very speedily changed my mind. I don't think I've shifted much on that since the early thirties.

Did the Fortune *experience have a lot to do with your changed view?*

I think a great deal. *Fortune* was a tremendous educational experience for me. Not only did I see the United States at Mr. Luce's expense, but I got to know really quite a hell of a lot about its goings-on. In our world there's nothing like a magazine devoted to business to let you know where the body is buried.

In one of your works, Poetry and Experience, *you talk about Yeats as being an example of a "public" poet, very unlike, say, somebody like Emily Dickinson, whom you refer to as a "private" poet. Could you comment on the difference between the two?*

Yeats's letter to Lady Dorothy Wellesley, which mentions an article of mine in the *Yale Review* which uses the phrase "public speech" in reference to poetry, says that he wants her to read the piece.

I wrote that essay when I was a law student at the Harvard Law School, about Yeats's conception of the public world and his use of the public world, his carrying of poetry into the public world. This was the time when the whole tendency was to talk about poetry and propaganda, poetry and propaganda, like a series of parrots; and that essay is published in one of my first books of essays. I didn't send it to him. I didn't know him. But Yeats saw it and said to her in the letter, "I think it's very important for us" (who us is, I don't know—anyway, Yeats). I remember reading that and saying, drawing a deep breath, "Well, what do you know!"

But it isn't a question of public or private poet. It's a question of to whom the poet is speaking and in what language. Is it a language so esoteric and private that only a few people with the requisite reading and education and taste can possibly understand it, or is it a language which is in the open air and which has open and public meanings? Do you face up to the light? "Public speech" also has to do not only with the language, but also with the world about which one is speaking; that is, is this again only the world of the emotions, or is it also the world of event, the world that Homer occupied? My question always is, can you exclude one or the other? I'd be the last man to say you must be in this world or you must be in that one! But if you take poetry seriously, can you exclude one of the vast areas you can experience, particularly in our time? Ours is a public age. The events that concern us are wars, the dangers of wars, the dangers of growing civilizations, and the destruction of the earth—nothing private about these views, objects, problems! What has always bothered me is the constant attempt to restrict poetry—to make it "recherché"—to make it precious—make it rich, deep, beautiful, crystalline, and the property of about eight people who can handle it! That means reading as well as writing.

One critic comments that some of your poems in the 1930s seem to be written for a much larger audience and thus are more public; that purpose had, he says, a tremendous effect on the language that you used and reduced

the quality of the poetry. Do you agree that writing for a larger audience
weakens the quality of poetry?

"Larger audience" is one of those phrases which implies that you're presently
engaged in hollering from a house top and that you're damned if you're not
going to be heard by everybody around. I'd rather go at it the other way. It's not
so much a question of larger audience, but it's refusing to be restricted to
a small audience—refusing to accept limitations. But when it comes to the
question of the effect of this kind of a turn, however you want to define it, on
the quality of the work, I think there's something tendentious about that
which one has a right to question. As one gets deeper and deeper into the
essential, which is the human situation in the world, one is practically compelled to use simpler and simpler language because the specialized terms, the
terms which pass current in the intellectual world, just simply won't carry
the emotional burden which must be carried by language which deals with
the human condition in a situation like, let us say, *Land of the Free.*[12] *Land of*
the Free is trying to find words for the purgatory of the Depression, for the
American hopes and expectations and what had happened to them. The actors
in the situation are, for the most part, the poor and the ignorant, and the language must be simple because otherwise it loses its meaning. It will turn into
a sociological tract very easily and if it turns into a sociological tract, it's dead.

I think one finds for almost all poets really worth reading that as they close
with the human issue, their language becomes more and more simple and,
therefore, if they are masters of that language, more poignant and more emotionally convincing. Emily Dickinson, with her very private world, and very
subtle and complicated thoughts, had her chief triumph in the fact that she
was able to stick with language that might have come out of a hymn book, and
a lot of it did. I think to say that more widely human reference makes a poem
qualitatively inferior is to make a totally unjustified assumption about human nature and what human beings are.

Could you perhaps tell us something about some poems of that period? For
instance, one of the really bitter poems in Poems, 1924–1933 *is "Lines for an*
Interment." Apparently you were writing about your brother. You had
written about him closer to the war, in the twenties; and here you are in '33,
writing about him again. Do you remember why you went back to the
subject?

Yes, I do. I remember that one quite clearly.

Lines for an Interment

Now it is fifteen years you have lain in the meadow:
The boards at your face have gone through: the earth is
Packed down and the sound of the rain is fainter:
The roots of the first grass are dead.

It's a long time to lie in the earth with your honor:
The world, Soldier, the world has been moving on.

The girls wouldn't look at you twice in the cloth cap:
Six years old they were when it happened:

It bores them even in books: "Soissons besieged!"
As for the gents they have joined the American Legion:

Belts and a brass band and the ladies' auxiliaries:
The Californians march in the OD silk.

We are all acting again like civilized beings:
People mention it at tea . . .

The Facts of Life we have learned are Economic:
You were deceived by the detonations of bombs:

You thought of courage and death when you thought of warfare.
Hadn't they taught you the fine words were unfortunate?

Now that we understand we judge without bias:
We feel of course for those who had to die:

Women have written us novels of great passion
Proving the useless death of the dead was a tragedy.

Nevertheless it is foolish to chew gall:
The foremost writers on both sides have apologized:

The Germans are back in the Midi with cropped hair:
The English are drinking the better beer in Bavaria.

You can rest now in the rain in the Belgian meadow—
Now that it's all explained away and forgotten:
Now that the earth is hard and the wood rots:

Now you are dead . . .

My brother Kenneth was one of the very first members of what later became naval aviation. His unit included some people who had very distinguished futures. For example, Bob Lovett, who was head of the naval aviation operation out of Dunkirk during the whole miserable winter of 1917–18 and later was one of the first secretaries of defense, was a member of that unit. And there was Dave Ingalls, who was a great naval ace and later turned into quite an important figure in Ohio. The men in the unit were also people who, because they were members of the same class at Yale, were good friends and kept in touch with each other. In 1933, they invited me to attend the annual dinner which they have in New York. I went and was filled with very unexpected reactions. Many of them—Lovett, particularly—were close friends of mine. But I was struck by the fact that these events of fifteen years before had become just that: events of fifteen years before. And why not? After all, life does have to go on. But I came out of that place boiling. Not at the men, but at the nature of memory and what happens to it, what happens to great hopes and great tragedies. And I wrote that poem.

Is it accurate to say that the poem "Elpenor (1933)" was written in response to the Nazi book burning?

No, I don't think so. The Nazi book burning had taken place and I had been paying a good deal of prose attention to that. What that poem is about is the subject which develops itself as the poem proceeds. One has to remember that was also a Phi Beta Kappa poem at Harvard, and a Phi Beta Kappa poem has to be read to the audience so this had to be a poem which could be understood in a public reading. It's constructed with that in mind; that is, the images at the beginning are static images of an impotent and paralyzed time, sinking deeper and deeper into the mire, the young playing no admirable part in it. And then it does move on to a series of metaphors of movement, of voice, new land, or new arrivals, discovery. I like that poem. I quite frequently read it aloud. It was meant to read aloud well and it does.

Doesn't the poem say "Do not look back to the past as a place to return to, but look toward the future and to some new and newly created freedom"?

Well, that's subtle, to my taste. During the early years of the Depression, the efforts of the government (in fact even before Mr. Roosevelt came in) were directed to a return to the prosperity of the twenties and the orderly and more or less pleasant life in America that Americans had been living off and on, with recessions in between every four or five years, for half a century. The direction was all back toward what we've lost. But Roosevelt's great perception was that that "warn't" the way to turn; that it's the other way; that we had to move ahead—we had to move ahead into a wholly new conception of the operation between government and people. Mr. Roosevelt is dismissed by the bright boys as not being quite intelligent enough to see that, but he was a lot more intelligent than they were. And he did see it very clearly. This was a point in time in which you really did have to make a physical effort to turn around and look ahead. Nobody wanted to look ahead; that way lay disaster. Each day was worse than the last. Banks would drop 50 points one day and 180 the next and the more you looked ahead, the worse things got. And people went out windows because they couldn't face the thought of what the next morning was going to be like. So at least part of "Elpenor" involves the necessity of an acceptance of the disaster and a move through it toward something out there, instead of hiding back here.

In the 1933 collection, several poems are dedicated to individuals; for instance, "The Night Dream" is dedicated to R. L. Who is R. L.?

An English novelist and poet. Her name is Rosamond Lehmann. I knew her very little, but she was a friend of some of my English poet friends and I had a conversation with her one day, a piece of which did turn up in a dream about a lion. So the poem came out of a dream. It has this dream element. You know how in dreams you are somehow informed that something totally irrelevant to, let's say, Rosamond Lehmann is relevant to Rosamond Lehmann. You're just given to understand that. So the lion figure, lion's mouth, has something to do with her. This was the only effort I ever made to recapture a dream. But you can't put dreams together. They move too rapidly. This did attempt to do that though and it took on the form of a love letter—a love poem, but an emotion I never felt for the body in question!

How about "Voyager" for Ernest Hemingway? The principal reference in that poem is not an obvious one.

He had a lot of trouble sleeping too. There always had to be somebody else preferably in bed with him and if not, if the sex involved made that not easy, then in the same room. Otherwise he did have these nightmares of horror, which I think came from the Italian war. That war as he saw it at the age of eighteen was not anything to give you good sleep for quite a while.

You said "he had a lot of trouble sleeping too." And the poem says "we." Do you have difficulty sleeping?

Yes.

Who was H.T.C., the person to whom "Pony Rock" is dedicated?

That's Harry Curtiss. Harry Curtiss was the man that Mina Kirstein married. They lived in South Ashfield; Pony Rock is on that farm in South Ashfield. Harry died. He had tuberculosis when Mina married him. His attachment to that place, and particularly to the Pony Rock, was very, very strong. Nothing I can really say about it. He wasn't particularly a friend of mine, nor would have been under any circumstances. His interests were wholly different.

A striking poem in the group is the one called "Aeterna Poetae Memoria." Is the poet you're talking about as the "you" Rimbaud or Verlaine?[13]

Rimbaud. Verlaine was about ten or twelve years older than Rimbaud, who was of course an enfant terrible and a human demon but also a very great genius, and they had an affair, which went on for a considerable period of time, in the course of which, somehow or other, Verlaine got himself shot with a gun which was either in Rimbaud's hands or it wasn't. The document in question is the document which refers to this very famous event in French literature, in fact in literature generally, the attempted (if it was an attempt) murder of Verlaine by Rimbaud. What's assumed in the poem is that this is a document which throws light on this famous situation. The reason for the Latin title is that only Latin is sufficiently pompous. The eternal memory of the poet is offered for sale by a man who deals in this kind of thing, and the contrast intended is between that nasty little piece of gossip and the actual quality of Rimbaud as poet, his real greatness. What the poem is doing is to place Rimbaud's real greatness as a poet against the nasty little interest in this document, which is going to be sold for a vast sum of money and the remark is, "men remember you, dead boy, lovers of verses"—the hell they do! It's a totally ironic poem.

"Nat Bacon's Bones" is a kind of ballad. Was there a specific occasion for the poem that you remember?

Somebody who really knows American history, one of those Southern historians who would know all about Nat Bacon, wrote me after that appeared to say: This is a very embarrassing letter for me to write because I ought to know the answer, but is there such a ballad? I had to say, no, there isn't such a ballad.

It's just there because it's a good ballad. You know who Nat Bacon was? He is the Nat Bacon of Bacon's Rebellion, which was a very considerable flare-up in Virginia before the Revolutionary War.

Was "Notes for a Dedication" written for a specific dedication or is that simply the title?

No, there's no particular occasion. The model is Professor William Lyons Phelps of Yale. He's far too good a man to be treated that way. I was at that stage in my life when the fame I got had not in all respects sufficed. . . .

In "Unfinished History" you make a distinction between what appears by daylight and by night, and there seems to be a relationship between the surface of a person and the depths that has to do with love. The image works centrally in the poem, just as it does in the poem called "Before March"; not in the same way but similarly.

Well, so far as your first question goes, it reminds me of a remark of Scott Fitzgerald's when somebody was talking to him about the title of a well-known novel of his. Scott said, "Well, night does a great deal for the title, *Tender is the Night*. Women are different by day and by night and night has its own particular relationship to love and always has had from the beginning of time. There is a difference in depth of a woman's face when she's defending herself in full light and in the dark, when she's not defending herself." That's what that's about.

The last stanza reads, ". . . how then will it change with us when the breath / Is no more able for such joy and the blood is / Thin in the throat and the time not come for death?" Now that it's still unfinished history, has it changed?

When I read that poem, which I very rarely do, I remember its saying that nothing is more remarkable than the little one knows even about oneself, and when one has reached middle age, no one knows what lies ahead, what one is going to feel. That would be my answer to you.

Was "Broken Promise" in response to a particular incident?

You see, one general comment is that not all poems, even lyric poems, are autobiographical by any matter of means. For example, there's a whole sequence there called "The Woman on the Stair," which was an attempt to write a novel in verse, and nobody in it is anybody I know well. This one is a poem which came out of a combination of images, the lintel of a door and a star. This is in the south of France, standing completely alone inside of a door with a star visible under the lintel of the door. The beginning of that poem sort of came out of that, but I can't explain why. I just happen to remember the association between those two images: the star and the lintel. And Ophelia is very naturally associated with the emotions with which that poem deals.

In "Critical Observations," why do you call them "bastards"—the "fawn-colored bastards of all of them"? Why are they "slick in the wrist"? Were you writing this with the idea that a great American novel would never be written? Was there a lot of talk about producing the Great American Novel?

There was more talk, I think, in that decade about the "Great American Novel" than has been heard since. Probably some great American novels have been written. There was a sort of assumption that some time—bang—it would simply appear. I would think that the first trochee is fairly clear.

Let us await the great American novel!

Black white yellow and red and the fawn-colored
Bastards of all of them, slick in the wrist, gone
Yank with a chewed cigar and a hat and a button,
Talking those Inglish Spich with the both ends cut:
And the New York Art and the real South African Music
(Written in Cincinnati by Irish Jews)
Dutchmen writing in English to harry the Puritans:

Puritans writing in Dutch to bate the Boor . . .
Let us await!   the great!   American novel!
And the elder ladies down on the Mediterranean,
And the younger ladies touring the towns of Spain,
And the local ladies Dakota and Pennsylvanian
Fringing like flowers the silvery flood of the Seine,

And the Young Men writing their autobiographies
And the Old Men writing their names in the log—
Let us await the late American Novel!

It's a bawdy cartoon of the literary life in New York and Europe.

A sonnet that you wrote that's included in this collection is called "The Revenant," the ghost, and you begin with the apostrophe to a "Too dull brain, unperceiving nerves." There seems to be a question on subject and verb and the way it's punctuated.

> O too dull brain, O unperceiving nerves
> That cannot sense what so torments my soul,
> But like torn trees, when deep Novembers roll
> Tragic with mighty winds and vaulting curves
> Of sorrowful vast sound and light that swerves
> In blown and tossing eddies, branch and bole
> Shudder and gesture with a grotesque dole,
> A grief that misconceives the grief it serves.
>
> O too dull brain—with some more subtle sense
> I know him here within the lightless room
> Reaching his hand to me, and my faint eyes
> See only darkness and the night's expanse,
> And horribly, within the listening gloom,
> My voice comes back, still eager with surprise.

The scene, I take it, is quite obvious. You probably have both been wakened at night by your own voice calling, as the writer of this had been. His brain, his nerves, his sense won't tell him what's happened but something in him knows. "I know him here within the lightless room / Reaching his hand to me." It was a dream I had about my brother after he had been killed. What helps the most is to relax and listen; let your ears tell you. It's when you begin wrestling with the *minutiae* of a poem and trying to derive meaning from it—abstract meaning—out of it, that you lose it.

In 1934 you collaborated in a ballet called Union Pacific. *How did that happen?*

Oh, that's very easy and very quick. Vladimir Nabokov had a first cousin whose name was Nick.[14] Nick turned up in New York in the early thirties. He was an irresistible man. He was just one vast chuckle about everything although he was exiled from his homeland; his family had been largely slaughtered and he had plenty of reasons for sadness but he wasn't sad. We got to know him very well. He was a composer. He never became as good a composer as he could have but that was largely because he devoted a great part of his life to the struggle against intellectual tyranny, the imprisonment, the censorship, and torture of writers and artists. He was one of the founders of the most effective of the organizations that have waged that war. He gave a great deal of his time to it. Well, in the early thirties, when I first got to know Nick, he suggested that he and I do a ballet. I said, "I don't know anything about ballet. I've never even thought about it." And he said, "You write an account of what you want to have happen on stage and I'll set it to music." Well, it wasn't quite as simple as that. I was at that time, of course, working on a piece for *Fortune* which involved me in a lot of knowledge about the Union Pacific Railroad which I didn't necessarily want and I decided to use that. It was a primitive idea. My friend Lincoln Kirstein, who is the papa of ballet in the United States, the real founder of the New York City Ballet, told me grimly that *Union Pacific* was not a ballet and shouldn't be called such on the program. And he was right. It wasn't a ballet. It was just a sort of a skit that had dances arranged for it. But Nick had arranged for a producer who called his troupe the Ballet Russe de Monte Carlo. His name was Colonel de Basil. He was a white Russian, ex-military officer. Gerald Murphy had a collection of American (what the British would call "music hall") music of the seventies, eighties, and nineties. Absolutely wonderful stuff! Nick had no ideas about America. He was here just because he had to get out of Europe so he didn't know where to turn and therefore Gerald's collection was invaluable to him and he used that music, which is incredibly exciting and foot twitching because of its origin, where it came from. My scheme for the ballet was based on the fact that the golden spike was driven by Mr. Morgan[15] on the top of Promontory Mountain overlooking the Pacific—the Union Pacific had been built from the Pacific up toward Promontory Point by Chinese workmen and, from the east, west by Irish workmen. So here were the Irish and the Chinese and all these beautiful music-hall ditties. The primary dancer and leader of the Ballet Russe de Monte Carlo was the marvelous Léonide Massine, who took this rather crude concoction of Nick's and mine, put it together and created something, which we went down to Philadelphia to see presented for the very first time. I can see the trip down. Nick and I met in the dining car and started to arm ourselves for the evening. We started on beer and worked down from there. The thing was put on. It was a wild success. It went to Boston—it was even a greater success in Boston. It went to Chicago, where it swept the town. It wandered around Europe for two years. Neither Nick nor I ever got a cent! Not one red cent! Colonel de Basil got all that! That's the end of the story. I told you it would take two minutes; it takes three! It wasn't any good, but it was a lot of fun.

*In the history of ballet, it was remarkable because it was one of the very first
ballets that focused on an American subject.*

Nick Nabokov told me that he had found that it was *the* first American ballet,
that there "ain't" no other; that is, American theme, American situation,
American writer, and so forth.

*You indicated that Mr. Nabokov thought it would be a very easy little thing
for you to do, to write up this ballet. Apparently it wasn't so simple after all.*

I had to form some idea what a ballet is and how it's written. I'd never seen
the written choreography of a ballet. It is a very complicated thing when it's
done professionally. It's all turned into a kind of sign language showing positions and so forth. I never got into that. I just wrote an account of what was
going to happen, about three and a half pages long, but what carried that ballet
was not my idea and not the dancing of the ballerinas of the Ballet Russe
de Monte Carlo; it was Gerald's music, which wasn't Gerald's but came out of
the music halls of forty or fifty years before.

Did you ever have the urge to do another ballet?

No, no!

We assumed your answer would be one word.

One word twice repeated!

You also wrote, in the 1930s, Frescoes for Mr. Rockefeller's City. *In* Frescoes
*you depict essentially the whole history of the raping of America and you
express, through the poems, tremendous rage over what has happened to the
land and the people. What kind of a response were you thinking of evoking in
the reader with these poems? They seem somewhat negative.*

"Landscape as a Nude" is a love poem to America. The Black Elk memories
refer to "Black Elk's Memories of Crazy Horse," recorded by Neihardt,[16] who
was quite an extraordinary man! The Crazy Horse role there is a very positive
role indeed, a heroic figure. What happens after Crazy Horse's death is, of
course, that the railroad goes through and you get some very bitter lines at the
end of it. The "Background with Revolutionaries" is pretty completely negative, not the revolutionaries but the little New York Marxists. But it's not

negative about the country or the effect of the country on the people who moved into it. These poems were written plumb in the middle of the thirties, at about the same time as *Land of the Free*, which I've already mentioned. It goes with them or, rather, would. *Land of the Free* came out of those marvelous photographs that were put together by the Resettlement Administration and done by Dorothea Lange and people like Ben Shahn, a very great painter who turns out to have been a marvelous photographer. Jim Agee's sidekick, Walker Evans![17] I remember a great many of them. These photographs were constantly under my hands as Librarian of Congress because we accepted them, kept them, took care of them, and so forth. There was a foreword to *Land of the Free* that says that it is photographs illustrated by a poem, which was not an attempt to be funny but to tell the truth. Those photographs do go together. They make a marvelous sequence. The poem is an illustration of them in the sense that it tries to give them a theme, a running, continuing sort of choral voice. Both *Land of the Free* and *Frescoes for Mr. Rockefeller's City* came out of the Depression. The Depression had the effect of doing lots of things. It ripped all the veils away. It stripped things naked that one had not before looked at nakedly. In other situations you sort of assume that, for instance, because people had said that New York was beautiful, New York had to be beautiful, so you wouldn't look very far. It did have its beautiful moments, but in the Depression you began to see the stinking, awful ugliness of the place. The South, which one had always thought of as being at least visually agreeable, turned out to be made out of largely eroded acres, millions and millions of eroded acres. The Resettlement Administration people were in the Department of Agriculture; therefore, they were directed toward this sort of thing, but their cameras caught something more than just eroded land. They caught eroded human beings, and then there was the whole story of the "Okies." I can't remember what the relation in time between John Steinbeck's wonderful *Grapes of Wrath* and *Land of the Free* is, but I had not read *Grapes of Wrath*[18] before I went to work on this. I think they more or less came along together. Also I'd been out in that country; I'd gone out to do the *Fortune* piece on Farmer Tom Campbell we already talked about. Being out there in Montana with Farmer Tom at the time of the harvest, you didn't have to know anything about the land or the elevation of Montana or anything else to know that there was trouble ahead. The combines moving through those enormous wheat fields just above the Crow Indian reservation moved through autumn sunlight and clouds of dust. It was perfectly obvious that something had to give, and I went down from there to Colorado and to the Texas Panhandle, the Oklahoma-Texas area, where the same thing was going on. This was Okie country and everything came together: the dust, the dryness, the breaking of the plains, the "breaking of the immemorial sod," and the human erosion and so forth. It was infuriating and enraging and sickening and deeply troubling, and yet I feel a great throb of hope in *Frescoes*. I don't feel much hope in *Land of the Free*. It was pretty hard to feel any hope about those people. They felt very little about themselves.

In Frescoes *you depict a country and a mural at the same time. Was this something you were consciously trying to do in the poem on Crazy Horse, for instance?*

No, I don't think so. They got their title after they were written and their title came largely from that incident in Diego Rivera's fresco,[19] in the big room at Rockefeller Center where the Rockefeller interests compelled him to delete Lenin from his mural. I responded to that with that title, but the poems had been written before that. This preparatory school called *Fortune* that I was going to at the time had a great deal to do with it. I had seen the high plains in the West when I was a boy of twelve. I went out to Wyoming and spent a long summer in the Little Big Horn on a ranch there, and had loved it. But I'd never seen it with the kind of scope the airplane made possible. Planes were flying around in the thirties and you could get from here to there fairly easily. So you covered a great deal of ground and that had its effect also. I like the *Frescoes* very much. They stand up for me all the time. They made a great many people very, very angry and that's one of the reasons I like them most: because they made the right people angry. This was also the beginning of my career as a "Fascist." I was pegged as a Fascist by John Strachey,[20] who was an extremely well-born, intellectual, agreeable, nice, big, tall Englishman, who had turned Communist the way a lot of people did. Auden turned Communist for a while, even Stephen Spender did.[21] John Strachey, who was no ordinary Stephen Spender, turned Communist. He came to this country, went up to Columbia and made a speech one afternoon. One of the researchers came rushing into my room and said, "Come here and listen to this!" Somebody had a small radio and Strachey was speaking into a microphone and some local radio station was picking it up and it was being delivered down to the Chrysler Building where we were. He was referring to me as a "Fascist," an "obvious Fascist," a clear supporter of Franco and Hitler, because in the "Landscape with Revolutionaries" I used some dialect lingo for the talk of some of my revolutionaries. I guess Strachey had a right to complain about that, but still I'd do it again if I had it to do again. There are certain short cuts you ought to be permitted.

*In "Oil Painting of the Artist as the Artist," you very swiftly and economi-
cally draw a picture of the artist who is, perhaps, European, in the sense that
he's very refined.*

He's a real expatriate.

*In relation to this person, you mention Horace, and you also mention James.
Why those particular figures in relation to your artist?*

First of all, this character's an aesthete; second, he's a transplanted American;
third, he loves Europe because the stock prices are all in Italian. The places he
goes to are mentioned in Horace or Henry James. These are aspects of his
quality as an aesthete and as an expatriate. He's ambiguous, including qualities that at one time, when I didn't know as much about the record as I should
have, I attributed to Ezra Pound. Pound was a great admirer of what he
thought was Jefferson. Jefferson according to Pound is not Jefferson, but
Pound decided that's the way Jefferson had to be. He was devoted to Jefferson
and had a great admiration for certain American notions that really were
never American notions. His first return from Europe after his departure very
early in the century was about the middle thirties, and then he stayed for
a very brief time. He had the sort of aesthetic snobbery about the United
States which I particularly objected to at that time; as a matter of fact I still do.
So that there are some Pound-like qualifications and qualities there, but
I wasn't thinking of Ezra. I had sense enough even at that time to realize that
that glove wouldn't fit his hand, but there were plenty of people of that kind
around.

*Did anybody ever accuse you in that poem of writing a self-portrait? You
were a classically trained person who had a European background. Did your
words in this poem ever come back to haunt you?*

No, not that way, I don't think. Because the total poem, which was also written by Archibald MacLeish, is rather adverse.

*In the middle of "Empire Builders" there is another of your beautifully
evocative descriptions of the grandeur of this country, addressed to Jefferson
from a Captain Lewis.*

This is the Lewis and Clark expedition, although the document from which

I quote doesn't exist. Nevertheless, the event did. For example, the appearance of the ship by which the letter is sent back is historically verified, and the route followed is very correct, but the language is mine and not Meriwether Lewis's.

How did you decide on the arrangement of the poems?

I can't answer that question at all. I don't remember.

The poem ends with an affirmation of your belief in what this country is coming to.

"There is too much light on my eyes to be listening" is the last line of the poem. That's light, continental light, continental sunlight.

One of the great collections of poetry that came out of the decade is Sandburg's The People, Yes. *How would you compare that work to* Frescoes?

They're not comparable simply because Carl's *The People, Yes* is, regardless of the way in which it is published, a series of short pieces: those wonderful sayings that Carl was always putting in the mouths of people and all this sort of thing. But there's plenty of rage in *The People, Yes*, as there is in *Frescoes*. I suppose rage was endemic in the time, endemic in the period.

You knew Sandburg personally, didn't you, even before this period?

Well, let's see. When did I first meet Carl? I think the first time I really got to know him was while I was in New York working for *Fortune*, early in the thirties. We had friends in common. I don't remember our meeting, but we took to each other right away. Very early on in our association, we had dinner together one night; either Carl suggested to me or I suggested to Carl that we go up to a convention of the Communist party,[22] which was being held in New York. At that time, nobody paid any particular attention to the Communists. There were very, very few of them and they were objects of mirth, rather than anything more serious. Also Russia wasn't the threat that it became later and Joe McCarthy hadn't been dreamed up and so forth. So we went and we were very happy boys, and we introduced ourselves and were met rather coldly. The convention was happening in a number of different rooms in the building. What the building was I don't know, perhaps a school building. We were allowed in—you wouldn't be allowed in now, of course, and you wouldn't go either—but with considerable reservation. Then when we tried to move around from one room to another where these discussions were going on, obstacles were put in our way. Finally, we found ourselves in a place where some perfectly incredible things were being said, incredible for their ignorance. These were statements being made by sort of grade-school intellectual types about the American situation, the American economy, American history but bearing no relation to what had actually happened. Carl and I got to laughing, and we were thrown out. We really were literally, physically, thrown out! We weren't kicked, but we ended on the sidewalk. We were still laughing! This established a real basis for friendship between us. Carl was a great admirer of my mother. Being in Illinois, he knew what she'd done in Chicago. He used to come out and see me, when I went home. Mother loved him. She loved to get him talking. Then I wrote a review of The People, Yes,[23] which was just one long halloo of delight and that cemented bonds. In the fall of 1939, when I became Librarian of Congress (I hadn't seen Carl for some time), I was trying very hard to get through some work on my desk. Carl was not in my mind. He hadn't called me; there'd been no connection of any kind. Suddenly the door opened. The secretary was sitting right outside the door, hadn't even telephoned me, nothing. There was Carl with an old felt hat, a moth-eaten blue coat that he had all the years I knew him, which must have been twenty-five or thirty. He had a burning cigar, which is not what you're supposed to do in the Library of Congress. He walked into the Librarian's office, which is a large office right in the middle of that old building, the most Byzantine-looking room you possibly can see. Pillars going up which are not supporting anything, a domed ceiling with nymphs, largely nude, floating around. Carl didn't say a word to me. He didn't even look at me. He walked slowly around the room. He went to the door and cleared his throat and said in that incredible voice of his, "Over the poet's coco was rococo." He walked out and I didn't see him afterward for years! He was a darling man!

How do you regard him today as a poet?

I'm furious at the critical attitude toward Carl Sandburg! It's largely the work of Bunny Wilson,[24] who was far from being the critic he's supposed to be. He was a very small-minded, petty, jealous, mean man and a stinker of the first order, and if I'm saying those words for all eternity, I mean them. He hated Carl. He wrote a review of Carl's enormous *Lincoln* which was contemptuous, demeaning, belittling, and, as for Carl's being a poet, he disposed of that in a couple of well-chosen sentences. Carl has his limitations as an artist, obviously; but there is a cadence which is definitely his own, which he made his own; there's a voice that is definitely his own. You'd recognize it anywhere. It isn't Whitman. It's a very tiny piece of Whitman, but it's definitely his own. Carl isn't going to be easy to get rid of and all the attacks that have been made on him haven't succeeded. I don't think Carl is a first-rate poet, but I think he is a poet without any question, and there are only five or six of those around at any given time.

Who else in the thirties would you say was doing something significant?

Oh, both Eliot and Pound! They were very good at this time. It was before Tom was ill and before Pound got wrapped up in the desert at the end of his cantos. Wallace Stevens, and, of course, Frost more and more. I didn't care much for Frost at the beginning of my association with him, my knowledge of his work. But I admired him more and more through that time. And Mark Van Doren. The thirties were an awfully good time. And as regards the general scene in English poetry, Yeats was at the top of his powers, and Yeats is certainly the greatest poet since Keats. It was a tremendous time. You sort of had to fight for air, there were so many other people breathing.

You mentioned not liking Frost at first. Or did you mean his writing?

I was talking to Bernard Malamud, who turned up here at dinner with Steve Becker at the end of the road,[25] and he said, "I've been reading about the things Frost did to you in the thirties." You know, he went to a Bread Loaf reading and lit the newspaper to break the thing up! Just behaved like a very bad boy.[26] I heard myself saying to Malamud (I'd never thought it before but it just came out), I said that I myself was astonished that I hadn't felt any indignation or anger about it at all and that probably the real reason was that at that time I didn't respect Frost's work so I didn't give a damn what he said or did. Later I came to respect his work very, very highly indeed, and by that time he was a close friend, so there may have been a connection.

During the 1930s you not only wrote a great number of poems but you also were writing verse plays. That certainly was then and is now an uncommon form. And why did you think of radio as the medium for two of them?

Well, somehow or other I had the sense, sort of by instinct, that radio offered an opportunity for dramatic poetry that should be seized. Almost a feeling of compulsion to take advantage of it. I had a scary feeling from the very start that it wouldn't last long—couldn't last long. I didn't foresee television. If

I had, I probably would have shot myself! I did have a sense of opportunity. You have to remember that radio for ordinary human use happened in the twenties. When we went off to France in '23, I'd never heard of radio. Probably a few people had sets but there were no regular programs or anything of that kind. I got back in 1928 and radio had firmly begun.

I can remember while we were moving into this house, which we did in '28, unpacking some things on the floor of what is now the dining room and coming upon a radio which didn't belong to me (a funny little object—small squat dark box which was sitting there on the floor). I don't know where it came from or whose it was but I twisted it around until suddenly some noise began to come out of it. My first reaction was one of absolute horror. You mean the world is going to be full of that noise? I was right. It is! Well, then I became very much interested in it as a possibility of doing things.

In any event, I'd done *Panic* in 1937. I have to talk about *Panic* first. It was a disastrous flop and it lasted only three nights on Broadway, but it was an exciting experience for several reasons. Exciting first of all because what it was dealing with was actually happening right around us. The worst of the Depression, looking back on it, was over, but we didn't know that at the time. Things actually seemed to be worse in the middle thirties than they were in the very beginning. Second, the communist theme, which is the essential theme in *Panic*, was playing itself out not only in New York at that time but in that theater, and third, of course, Orson Welles, who was nineteen years old, was playing the tycoon, the hero victim of *Panic*. He was a fabulous creature, an extraordinary man, more interesting then than he is now.

But the question in my mind, looking at it now, is whether *Panic* makes drama of the ideas with which it deals, or whether it is simply submerged in those ideas and ceases to be drama? What I was concerned with in the play was the intellectual war which in the thirties was waging itself at a pretty abstract level in New York. People like Sidney Hook, who is now a respectable professor of philosophy somewhere, was at that time a very effective Marxist dueler, deep in the dialogue of Marxism. I don't think he was ever a Communist; he was Marxist in the philosophic sense.

What motivated me, as I recall it—I'm sure I'm right about this because I can still feel the rumbles of anger about it—was the Marxist conception that ours was a predetermined destiny. Marx had discovered what the laws and the rules were so that he knew how the tennis game was going to come out, and it was dialectical materialism which was going to resolve everything. At that point—being at that time way over left myself, as you tend to be in your younger years (I never thought of joining the Communist party but I knew an awful lot of Communists and knew them in a friendly way)—I thought the

Great Depression of the thirties was one of the most dreadful, contemptible, horrible mismanagements of the society I'd ever heard anything about. You can see its origins in the twenties. You can see where it all came from. But when I began to be told that the answer to this was dialectical materialism, that we had to submit to a preconception of man's fate, I began to boil and that is what that play is about—that we're hopeless and helpless and can't do anything about it. McGafferty, who is an oaf and a slob, does become some kind of a hero because he refuses to accept this; and the pathetic voice of the blind man, who is, I suppose, the part of Tiresias, like so many borrowings of that kind, is far from being heroic because all he is is a parrot.

Now when I think back over it, the whole intellectual aspect of this is changed. What one has to remember about that period is that Marxism at that point was a cause in which young hopeful people believed. Nobody in his senses now believes in Marxism. It means Russia, which means the most despotic police state, the most destructive, cruel, brutal society ever conceived, but in the thirties they did believe, face to face with the ignoble collapse of capitalism—stupid, ineffable, ridiculous, and brutal. It made you rage to look at it! It could have been avoided. There was nothing inevitable about it. So the blind man of that society is a formidable figure. He's not, anymore. If you could say of any play that it was dated, that play is dated and I think that's what more or less kills it.

One anecdote about it which brings all this out and really is worth talking about for five minutes is this: the play was not put on like any other play has been. There was no producer who said, "I'll raise the money and I'll put on the play." There was Jack Houseman,[27] who was feeling toward the Mercury Theatre, which he and Orson set up later, who said, "I would like to produce this play but I haven't got any money." There was no money available. We were plumb in the deep middle of the Depression. But I did have a friend, one of my very close friends, a very conservative man, a great American public servant later on, a man who was a friend of mine at that time because he was in the same class at Yale as my brother. This is Bob Lovett, whom I've mentioned before. Bob felt peculiarly close to me and he did have some money. He had no interest in the theater, but for reasons which I have never understood, he financed this.

Now, when you say financed, it doesn't mean at all what it means now. Financing a thing now, anything, means at least a hundred thousand and perhaps a quarter of a million. I think Bob put in four or five thousand, maybe a little bit more. I'm sure not more than that! The whole thing was done on a shoestring. We opened it and it was directed by Jimmy Light,[28] who had a long experience of directing O'Neill plays. He was one of the principal directors of the Provincetown. He was, as he would have been the first to tell you, somewhat given to imbibing alcohol and that made things difficult for him, but he took this on, on a shoestring. Orson did it for next to nothing. He and his wife would turn up at the theater at about eleven o'clock in the morning and begin on his makeup, which was not going to be seen by anybody until eight o'clock that night. He was devoted to the play and devoted to the possibility. Very excited! I never heard of Martha Graham getting paid for this or any of her dancers. They probably were, somewhat; three or four dollars.

But the theater in New York was at that time at absolute gravel level. An opportunity to play was a miracle. This was at the very beginning of Harry Hopkins's[29] operation through government funds of raising theater in New York. We opened and it was clear that we were going to close almost at once. We'd always expected that, so that was not bad. But after the first performance and before the second (and this is the point that I'm coming to) the Communists in New York—with whom I was at that time on fairly good terms (I knew quite a lot of them), although I was engaged in writing attacks on them, which appeared in various publications—the Communists turned up and said as follows: they would take over the theater for the third night, 50 cents a seat, something like that, if I would submit myself to cross-examination after the performance. We had nothing to lose but our chains, and so said yes, of course, delighted.

So we played the third performance and really it went very well that third night. Our theater was quite full of, I suppose, Commies, and after the final curtain came down without too much applause, we gathered on the stage. One of them was a man named Jerome. I have forgotten what his first name was but he was agitprop; that is, he was the head of "agitation and propaganda." He and a brother of Earl Browder (Browder was then the head of the Party) and a number of other people who were in the Party and proud of it and talking about it were on the stage.[30] And so was I. I had a fever of 103 degrees. (I don't know why or what from, probably from strain, because it only lasted three or four days.) Practically none of the audience had remained to see this great crucifixion of the playwright, but right down in the front row, guess who! One of the memorable events in my life. I looked down and there was Eugene Meyer, a very wealthy publisher of, and really creator of, the *Washington Post*, with his wife Agnes, who was later a great friend of Thomas Mann, and his beautiful daughters, one of whom was Kay, who is now running the *Post*, Kay Graham. They were all down there in a row and a few scatterings of other people, and I went through a cross examination about my theories about dialectical materialism and the communist conception of definite and unavoidable fate; capitalism is going to fall; communism has to rise; the victory is ours and so forth, and here was I. "Why does this man who talks this way have to be blind, Mr. MacLeish?" That fever of 103 didn't stop me! I said, "Because he *was* blind. He was talking about something he couldn't see and didn't know." No newspaper ever reported this. It's an event totally unknown except to a few people now alive, like Jack Houseman and Orson; but they weren't interested in it. I mean they'd had their third performance and what more was there? They didn't care what happened!

The Communists might have applauded the play simply because the chief capitalist crumbles.

Not at all. What got to them was the fact that the prophet was a false prophet and they just couldn't take that. They saw it as an anti-Communist play; but that play, when I was up for confirmation as assistant secretary of state, was back there. So it stuck in some people's minds, which is one proof perhaps that it wasn't as bad as it could have been.

You said it was a dated play, but it seems to hold up pretty well as an example of Greek tragedy.

This is what it was supposed to be! *Oedipus* is obviously the model. I say that and blush when I say it, because you can't be as far short of a model as that and claim it as a model, but that was what we were after. McGafferty was *it*, you know . . . and there were lots of examples. They were going out of twenty-second-floor windows all over Wall Street! So far as I know that's the only play which ever dealt with that problem, so I'm not ashamed of it. And also nobody who ever played in that play has ever forgotten it. My one tie to Martha Graham is—and I'm very proud of any tie to Martha Graham—that she was crazy about it. She thought that's the way you ought to write a play. But of course her reason was that her chorus played an enormous part, her choreography was adapted perfectly to the sense of time and place in the ¬lay suggested by the Flatiron Building in Times Square, which was part of the set.

The review in Theatre Arts *said that the production itself was very fine, that the set was ingenious, that the whole movement was beautiful.*[31]

The newspaper reviews, which are the only important ones, were encouraging, but the drama critic of the *New Yorker* at that time was a famous son-of-a-bitch, and he really let himself go on this one.[32] The day after the play closed, Ada and I set out for England where I had a *Fortune* job to do; that review caught up with me in England and it really made me sick. I wish I could remember his name. Perhaps it's just as well that I can't.

Were you involved in any way with the preparation for that production?

This was the most informal production you ever saw in your life. Everybody put in his two cents' worth, even the carpenters. In fact, we were minus two chairs for a scene, and so I borrowed some money and hired a taxi and went down below the Village, where we were living then, and took two chairs out of my apartment. The taxi driver got interested in this, helped me put them in the back of the car, and we drove back to the theater. I paid off the taxi driver and that was all I had. There I was with the two chairs, and I started to carry them into the theater and somebody, I think it was Jack Houseman, said, "For God's sake, what are you doing? Do you realize all the union help will walk out if you carry those things in?" One of the union help said, "Ah shit, to hell with that!" They carried them in. It was a friendly production.

You've talked about some of the ideas that led to the writing of the play. Do you remember what made you decide to do it?

All you'd have to do would be to spend a couple of days in the library reading not the *New York Times* but the papers that reflected what was going on in New York to realize why it was written—this debate with the Marxists (I'm not saying Communists. They weren't. Many of them never became Communists), the boys at the *New Masses*. [33] The only vehicle that was even available to anybody on the other side, and I was on the other side, was what was then called the *Saturday Review of Literature*. It was the *New Masses* against the *Saturday Review of Literature*. They both pretended that they weren't engaged in doing anything, but they actually were. And this conflict went on and it got very dramatic in the end and it finally just turned into a play.

Was this your first meeting with Mr. Welles?

I'd never heard of Orson! Neither had anyone else. Orson was nineteen at that time. Orson, as a nineteen year old, was a duck. He was wonderful. He had a beautiful voice. He didn't know how beautiful it was, so he didn't spoil it. He was a wonderful amateur actor. He did all the things amateur actors do; I mean he overdid everything, but he learned awfully fast. Jimmy Light, who was at that point about forty or fifty and had great authority, was one of his great teachers. Houseman is a remarkable character. Houseman, so far as

I know, never opened his mouth from the beginning to the end of the thing but his presence was a little like knowing that there is God somewhere. Jack has a real genius for theater.

Why is the play dedicated to John and Katy Dos Passos?

Partly reasons of affection—I'm very fond of Dos and Katy—and partly because Dos was by the time of *Panic* engaged on a long journey from left to right, which was going to take him just where it did take him: to the point where he thought that Bob Taft was the salvation of the Republic. It was relevant to that. Dos didn't like it and didn't like what it was saying and Katy was wholly indifferent to it and those two considerations seemed to me the best possible reason for dedicating it to them!

You wrote this play in '35. There were radio plays after this, for a time, but nothing for the stage for years.

After what happened, you begin to feel it's not meant for you. From the theatrical point of view, *Panic* was a disaster. The fact that it's still alive (I don't mean by that it is still in print. I mean the fact that a few people still remember it) is quite important. But Lovett lost everything he put in.[34] I never got a cent out of it. Neither did anyone else. A few salaries were paid. That was about it. And in the theater, as you know, that's one of the important things—you have to pay the help, at least! So I wasn't tempted to go on with that. Radio avoided all this. A radio production costs next to nothing. You don't put in a penny; you don't charge anything. You just take over the machine! But what I was leading up to was that nothing that happened in connection with *Panic* was of a sort to encourage me to go on. But having started doing this, having a sense of what it was like to write words for the stage and actually to hear them on the stage, there was no return; you've got to go on with it. It's just too good! So, the two things—my curiosity about radio and the *Panic* experience—came together in my mind. And also what was happening in Austria related to *Conquistador*. These four things went together.

The relation between *Conquistador* and *The Fall of the City* was this: *Conquistador*, of course, has as its ultimate setting Tenochtitlán, Mexico City, and particularly the great square in the center of Mexico City, and my mind was full of that scenery from my trip to Mexico in '29. That was a sort of a residue in the back of my head. Something, someday, to be used—the Zocalo, that big square. Second, what was happening in Austria suggested the theme and concern because the *Anschluss*, the takeover of Austria by Hitler, had been projected but hadn't yet happened[35] and the theme of *The Fall of the City*, which is the proneness of men to accept their own conqueror, accept the loss of their rights because it will in some way solve their problems or simplify their lives—that theme had also been projected in terms of Austria. Then there was the *Panic* experience and the great deal of concern and thought about words and audience and so forth, which is what's in the foreword, and those things sort of hitched up together. The play was written in a, for me, relatively brief period of time. Nor did I pay much attention to time in writing it. Of course, writing for radio or TV now, you've got to be within a second or a few seconds of where you're supposed to be. I learned, to my surprise, that it was exactly the right length, which was an intervention I guess of God because I'd never thought anything about that. In any event, the theme of the scene is one of the great Aztec myths which can, I think, almost be verified because it was still floating around in Mexico at the time after the conquest; Bernál Díaz picks it up. That myth was a myth that just before the Spaniards came, a woman who had been buried in a grave at the edge of the Zocalo had risen from the dead and had spoken. I have forgotten what it is that she says in the prophecy. In my play, of course, she says, "The city of masterless men will take a master." I'd borrowed that from the *Conquistador* world and I got the contemporary scene, which is the matching one. After all, Cortés was accepted even by Montezuma when he originally came. He might have gotten away with it, without the awful massacre of the *noche triste*, if he had been a little wiser. So that there is a common theme between the two of them. The play was written quite, quite rapidly for me as I said—in a matter of several months. It was then put on by the CBS experimental theater very shortly after it was finished. There was a man at CBS at that time who was running that theater and playing with the possibilities of dramatic verse on the air. His name was Irving Reis. I took this around to him and he immediately said he would do it. CBS was then a much simpler organization than it is now and they backed it. It was a little cheap compared with television shows. It was expensive for that time though and expensive for radio because you had to have a mob and you also had to have two or three thoroughly good actors. Those two or three were Orson Welles, Buzz [Burgess] Meredith, and Adelaide Kline, who did the voice of the dead woman; and they had to take the Seventh Regiment Armory in New York to do it. So it was fairly expensive. And about a year later they broadcast it again from the Hollywood Bowl. Nothing got broadcast coast to coast in those days but this half hour verse play was broadcast coast to coast twice by CBS! Everything about it worked well. The production was a beauty.

Did you get any kind of response from the audience?

Oh, heavens, yes! One letter I remember very well! I can paraphrase it. It was from a man in New Orleans. It was sent to CBS to "whoever wrote that thing! At 7–7:30!" He said that he had a regular established habit that on Sunday he went out and played, I don't know, golf, tennis, whatever it was; he named the hours, and said he played until he got tired and then went home and filled a bathtub and took his radio and put it on a chair where he could hear it and got into the bathtub. In the letter, he said, "On this day I played my game and got tired, came home and filled the tub, turned on the radio, got into the tub, and the goddamn thing began spouting poetry at me! And if I could've got it, I'd have choked it, but I couldn't! And you want to know something? It's great!"

Were you able to do any rewriting during rehearsals, or did you just have a finished script?

I never changed a line and nobody ever asked me to. We had only one rehearsal! It turned out to be the right length, as I said. I think we had some premeasurements of time so we were quite sure, because we had all these schoolchildren. However, from the point of view of modern television, it was still the most slapdash thing you ever heard of! The reason I'm talking about time here is that what I next want to refer to is very much a matter of time. The day or the day after the day following the second performance, I had a telephone call from a classmate of mine at Yale named Charles Andrew Merz, who was the editor of the editorial page of the *New York Times* for many, many years, and who said to me, "I heard your *Fall of the City*. I was very much interested in it but I'm much more interested in something else. In fact, I've never been as much interested in anything as I am in this! Did you know that the Nazis were going to enter Austria and just at that time?" Here's where I've got to look things up! Whether the *Anschluss* happened a few days before that broadcast or a few days after or longer, I don't know, but I know in Charlie's mind the two things were closely linked together.[36] I said, "I only know what I read in the *Times*, Charlie." He said, "Well, we didn't know, but what happens in your play is exactly what happened in Austria and I want to find out from you whether you have prophetic gifts or whether you're a phony who stumbled on secret information and made use of it." I don't think I was as much impressed by that at the time as I was later because what chiefly impressed me was the way the thing worked. Audiences, of course, at that time for radio were not as carefully measured as they are now and also very much less was known about the way of measuring them but I remember that CBS figured out, with great astonishment, that *The Fall of the City* in its first performance, broadcast from New York from the Seventh Regiment Armory, plus its second performance, broadcast from the Hollywood Bowl, reached an audience which was well over one million souls. It probably was much larger than that and was still very small, you know, but at the time these figures were just mountainous! The whole thing brings together so many candled threads and so many coincidental things that it is sort of a mystery in my mind, as you can see from the way I'm talking about it. It's not at all as clear to me as it ought to be even now, but it was clear enough to persuade me that I had to go on, I had to do another one, and I did proceed to do another one of the same kind, *Air Raid*, the next year.

The Times *called the play one of the most ambitious radio presentations ever attempted.*

You have to remember that very few had been attempted! *Fall of the City* was the first verse play ever written for radio, unless Louis MacNeice[37] beat me by one day!

Did you become involved in the preparation for the broadcast?

Very much. We were all feeling our way. Orson was, because of his voice, just a natural for the narrator. And you wouldn't have allowed anyone else to do it, anyway! He was on pretty sure ground. Some of the other actors had had radio experience; Orson only a very little. And the crowd was made up of women and schoolchildren from New Jersey. I don't know why from New Jersey; don't ask me. They all turned up in the Seventh Regiment Armory. They only had one really full rehearsal. I came the preceding day and then they came back on that day. The question of how to produce the kind of effects that we knew we wanted but didn't know how to go at was very, very difficult. For example, the conqueror. The conqueror has to be heard. The narrator keeps talking about his coming. He can see him, you know; he sees him coming down the street. Well, the conqueror has to clank a little, but how to make him clank without making him sound like a bag full of tin cans was a problem. This sounds more pretentious than it is because there was so little time and we also had next to no money. I think I was paid a hundred dollars for it. I think that was my fee for the whole thing. I'm sure it wasn't bigger than that! It may have been smaller. There wasn't very much money to do any of this. The schoolchildren all contributed their services. They were delighted to be on the air, so to speak.

So it was rehearsed briefly and then done live.

Everything was done live then. There was no taping. There was and I think still is a glass record of *The Fall of the City*. CBS also had a recording of it.

In Theatre Arts *there was an article by Oliver Larkin who designed a set for a dance drama presentation of* Fall of the City *at Smith College.*[38] *Apparently there were other productions of this same dance drama and Mr. Larkin, or the note to the article, said that you were involved in the production, at least by giving your blessing and by coming to some of the rehearsals. Having seen the dance drama and having listened to it on the radio, what did you think of the transfer to stage? How did it work?*

I remember the Smith production very vaguely. I think it was done in the one big auditorium they have and not a very good stage. What I remember largely is what Mr. Larkin talks about; that is, the choral dance movements of the crowd and of the coming of the conqueror and so forth. I realized at the time how much *The Fall of the City* owed to not being seen, how much it owed to the fact that the imagination conceives it, because these choral figures kept getting terribly in the way of what I had seen in my own mind. This is not a reflection on dance on the stage because one of the things I mentioned in connection with *Panic* is that although it's not a very good play, the dancing chorus coached by Martha Graham and danced in by Martha Graham was the great moment of that play. The scene of *Panic* at the beginning is Broadway at Seventh and 42nd and the Flatiron, that little Flatiron Building with the news that marches around it. These dancers were taking their movement and beating their time to the alleged movement of the news. The building was there or suggested—obviously the letters didn't go around. And that was extremely effective. But when it came to *The Fall of the City*, I didn't like the Smith production very much. There were several stage productions that I saw, but I didn't like any of them.

One question about thematic content. Two articles suggested that the conqueror was fascism. What is your response to something as limiting as that—or was that what you really had in mind?

The end of the play, after the helmet has been found to be empty, does not refer to the conqueror. The conqueror is not the central figure. It's the people, crowding around and approaching him. He mounts the pyramid. At this time, an instant of breathless silence and then the voice of the announcer:

There's no one! . . .
There's no one at all . . . No one! . . .
The helmet is hollow!
The metal is empty! The armor is empty! I tell you
There's no one at all there: There's only the metal;
The barrel of metal: the bundle of armor. It's empty!
The push of a stiff pole at the nipple would topple it.
They don't see! They lie on the paving. They lie in the
Burnt spears: the ashes of arrows. They lie there . . .
They don't see or they won't see.
They are silent . . .
The people invent their oppressors: they wish to believe in them.
They wish to be free of their freedom: released from their liberty:
The long labor of liberty ended!

It's a play about the way people lose their freedom. It's not a play about the Fascist master. You know, that's really extraordinarily good verse! I think that in a very real sense the verse in *The Fall of the City* does, more successfully than I ever was able to do it again, what I was after—that is, using the rhythms of an excited voice, rhythms which are motivated by the excitement, and making the excitement the author of the rhythm. I have here a letter I wrote to Buzz Meredith a year or two ago apparently. It reads:

Dear Buzz, I'm glad you are reading *The Fall of the City* in Washington. Memories are short, even in a century like this one, which sounds more and more like a stuck record as it plays on and on. Everyone knows now, thanks to the courage of the Soviet dissidents, that the modern police state is the bloodiest, most brutal instrument of human oppression ever devised, but not everyone remembers how the police state comes to power. That's really the point. That's what it is, and that of course is what *The Fall of the City* is about. It was written in '36 during the events which led to the Austrian surrender to Hitler, without a battle fought. Its scene is Tenochtitlán, the Aztec city of Mexico, which permitted the peaceful entrance of its destroyer Cortés and his Conquistadors. Which is all ancient history, of course, or would be except that even ancient history repeats itself with us. A year ago it would have been Portugal if the Portuguese people had not found the courage to resist. A year from now it may be Italy and after that . . . what, France? You who played so brilliantly in both the CBS productions of *The Fall of the City*, to say nothing of the part you have played in your time, need no reminder of all this.

Apparently he asked me to write something that he could read before he read the play.

The Fall of the City *was topical. Wasn't* Air Raid, *also?*

Yes, *Air Raid* was too. It in many ways is a less interesting operation. I mean in external and internal ways. The relation to events is very much the same, much more deliberate in this case. That is when Guernica had happened and it was quite natural to try to imagine a city which was going to undergo that kind of an attack. You keep thinking of the horse who breaks into the right-hand side of the picture—rumor, fear, terror.[39] *Air Raid* has actual characters in it and some people who simply play a role in the tragedy in the classic form, a boy and his mother and so forth. Because of my own deep personal concern in and about the Spanish war, the apprehension at the beginning, the sense of coming—in this case the planes coming, not the conqueror—is more moving to me than the beginning of *Fall of the City* but, nevertheless and notwithstanding, the play *Air Raid* just doesn't do the same thing. I don't know why. I think it's good and there's some verse in it that I like, but it doesn't have the quality of *Fall of the City.* I was really doing the thing over but in a different way. It was a better performance; we knew much more clearly what we were doing at that time than we did in *The Fall of the City*, but it just doesn't work as well.

Could you talk about how the play came to be written? Was this another product of the Columbia Workshop?

My answer would be yes. But would I be right? It was published by Harcourt Brace (I went whoring after strange publishers at this time in my life), and its first performance over the air occurred Thursday evening, October 27, 1938, from 10:00 to 10:30 eastern standard time over the CBS network. It was CBS but it wasn't the experimental theater. But to go back to the question: How did it happen to be written? It goes back to the beginning of the Spanish war, partly due to my very close friendship with Hemingway, partly due to the fact I'd been in Spain, mostly with him, quite a bit during my years in Paris, and also because just shortly before this, a group of us, Hemingway, Dos Passos, Lillian Hellman, and I, had formed ourselves into a corporation which we called Contemporary Historians to do a film of the Spanish civil war. This was a film called "The Spanish Earth," which was photographed by a Dutch photographer, a Dutch motion-picture maker, Joris Ivens. Ivens was the great

MacLeish in his *Fortune* days.

MacLeish in Montana with farmer Tom
Campbell, 1934.

Archie and Ada, 1935.

Robert Frost and MacLeish at Bread Loaf, 1940.

A meeting with the officers of the Library of
Congress Union, Library of Congress cafeteria,
1940. MacLeish is second from left.

State Department, 1944. *Left to right:* Bill Clayton,
Dean Acheson, Joseph Grew, Edward Stettinius,
MacLeish, Nelson Rockefeller, and James Dunn.

camera man of his time, an absolutely fearless man, a passionate and convinced Communist, who was as mild as your grandmother, really quite a lovely guy, except for that knot of wrong conviction in the center of his liver! The Spanish war meant what it did to my generation because every one of us who was willing to face the facts was aware that this meant another world war. You couldn't avoid it. This was the great try-out of Hitler and Mussolini, the preparation. All this means that this is much more of a journalistic operation than *The Fall of the City*. I mean it is very much as of now, about now.

In an interview done by Orrin Dunlop, published in the Times *on October 30, 1938, you indicated that you worked for four months on the play, and that the expenditure of four months' work for one half-hour broadcast made you wonder about the personal cost of doing this kind of thing.*

I think in this case too my fee was just about the same as *The Fall of the City*, a trifling sum. *The Fall of the City* took longer because the whole thing had to get itself invented. I should have mentioned this before; I'm sure it's obvious: the really inventive technical development is the use of the natural paraphernalia of the ordinary broadcast, that is to say, an announcer in the studio and a reporter in the field. I used that in both *Fall of the City* and in *Air Raid*, and a very successful device it turned out to be. It gives you a Greek chorus without the rather ridiculous self-consciousness involved in carting a chorus in and standing them against the wall and having them recite. These people have a function; they are recognized by large audiences of nonliterary people as being proper participants.

You remember the broadcast of Fall of the City *and you were very pleased with that. How do you feel about the broadcast of* Air Raid?

All I remember has to do with time. *Fall* was exactly long enough, but, on *Air Raid*, I made no attempt to pace it. I knew I only had half an hour and I knew roughly how many pages that would be. I was told by the official at CBS who was in charge that after about ten minutes into *Air Raid*, he began to worry that we were going to be short. And what in hell were we going to do then? It was going faster than he'd thought it was going to go. But it came out within eight seconds of half an hour! God must have had something to do with that!

One magazine article said the radio effects in Air Raid *were even more adventuresome than those in* The Fall of the City. *Perhaps they were talking*

*about the curves of sounds for the aircraft and the sounds of the voices, the
women's voices particularly. Do you remember how the effects were
decided upon and created?*

This was a case in which having had the experience of *The Fall of the City*,
I didn't hesitate to write what are, in effect, stage directions, not for the
movement of characters on the stage but for sound. If you look at the text,
you'll find these things are all the way through it.

*You talk of the scale of the women's voices rising. Did you think of these
effects as the text was written or were they added afterward?*

Take that woman's voice—at its shrillest it parodies the rise and fall of
a wartime siren. It also relates to a song which rises and falls. It relates to fear,
to ecstasy. It has all these possibilities, and it's used thematically as a sort of
base to come back to emotionally. Incidentally, it's my impression (I don't
listen to radio plays very much but I listen to television plays occasionally)
that neither radio nor television has made much progress over where we were
in the middle thirties. In fact, we got off to a better start than I think we're getting off to a finish.

Since your arrangement with Fortune *was such a good one, and the years
there were so obviously productive—the two verse plays for radio,* Panic,
two books of verse, a ballet, Land of the Free, Public Speech—*why did you
move from the magazine to be curator of the Nieman Foundation at
Harvard?*

I had been working my head off through the thirties, from 1929 through 1938,
and profiting by it a great deal myself. I got more writing done in that decade
than any other in spite of the fact that I was working full time with *Fortune*.
I was aware of the fact that I was getting, at Mr. Luce's expense, a magnificent
education not only in North America, but in South America, Europe, Japan,
various other places—very happy about all that, but there was a feeling about
Time Incorporated, the whole complex, which became very trying to me in
the years of the Spanish war. *Time's* foreign editor, a man named Goldsborough, from the ancient Goldsborough tribe in Baltimore, was really pro-
Franco and, although I hesitate to say it of the dead, I think he was pro-Fascist!
At least he sounded as though he were, and a good deal of his work suggests it.
And Harry and I had a number of run-ins about it. It had nothing directly to do
with me, since I was working for *Fortune*. But nevertheless, I was working for

Time Inc., and I felt deeply about the Spanish war. It's the one thing about which in my entire life I had sound prophetic feelings. It was perfectly clear, as I mentioned, that the war was, from the point of view of the Germans and the Italians, a warm-up for a second world war. You couldn't avoid seeing it unless you shut your eyes! Most people did shut their eyes! But there were some in my generation who didn't. I felt very strongly about it.

And there were some questions of personality. Time Inc., as my son Kenneth discovered as well as me, is a real rat race, or was.[40] Highly competitive. People would cut your throat as soon as look at you in the competitive run! There were great prizes in terms of money to be gained, and perfectly decent people became unscrupulous—and I hated the atmosphere of it. At the same time, I had, throughout this entire period, a very conscious admiration of and gratitude to Harry Luce, because through this entire period he stuck by that original contract we had, which provided that I could work for *Fortune* as long as I needed to any year to pay my bills, and then I could quit for the rest of the year and go about my own business. So that I was in a sort of confused state, increasingly fed up, and at a period in the year I can't place—it must have been fairly early in the summer—Jim Conant, whom I knew somewhat, and who was then president of Harvard, a chemist, a great public servant through the whole atomic business in the war and afterward, came down to see me and told me that Harvard had received a large gift from Mrs. Nieman,[41] in memory of her husband. The only terms were that it should elevate the standards of journalism, and Jim said that he had spent quite a lot of time worrying about the gift and what ought to be done with it. He felt very strongly that Harvard should not have a school of journalism. There were schools of journalism all over everywhere, and none of them, so far as I know, was ever much good, including even the one at Columbia.

So I began to pick up my ears when I heard that. And I asked him what he proposed to do with the money and he said, well, he wasn't altogether clear, but he thought he would use it for a series of stipends to a number of young newspapermen not above a certain age (the age limit was later removed) to enable them simply to use Harvard University any way they wanted to use it for the course of a year. No examinations; no degree; no anything! Just a year off to use the world's greatest university. I let out a hoot, and he said, "Well, I might as well come to the point. We have a provision in the budget that we've worked out for this thing for a man to run it. There's got to be somebody responsible for it—we can't just turn fifteen people loose and lose sight of them and meet them again at the end of the year—somebody's got to be in charge and seeing that they find out what they want to find out about Harvard. And," he said, "you know a good deal about Harvard in various ways and I'd like to ask you to do it." "Well," I said, "what is the amount you've set aside?" And he said, "Five thousand dollars." I was then earning at *Fortune* around three times that, which was pretty good newspaper salary at that time. And to my astonishment, I heard myself say I would do it. It was a ridiculous thing to do financially because it meant that my wife and children had to go back and live with her parents in Farmington while I lived in Cambridge with Ken and his new wife. (Ken was staying there for a year to take a master's degree in anthropology.) And we just eked the thing out the best we could.

Why I did it—what the positive reasons may have been—is something I've often puzzled about. The negative ones were that I'd had enough of Time Inc. and this was a way out that Harry, who was a great respecter of journalism and a man who knew a great deal about journalism himself, would respect, as he did. He made no complaint about it at the time.[42] But what my positive reason was I don't know because all I wanted to do was to find a way of supporting my family without doing anything but my own writing. I think it was partly this marvelous conception of turning fifteen youngsters loose in the university!

So I went up on that basis and that's how it came about. The office had no proper name. Jim, who was not without a sense of humor, decided to call it "curator." So the man who runs the Nieman Foundation is the curator of a flock of journalists, now foreign as well as domestic! And the thing has worked. I went down to their end-of-the-year dinner last spring and was enormously impressed by everything I saw. It has worked. It has been copied in other places, not as well, but it has been copied. And it's changed! We were poor relations then! We had no standing, no status. It was very difficult at the beginning. In fact, my principal task was to persuade the best of Harvard professors, the ones who should have to do with the Nieman fellows, to accept them as auditors in their courses. By the end of that year, it was such an obvious success that professors were falling all over themselves to lure Niemans to come and sit and listen to them! It was a success largely because of the support of two men who had been friends of mine for some years on the Harvard faculty: Felix Frankfurter in the law school, and Arthur Schlesinger, Sr., the historian, a very admirable gentleman. Both of them were excited about the idea. So was Walter Lippmann.

Anyway, overcoming that initial resistance was one of the problems we had. Another was the invention of some sort of device that would keep these people in relation to each other because they could teach each other a lot! In fact, that's the way I have often thought is the way a boy or girl learns most in undergraduate work. So we devised a dinner once a week—I'm a great believer in dinners. I think dinner's the best possible way of getting conversation going—and that money was made available by the foundation to make this possible. And we also made arrangements with a restaurant in Boston. We got a back room. I would invite various types of people to come, usually other journalists who had nothing to do with the Nieman Foundation. Walter Lippmann, first of all, who had a great deal to do with the Nieman Foundation because he was a Harvard man and an adviser on it in the beginning. Then we got members of the faculty who were in the same general field of this guest so that you had a central discussion going and then let the reporters fall into their reportorial habit of nit-picking and questioning and getting their ears pinned back. It was very good for everybody. I think that was my invention, but there's a view that it wasn't—that it was Jim Conant's. And Jim is dead, so we can't find out!

But it was a useful year—gave me time to write, although I didn't get an awful lot done. And the institution itself has turned out to be most successful—I should say immensely! It now has up to six or seven foreign journalists in addition to eight, nine, ten domestic, and it has anywhere from five to seven or eight women every year. So it's a good mix! When I went down last spring, the real center of interest was a South African black journalist, who is erudite, sophisticated, a deeply feeling man, a man whom the rest of them obviously respected beyond words! And conversation kept going back to him.

How were you able to get things done if you were living with your son? Did you have a place in his house where you could work?

I had an office on campus, and since the Niemans were never around the office except toward the end of the afternoon, it turned out to be all right.

What kind of writing did you do that year?

In fact, I did a good deal of writing that year, but not as much as I wanted to do. I got started on what turned into *America Was Promises*. I know that because I was still working on that the next summer when Mr. Roosevelt called me up and told me I wanted to be Librarian of Congress!

The Poet in Government

1939–44	Librarian of Congress.
1939	*America Was Promises* (poetry). Duell, Sloan and Pearce.
1940	*The Irresponsibles* (prose). Duell, Sloan and Pearce.
1941–42	Director, U.S. Office of Facts and Figures.
1941	*A Time to Speak* (prose). Houghton Mifflin Co.
1942–43	Assistant director, U.S. Office of War Information.
1942	Rede Lecturer, Cambridge University, England.
	American Opinion and the War (prose). Cambridge University Press.
1943	*Colloquy for the States* (poetry). Houghton Mifflin Co.
	A Time to Act (prose). Houghton Mifflin Co.
1944–45	Assistant secretary of state.
1944	American delegate to the Conference of Allied Ministers of Education, London.
	The American Story (broadcasts). Duell, Sloan and Pearce.
1945	Chairman of the American delegation to the London Conference of United Nations to found UNESCO.

In 1939 you were appointed Librarian of Congress by President Roosevelt. You had written an article in 1933 for Fortune *on the New Deal Concept.*[1] *Was that your first association with Roosevelt?*

I think so; I can't remember anything before that. Then one of my contributions to *Fortune* in that period was an article on inflation which, needless to say, was the work of a total noneconomist and a man ignorant of the literature of inflation.[2] The Great Depression was a modern-type depression in which you get both unemployment and inflation. Although prices were dropping, particularly for farmers, there was inflation in other sections of the economy and inflation was very much discussed. So I took advantage of my position as an editor of *Fortune* to go down to Wall Street and talk to all the business authorities on inflation, and the more I listened to them, the more I read. I read everything there was on the subject at that time that I could understand. The more I read the more completely confused I became and the more I decided that there was only one possible attack on it and that was through the methods and methodology of fairy tales. So I took off from the fairy tale about the giant whose heart was in an egg, and the egg was in a duck, and the duck was in a well, and the well was in a church, and the church was on an island, the island was in a lake, the lake was in a forest. And the giant was all right until something got hold of his heart and squeezed it, at which point he would expire. This made it possible to examine the theories of inflation, you see—the gold standard, etc.—and for some mysterious reason the president read that and I got a terribly nice note from him, which was my second contact with him.

There had also been a third of a very different character, which was later. As I said before, at the time of the Spanish civil war, a number of us were outraged by the whole business and horrified because it was perfectly obvious as we looked at it that this was much more than a Spanish civil war; both Italy and Germany were involved in manipulating Franco and it was perfectly clear what was happening. So we set up a sort of informal organization to try to do some clarification. Bob Sherwood[3] was a member; I was another. And we eventually went to see the president to protest the failure of the United States to do anything to aid the not only duly elected but patently democratic government of Spain, as it was prior to the civil war, against a mutiny, which was being manipulated by the Fascists. And Bob and I had a very unpleasant interview with the president, unpleasant because neither of us had sense enough to realize that the president's hands were tied by the Neutrality Act and that there was nothing he could do about it, whatever his sentiments were; that he wasn't going to tell us self-acknowledged publicists that he had the same view as we had (that was the last thing he was going to tell us). So he took it out on us. And that, as I recall, was the last time I saw him before the Library of Congress business came up, which was one reason why I was flabbergasted when it did. I didn't expect it; I expected nothing but crates of bad eggs from Mr. Roosevelt from that time on.

You were invited to a luncheon in late 1938 that had to do with establishing a Roosevelt Library at Hyde Park, prior to the Library of Congress offer. Five or six people were invited to that luncheon; some of them were librarians. Keyes Metcalf,[4] for example, was there. Nancy Benco, in her recent article in the Quarterly Journal of the Library of Congress, *said that the librarians there felt that the future Librarian of Congress was among them.[5] Did that thought occur to you at that time?*

No, it didn't occur to me; I remember nothing about the luncheon except that I was profoundly bored by it. I was at that time running the Nieman Foundation up at Harvard and I couldn't see why I was there. And, until I saw Nancy Benco's piece, I'd never put the two together. I see now what she means.

Yes, apparently at that time Putnam[6] had already announced his plans to resign as soon as he could be replaced.

That puts it diplomatically, but not quite accurately. The last thing Mr. Putnam wanted to do was to resign. He had been there forty years, and he couldn't conceive of a life without the Library and it had taken a good deal of maneuvering to bring him to the point where he would consider retirement. It was very necessary that he *should* retire; this was well known but carefully concealed in the librarians' profession. None of the librarians would talk about it, but once I got on speaking terms with them, the first thing I learned was that they had felt for a long time that the situation was, as we discovered in the Library when we began to reorganize it, not good. The Library was years in arrears in its catalog cards; it really had fallen apart. I have the greatest admiration for Putnam. He gets very high marks for what he did, but it's just another case of a man staying on too long.

You were first approached directly by Mr. Roosevelt a few months later—around March 1939?

Yes. I had always assumed that the suggestion that I should be Librarian of Congress must have originated with Felix Frankfurter. I couldn't see anywhere else that it would originate and I now know, now that the Frankfurter-Roosevelt letters are published,[7] that the suggestion came from the president and not from Frankfurter, although Frankfurter was loyally true to his old student.

Were you surprised at the offer?

I was flabbergasted. You see, I had gone through one crisis of this kind; I had walked out of the law, and I had decided, at the very point at which Choate, Hall & Stewart had decided to make me a partner, that I couldn't be a lawyer, and that was a pretty agonizing experience and it left many aches and pains after it. Having gained my independence and having some reason to feel that I was now engaged in what I really wanted to do, it was alarming and really distressing to me to have anybody come along and say, "No, what you want to do is run a library." I am not a scholar; I had no interest in libraries as such, that is to say in the mechanism of libraries. My interest was in books, which is a totally different thing. And so I was unprepared and I was opposed to it for a number of reasons, the principal one being that at the time when Mr. Roosevelt wrote me, I was deep in what turned out to be *America Was Promises* and felt I had to complete it and had no ideas beyond that.

Your position at Harvard was a lot less demanding of your time than Fortune *had been?*

Yes, it was much less demanding of my time, but it also didn't pay me enough to live on. Which meant that, if the Library of Congress hadn't come along, I would have had to go back with my hat in my hand and say, "All right, Harry, I'll start again." But the last thing I wanted on earth was to get into an administrative position. I knew there would be no time for writing, and there wasn't as it turned out.

Yet somebody told you that there would *be time.*

Mr. Roosevelt. He said you can run the Library before breakfast every morn-ing. I don't think even with him it would have sufficed. So far as the re-organization was concerned, he would have had somebody else do that. But that wouldn't have worked. To reorganize the Library as it had to be re-organized, a responsible man had to make the decisions every day as you went along. Each decision entailed ten more. You had to be there. There was no way to avoid it.

Is Mr. Roosevelt the one who did convince you to accept the position or were there other things that came into play?

The sequence of events was that I was told by Tommy Corcoran that I was lunching with the president the next day,[8] so I went down, lunched with him in the Oval Room, where we had a very pleasant time; he told me that he wanted me to be Librarian of Congress. And I told him that this was a total and complete surprise to me and that I would have to have time to think about it and I would have to talk to my wife, Ada. And he said, "Of course you do and I'll expect to hear from you in a couple of days." We parted very amicably and I went, my heart sinking all the way, back to Farmington, and I found Ada in exactly the same shape; she had exactly the same view about it, and we duti-fully spent two days, but we knew where we were going to come out. Then I wrote the president the nicest letter I could, telling him I just simply couldn't do it and I thought that was the end of it, but two days later I got another call from Corcoran, who said, "You are lunching with the president again tomorrow." And that happened and Mr. Roosevelt, as he could, turned on a combination of charm and authority which was absolutely irresistible. And after he talked with me for a little while about it, not taking anything for granted, talking about what he thought the Library of Congress was and could be, ought to be (he saw it as a great, quasi-educational organization and not for scholars, but the country at large—fleets of Library of Congress bookmobiles in the illiterate South; he had a real vision of it), I couldn't say no.

None of that ever did happen, though.

It never happened because the war happened.

But it has never been picked up by anyone else either.

No, never. He and I never really talked about the Library after I became Librarian. From that time on I began seeing him on other matters in connection first of all with aspects of the growing crisis at home, and then in connection with the war. But you are absolutely right; nobody has ever picked that up. And, of course, I don't suppose the situation would be appropriate now. The South has changed entirely. Education in the South has changed. Had the war not occurred, though, something of this kind might have been done, and it might have had real consequences, particularly in view of the fact that we had the folklore center in the Library of Congress. That gets your foot in the door right away. You can go into a prison and begin taking down songs of all the Negro singers among the prisoners, which is what the Lomaxes did, father and son,[9] and that opens up the whole black community to you, where all the memories are.

To get back to your second talk with Mr. Roosevelt; you didn't accept the offer right away then either, did you?

No. I had to say again, "You've asked us to reconsider it; of course we'll reconsider it. I'll have to go back and discuss." And he gave me an odd look which almost said without words, "I'm married to a woman of force, too."

In his recent article in Pembroke *magazine,[10]* Keyes Metcalf *makes the statement that he was asked by the American Library Association to dissuade you from accepting the position. He felt it his duty to do what they asked him to do, so he called you, told you what they were saying, and you said, "If they don't want me to accept it (and I had about made up my mind that I was going to say no), I am going to change my mind and I am going to say yes." Is that true?*

That's one of the two things that I do remember very clearly because Keyes's telephoning me made a great impression on me. I thought it was a shocking thing for him to do. I knew Keyes quite well. I had seen quite a lot of him, in my Nieman incumbency. He's not that kind of man. But he called and at the time, the president had already sent my nomination to the Senate. The ALA was meeting in California and the proposal was that I should withdraw my name. And I said, "Keyes, have you really thought about what you are asking me to do? The president has, with my consent, sent my name up to the Senate and you're suggesting that I should now undercut his nomination and go back on my commitment?" And Keyes said, "Well, I see the point." He was very much embarrassed. He obviously didn't like what he was doing a bit, but I never said, and it wouldn't have been true, that I had made up my mind to pull out and that they forced me to change my mind. I couldn't have done it after I told the president he could send my name up. Keyes has just forgotten, I think.

There was a lot of controversy when the appointment was announced and you were attacked for a number of reasons by different people. Part of it, of course, was because librarians said you simply were not qualified. Some of the press were against the appointment for other reasons.

Only the *Herald Tribune* in New York. The editor of the editorial page was a man who later became one of my dearest friends, Geoffrey Parsons. Geoffrey greeted the president's nomination of me to the Librarian of Congress with an editorial which mixed no metaphors. It was entitled "A Shocking Appointment." It was largely on the grounds that I, although doubtless quite a nice fella, knew nothing about libraries and this was the greatest library in the world. Then there were elements in public life in America who regarded support of the democratic government of Spain as equivalent to membership in the Communist party because the Russians had intervened in Spain, once Hitler and Mussolini had intervened on the side of Franco. So there was a good deal of yammering on the ground that I was probably also a Communist. And then there was, just as there was when I was nominated to be assistant secretary of state, some opposition simply on the ground that I was a poet and that poets are unfit for public office.

Was the hearing before the Senate Library Investigation Committee routine procedure?

I don't even remember the meeting before the Senate. The Senate has a committee on the Library, or a committee the responsibilities of which include the Library, which almost never meets. It never met again while I was Librarian. It met only for this purpose. I vaguely remember being there, but I don't remember what happened. I don't think it lasted more than three or four minutes.

Once you accepted the position, you were sworn in here in Conway.

I was, indeed. The committee acted; I don't believe there was any dissent. The

Senate acted at once, and if there were any votes against, there were only a few.

That was on July 10, 1939.

I then received the necessary documentation indicating that I was Librarian. Prior to that, in my final letter of acceptance to Mr. Roosevelt, I had asked if I could take office in the fall, and he told me I could. And, therefore, I had this summer before me. I didn't want anything to take me away. I wanted to finish that poem. It was suggested to me that I ought to complete the formalities and so I went down to the post office one morning. Charley Dacey, the postmaster, was there; there was nobody in, and I said, "Charley, would you mind taking my oath. I'm going to be Librarian of Congress" and I gave him the documents. We did it through the wicket at the post office.

Did you need a witness?

Yes, I think Sidney St. Peter, who is the postmaster now, was there or was called in.

It happened on the spur of the moment?

Yes, it wasn't very bright of me. I probably should have thought of something a little more dignified to do, but the idea was simply to complete the formalities so that I could get back to work.

So even the Greenfield Recorder *didn't have a write-up on that event?*

Not a word, not a word about it. This becomes very interesting when you consider that the present Librarian, Dan Boorstin, has quite a sense of the dignities of office. When he was sworn in, he had a ceremony in the Great Hall of the Library of Congress and the president was there. President Ford came up. And he had quite a crowd of people, a lot of congressmen. Didn't do him any harm with Congress. In fact, it was a very good thing to do, I think. When I heard about that I thought about Charley Dacey and me talking to each other through the wicket.

So you spent the summer finishing America Was Promises, *and then you got set to go to Washington.*

Finished that and went down. Mr. Putnam came up to stay with us, or came down; he was in Maine. I guess when you come to western Massachusetts from Maine, you come down. He turned up at the front door with his automobile boiling from the ascent of the hill, and he stayed with us for two or three days. Absolutely lost his heart to Ada. In our relationship, everything was roses until I got there and discovered that he had fixed himself up with an office not more than 100 feet from mine, down the corridor of the main building, and expected to play an active part in what he assumed would be the continuation of the routine governance of the Library. That, then, became very embarrassing. I don't know whether he was at the top of his judgment at that time or not. I think perhaps not. But it never occurred to him that as long as he was there, he having been the feudal head of the Library for forty years, everything would naturally go to him, and there would be two chains of command going on. It was very, very awkward. It lasted a number of months until the Carnegie Institute gave me $100,000 for a scientific, librarianlike examination of the Library and I got a group of people, of whom Keyes Metcalf was one, to come down and undertake it and this, to Mr. Putnam, was outrage. It was an attack on him and so he came less and less often and finally didn't come at all. Another thing, before we reorganized the Library, I set up a group of principal officers of the Library to meet in my office every morning at nine o'clock, my own council, and I didn't include him. And his feelings were mortally hurt. I couldn't have included him; he would have been sitting there listening to talk about himself which he would take personally.

Did other people who had been on the staff for quite a long time also feel some resentment at your establishing a council?

Yes. You see, this violated the steep feudal pyramid which came down from Putnam. When the Civil Service people investigated the structure of the Library administration for me, they found that there were thirty-five different organizations in the Library which reported directly to Mr. Putnam. There were the peasants at the bottom, their officials, and then the king on top. There was no organized representative discussion of Library problems. One other thing that I wanted to add about this, as a sort of sequel to Charley Dacey, is I told the president (nobody else was interested) that I'd come down the first of October. I sort of thought that "they" were waiting for me. "They" weren't waiting for me at all. They were just going ahead the way they had. If I had gone down at once after the appointment went through, there would have been a big hullabaloo, but since I didn't turn out for four or five months, nothing happened. But I didn't know how to proceed, so we went down a little bit before the first of October, got a house, moved in, and then on the first of October I got into my car, found my way to the Library of Congress (fairly difficult because I didn't know the road), and to the parking lot, which was back of the main building. There were two white lines for the Librarian, so I drove in between the two white lines, whereupon one of the members of the custodial staff, wearing a sort of policeman's uniform, came out of the door and said, "Hey, you can't drive in there. Can't you see? It's reserved for the Librarian." I nodded my head, and he said, "Jesus Christ!" That was my greeting!

So your children were put into school in Georgetown?

Mimi, yes. She was seventeen. Bill was ten or eleven, and he was put into a school, in connection with the cathedral, called St. Albans. I don't think that's quite right, but it's something like that.[11] Ken, of course, by that time was out of Harvard.

Did they mind that disruption in their life?

My aunt, Mary Hillard, as I told you, was the head of Westover, in Middlebury, Connecticut, outside of Waterbury, where my wife went, where I met her, actually. And Mimi was at Westover, so that she didn't have to face the Washington change until the end of the school year.

You assumed your new position and started a council, faced a certain amount of resentment, but began to get things reorganized. A lot of the changes you made have been much documented by different people.

They have been. The reorganization of the Library is covered by a special report which is in print, and that is pretty comprehensive and pretty accurate. It's as short as I could make it; I wrote it myself. There may have been some contributions by specific members of that council, but I think it covers the whole situation. I noticed in the *Library Quarterly* account of my successor, Luther Evans, a very nice phrase of his which nobody had ever been kind enough to tell me about. He said, when he retired as Librarian to go on to UNESCO, talking about his reorganization, that the astonishing thing was that there had been so little to change. That I treasured because he was a man from whom kind words came with difficulty.

"There was so little to repent" is what he said. What do you feel was the most important thing you did at the Library?

It's almost impossible to answer that question because you would have to take the word important and say important to what? From one point of view, you can make a very strong case for the proposition that the most important thing was to move the Library of Congress forward into the twentieth century. For one, its salary levels, for reasons which I never have come to understand, were way below that of the rest of the government. I think Mr. Putnam had it in mind that there were a lot of women in the Library of Congress and women got lower wages and that was all right and nobody complained. The Civil Service people were outraged when they discovered what was going on. The Library of Congress wasn't under the Civil Service. It's a legislative organization, not an executive one, and the Civil Service covered only the executive at that time. The reason I say that was important was that it not only made it possible for the Library of Congress to get people as good as other libraries could get, but it lifted the whole level of librarians' salaries throughout the country. All libraries in the country had to come up when the Library of Congress came up. The Library of Congress had been depressing them.

A second change that could be regarded as important from a totally different point of view was the attempt to bring the Library of Congress into contact with the scholarly community. Widener has the Harvard faculty, for God's sake, and the New York Public Library has Columbia and N.Y.U. and C.C.N.Y. and so forth. The Library of Congress had absolutely nobody to relate to. The various institutions of higher learning in Washington were quite insignificant at that time. Our attempt was to bring the Library into contact not only with the scholars who came there to work, but with scholars who would work for us. And that was accomplished. It was done in part by such accidents as getting Alexis Léger there as an adviser on French literature. That was partly with Hitler's help, of course. But, from Alexis all the way down to young specialists in all sorts of fields.

Thomas Mann was there.

We had not that kind of connection exactly with Thomas Mann, although he came there to speak on various occasions and became really a well-known figure at the Library.

How did the Chair of Poetry develop?

When I was sent down there, there was a Chair of Poetry. It was established by the man who founded and funded the National Institute of Arts and Letters and the Academy of Arts and Letters. This was through Putnam. Putnam did a lot of things of that kind. And this man had set up a Chair of Poetry and it was held by a man named Joseph Auslander,[12] at that time somewhat known as a poet. He wasn't particularly good, but he had a reputation of sorts. He had a very nice wife, and they just settled in there for all time. He was going to be the incumbent of the Chair of Poetry. And it seemed to me that this was not a good idea for many, many reasons. Well, I got to know them, and liked them very much—they were very nice people—and finally suggested to them that this was a bad idea for them and a bad idea for the Library. That what we ought to do was to take that chair and rotate it. We would that way be able to bring in people representative of the art throughout the country, various ages and so forth. And they acceded. They were very decent about it. We found something else for them to do, and the first incumbent, as I recall it, was Allen Tate.[13] Red Warren was very early; John Peale Bishop was there, Katherine Anne Porter. It goes down through a long list of people, and it has been, I think, really very useful.

One was a critic on the *New Yorker* magazine named Louise Bogan, or Bogán, as some people pronounce it, and she was a consultant in poetry while I was still there, which must mean that she was the third or fourth, and she had written a *New Yorker* review of a book of mine about a year before she was appointed which was a zinger.[14] And after she arrived we did what we did with all these people. We had a cocktail party for her and she turned up and you could see that she had come armed *cap-à-pie*. She was just going to brazen this thing out. Ada treated her as she treats everybody, with great charm. We got a couple of drinks into her. Finally she relaxed a little, and said, "I can't stand this anymore. Why did you do it?" And I said, "Why did I do what?" and she said, "Well, now, don't be coy," and I said, "Well, I really don't know what you mean. This cocktail party?" "Oh, no," she said, "I didn't mean that. I wouldn't be as rude as that. But why did you appoint me to this?" And I said, "Because you seemed to be the best qualified person available." And she said, "But don't you know?" And I said, "Yes, I know. I read, and I don't think it makes the slightest difference. That has nothing to do with your capacity as consultant and it really has nothing to do with my poetry."

So, in other words then, it was you who appointed the person.

The first few, naturally. I mean, after all, that's my corner of the world.

But there are people that I would have liked to begin with. Old Robert Frost, just because it would have gotten the thing off to a great start, but I knew better than to ask him. He would not have regarded that as a compliment, to be asked to be a consultant in poetry. If I had offered to step aside and let him be Librarian of Congress. . . . And Carl, I would have liked to have Carl, but I knew that Carl Sandburg would have been absolutely no good at it at all. He'd have been off with his "geetar" all the time.

Did Carl Sandburg give a poetry reading?

He did, indeed, and he used his guitar in that, too. Tremendously successful.

How did the poetry readings come about? Is that still carried on as a custom?

I was invited to give one last spring. I hadn't been back for years. Not their fault, particularly, not mine. With the experience of Mr. Putnam behind me, I was determined not to be around there. But they asked me to come back last spring, and it was one of the most heartwarming things I've ever gone through. How it started was that Elizabeth Sprague Coolidge gave money for the Coolidge Auditorium, which is a beautiful auditorium for chamber music. It seats around 280–300 people. And at the time when I was Librarian, we had a Budapest quartet with money provided by the Coolidge Foundation. Those concerts were open to the public; they were full, but in some mysterious way, they were never overcrowded. And the Library, through that, became a cultural center which Washington badly needed. And it was a natural step to amplify that and include readings. We had a number while I was there: the one you asked about, Carl Sandburg, Robert Frost, and also Robinson Jeffers, who was then very much at the top of his bent, and quite a number of other people. And the development of the Chair of Poetry, it all worked in together. It made a whole.

There was a difference, wasn't there, between the Chair of Poetry and the fellowship program for young scholars who recommended acquisitions within their own field?

That's right; that's a totally different thing.

And it's something that doesn't even exist any longer.

No, the fellowship program stopped existing very rapidly. It was financed by money from, I think, the Rockefeller Foundation, but it worked like a breeze. This was what I meant, a little while ago, when we were talking about the fact that the Library of Congress has no relation with a faculty of any kind to recommend books. At Harvard that just takes care of itself. Everybody sends in titles. The Library of Congress had no such arrangement. In fact, under Putnam, for years, the books to be bought were determined by a man who I think had no university education at all, an administrator who chose books by going through catalog cards and reading the titles. He worked all night, and all day; he worked like hell, but it wasn't good at all. Well, in order to make that up, we got the Rockefeller Foundation to finance a group of young scholars and therefore probably full of beans and not expecting so high a stipend. And that worked extremely well. The gaps that turned up in the collections were chasms, not gaps. When Alexis got there, Alexis Léger, he found there was something like three hundred years of French literary history not represented by a single title in the Library of Congress. These youngsters did a marvelous job; almost all of them were excited at being in Washington, and they liked the Library. You couldn't help liking it; it was a wonderful place to be, work. But, at the end of three years, the Rockefellers said that they thought they had done all that they should do. And they suggested that we should put it into our budget. Well, our budget was then being whittled down.

You never got anything you requested any year, did you, for a budget?

Oh my, the difference between our budget and what Daniel Boorstin gets now makes me sweat. It's just terrible.[15]

So that program just ceased to be after a while.

Daniel tells me he's going to renew it. And I recommended to him that he renew it at the other end of the academic scale. Instead of getting youngsters, fresh from the Ph.D. mill, that he take people who were being forcibly retired from the universities, at the age of sixty-five or seventy, most of whom have fifteen or twenty years of wonderful work left in them, bring them down, and that he then would have something. And he told me he was almost certain he could raise the money. He may do it. What Daniel proposed was a grant that would really enable a man to supplement his retirement allowance, which is always inadequate, and live very well in Washington and to enjoy life. Such scholars have been used to taking for granted their knowledge of the literature in their field, whatever it is. A little pressure with the book-buying techniques of the Library brought to bear on them will bring out information they didn't know they possessed.

Another thing that you did was to begin the Quarterly Journal of the Library of Congress.

It wasn't so clear at the beginning that it was going to be useful, but it has turned out to be; and another thing that has held on down there under various different names was an organization of the professionals on the staff: professionals in cataloging, in classification, in reference, and so forth, who would meet at regular intervals and be given an opportunity to raise questions they thought the administrative officers ought to be talking about and weren't. Those meetings used to be very exciting, very good. They petered out after I left, but they picked up again and now I believe are very effective. You see what they need at the Library (it's a huge staff) is some sense not that they are appreciated, but that their views are.

One of your purposes in establishing the Quarterly Journal *was to make your own reports more readable, rather than simply a list of facts and figures: how many books were acquired and that sort of thing.*

The one thing that I never was able to accept in that brief job was that anybody else should write any part of the report for me except those parts which were specifically and by title the reports of the copyright office, reference department, rare books, whatever; but the part of the report which dealt with the Library as a whole had to be written by the Librarian, and this perhaps is a weakness in my character, because one ought to be willing to let somebody else do that kind of writing for him. And yet it seemed to me so important that this should be said in the words that I wanted to use which expressed what I thought I was doing. It was a hell of a job writing one of those annual reports.

You made a number of speeches, of course, during the time that you were in that position and one of the themes that came back again and again was the role of the librarian in a democratic society. You saw the librarian's role as being very much that of an educator. What do you think a librarian can do, outside of stocking the books, to educate the people?

This was the period which ended by producing McCarthy and the great revulsions against democratic societies and against individual freedom, procensorship, the whole awful mess of stuff that turned up in the late forties and early fifties. And by the time we got around to active McCarthyism, this was all a lot plainer in my mind than it had been back in the early forties, ten years before, because by that time you had vigilante committees made up of old ladies from Chicago determined to get certain books off the shelves of the libraries—in other words, determined to censor what a free people were to read. And this immediately raised a terrible question for librarians. Some of the mostly unsung heroines of that period were the librarians; that is, people who refused to put up with the censoring of books on their shelves, who insisted on the right of a free people to read as adults and make up their own minds.

And it was at that time (this is not really a response to your question, but I'll try to get back to it) that I began talking about the librarian's position as an embattled position which was really *the key* position in American culture. I dedicated a library at Carlton College out in Minnesota with a statement of that kind, which was, I think, to me at least, the best statement of the situation which I was able to produce. It was really a piece about McCarthy against the lady librarians. And it made sense and it went rocketing around the country. It banged back and forth, repercussions everywhere.

Now earlier, McCarthy hadn't appeared, but very shortly after I became Librarian, we were on the verge of and then in a war with fascism, which means the struggle between free and authoritarian governments, and the library again becomes the great metaphor of that situation. It's the dramatization of it. What the librarians could do and did do (a great many of them did do) was simply to stand by their guns and insist that they would not yield to censors of any kind, even the people who paid the taxes which kept their library going, and a lot of them paid for it.

I think if I had become Librarian twenty years earlier, it would have been very difficult to talk about the librarian's profession the way in which we found ourselves talking about it—I don't know why I should use the plural—I found myself talking about it in the thirties. All of the political things that were happening in the thirties were related. You could follow them down to things that had to do with the life of the individual, the freedom of mind, freedom of speech of individuals, and, of course, the library is the mirror of all that.

You mentioned again and again that the most important way to avoid fascism and fascistic thinking is education. What do you see as being the most important subjects for students to be taught in a democratic society?

Would you say history, for example? Did you see Bill Moyers's interview with Robert Penn Warren? It was shortly after your own and that was one of the points that Mr. Warren made, that history and the whole sense of history seem to have been lost in this country and that we need to do a great deal more teaching of history. Do you feel that way too or would you add poetry?

I would add poetry, but from another point of view. I don't know that the teaching of poetry becomes as relevant to the great fundamental issue of human freedom, when you are talking at this level, in mass society, and individuals of all ages. History certainly has a very great deal to do with it. I would agree with Red. I agree with both parts of it. I think that the teaching of history has been lamentably academicized. There are very few Henry Steele Commagers who still use history as a weapon, and it should be used as a weapon. My God, life is a fight, and if you pretend you are not in a fight, you aren't talking about life. I would insist on the uses of poetry in a rather different dimension. What poetry, a constant reading of poetry, keeps alive in almost any reader, young or old, is a sense of human dignity, the importance of the human creature. After all, poetry is the inward of the thing that history is the outward of. Poetry is constantly examining the human possibility. It is constantly examining the emotional life, which is by far the most moving part of human life. It's constantly in search of the question of man. What is man? What is man? What is man? History sees the end result. It sees what happens when a Franco collapses power down on a country like Spain. Poetry is inside that and sees what the destroyed possibility would have been, because a great part of our past is the past of failures.

When you accepted the position of Librarian, did you see yourself taking on a long-term commitment?

One of the reasons I dreaded it was that I saw it as a long-term commitment. And I didn't see how I could go through all the struggle of accepting it (put the president through the struggle of getting me accepted and so forth) and pull out short of quite a long period of time. But I think that I really did what I'm afraid I've done quite often in my life, finding myself faced with a problem that I couldn't solve, that is the problem of the length, the duration ahead of me. I just stopped thinking about it. I decided to take it on and do what I could do as well as I could do it and stay with it. I didn't foresee the war. I won't pretend that, but I did know that there was a great likelihood of war. And, when you have a war ahead of you and you're in a government position, you do well not to try to think about the future very much. So, I think it was a combination of a kind of feeling of sick horror about losing a great part of my life, doing something that was not what I desperately wanted to do, plus the recognition that worrying about it wasn't going to help much and so I didn't think about it.

There is some evidence that you did attempt to resign after a few years in office.

Apparently; it seems to be true. Some of the things Nancy Benco dug up in my correspondence with Mr. Roosevelt—that I must have asked him to try to get me out of the position along about 1943—I have no memory of and that alarms me. I can remember almost everything else. That is almost the most important thing of all to remember and I don't remember it. I clearly did do it and by that time of course I had gotten to know him very much better.

We had, first of all, a kind of family relationship. We used to go round to meals at the White House quite a bit, and the president liked to go out weekends on the Coast Guard cutter they had given him and he liked to have Ada along to sing for him and keep him talking. And he occasionally talked to me, too. We had also by this time gotten to know Mrs. Roosevelt really quite well and feel the kind of almost reverence for her that everybody did feel that knew what she was doing. And I may really have talked to him about it rather than writing, although Nancy Benco says she found a letter from him which indicates that I had written.

Anyway, let's just accept the fact that I did somehow communicate this to him. The question then is, why did I feel that way? And the only answer I can make to that is that my experience at the Office of War Information was so repulsive to me that I just wanted to get out of everything I was doing and clear out. The Library of Congress position by that time was really running itself quite well. The big decisions there were ad hoc decisions like should we or should we not send the Constitution and the Declaration to Fort Knox and the reorganization, so far as we could do anything about it at that time with limited funds, was accomplished. There was a great deal still to do, but there was no money to do it with. And so the relation with the Library of Congress was sort of hung up and I was left with O W I and all the misery of that.

In the earlier years in government, there was a broadcast in 1941 of a play called The States Talking. *What is the relationship between the poem "Colloquy of the States," which appeared in the* Atlantic *in 1939 and the play? They're just about the same, but there are some additions: introduction by the narrator, who was played by Burgess Meredith, the Hitler voice that acts*

*as a kind of obbligato to the whole thing in the play, and the sound
effects—all primary additions to the broadcast script. Is the theme the
same? The criticism of the "impure" American by the Dictator Hitler?*

Well, it is a colloquy. That is, the states are talking to each other, a voice that
keeps being heard, and the states can't quite make out what it's saying.
They finally get the idea that it's pretty derogatory talk—condescending and
derogatory talk. They finally work out the gist of it and the voice is never
heard except as they talk about it. Without replying to it, they pretty well
dispose of it. It never really was a play. It would be very, very short for that. It
wouldn't take more than about fifteen minutes, don't you think, at the most?
I see when they published it [*looking at* Best One-Act Plays of 1941] they've
just simply broken down the verses. At the beginning, " 'There's talk,' says
Illinois. 'Is there,' says Iowa." That's the remainder of the line but they published, they printed it, right under the first line. " 'Talk about what?' says
Dakota," then they go back to "says Kansas, says Arkansas." I had nothing to
do with that! But this has to be me! "A sound, a woman's voice, an untrained
simple girl's voice, singing the first bars of the opening, 'As I was going to
ballyhoo the day I well remember.' " That's the song my wife Ada used to sing
all the time in those days. Actually, I have no memory of this script or the
broadcast at all. I remember the poem. It's one of my favorite poems. I read it
quite a lot. But I remember nothing about that production. At that time, you
have to remember, I was running the Library of Congress. I don't think I was
altogether aware of what was going on.

*All during the thirties you experienced a great deal of inner conflict about the
role of the poet and the poet's responsibility to art as opposed to his responsibility to the people and society. You ultimately resolved that conflict in* The
Irresponsibles *(1940)[16] in which you suggest that you feel that you had
avoided your responsibility to society and certainly saw other writers as
having also done so. You urged that it was time to become involved and to
fortify convictions. Do you agree that you had a strong inner conflict that
was resolved by what you saw coming from the European war?*

That's very shrewd and certainly worth thinking about. If you had simply
asked me the fundamental questions involved in that statement, I would have
said I'm sure that *The Irresponsibles* was written with a good deal of feeling to
try to make a point which my academic and writing friends, but mostly academic friends, refused to make. They were doing the opposite of what is done

by the generals who get ready to fight. They were getting ready to have opinions about Hitler in terms of the last war. They were damned if they were going to be sold down the river again; they weren't going to be caught again by anything like Mr. Wilson's rhetoric; they weren't going to wait as we all did three or four years after the First World War to discover we'd been had, and they were simply, totally, against the war against Hitler, not realizing that in this case we had no choice, and that the war, instead of being what the First World War was, a vicious deceit, was a war that had to be fought, as I think most of them would now agree and would have agreed to shortly after the war. That was what my conscious mind was concerned with. I think that what you're suggesting may be a considerable part of it because I was going through a period of a good deal of anguish about the relative values involved in one's commitment at that time. What surprises me, as I look back on it, is the fact that I was so certain so early, first of all of what fascism was and second what Hitler was really up to. One of the constant subjects of discussion among the new group of friends that I was making in Washington and myself and eventually between Mr. Roosevelt and myself, when I could get his attention, which wasn't often, was that group of questions: the real nature of the conflict and what Hitler was really up to. There were a great many people who believed that it was impossible that anyone, particularly the prime mover of a country which had been terribly defeated and crushed and humiliated, could possibly dream of conquering the world. Yet, now it is perfectly obvious that he not only did, he D I D. And he believed in it and he was within gunshot of pulling it off. If we'd failed at Normandy, he could have. He could have done it earlier too. At the time of *The Irresponsibles* I felt a considerable responsibility myself for the formation of the opinion which the America Firsters[17] held and which a great many college undergraduates held, and held violently, passionately. My concern was my responsibility for the beginnings of that, because a good deal of what I wrote in the thirties was along that line, too. I was so sick about the First World War that I couldn't cleanse my mind of it. I think one could make a case for the proposition that you are right; although I never thought of it before and I wouldn't myself put it that way.

You write in Actfive, *"The responsible man does what must be done." Is that how you felt about the position at the Office of Facts and Figures? It had to be done?*[18]

Well, it had to be done, but not for as high a ground as that! It had to be done because the boss told me to.

Was the Office of Facts and Figures somehow related to the Library of Congress?

In no way whatsoever. OSS (Office of Strategic Services), which had nothing really to do with the Library of Congress, was yet very closely related to it, and what we did about OSS was not something that Mr. Roosevelt himself told us to do. Mr. Bill Donovan[19] simply came around with word which he said was from the president, and I guess it must have been, I never heard anything to the contrary, asking us to help him set up the very first part of OSS, which was their office of research and analysis. He wanted us not only to house it in our new annex, which did have some room in it, but he wanted us to pick the people for it. And we did that, so that we had the head of the office of OSS in there to the neck as a part of the annex that I couldn't enter.

But that's a different story. What happened with OFF was that word was sent to me by a very high official of NBC, Robert Kintner. He came around with The Little Flower[20] who was working in Washington. He said that they and Mrs. Roosevelt were very much concerned with a federal office of information, not a departmental office of information such as there existed and still exists in every department, each one tooting its own horn and none of them interested in the overall picture. They had made considerable progress in putting it together and they wanted me to run it and I made a gesture with my arm toward the huge building in which we were sitting and they said that didn't make any difference because I could, of course, do the two together.

So then I got in touch immediately with either Missy Lehand or Grace Tully,[21] probably Grace. (Missy was the person really to get in touch with because she knew what the president thought; Grace Tully just knew what she heard.) I think it was Grace I got in touch with and she suggested that I should see the president. And I said I'm not going to ask him for an appointment to see him about something that somebody else has told me he thinks; if he wants to see me, I would of course be just too delighted but I'm not going to ask. The result of that was that I was asked to come down and I was told, very briefly, that that was what I was going to do. I complained that we were in the middle of a reorganization at the Library of Congress (I had become Librarian in '39 and this was '41, just two months before Pearl Harbor). Everything was going on, nobody was secure, nothing was secure, everything was in the process of floating around and trying to attach itself somewhere.

Mr. Roosevelt said, "Well," he said, "you'll remember that when you became Librarian of Congress, I wrote you that you could run the Library before breakfast." And I said, "Yes sir, you weren't right about that." And he said, "I didn't expect to be right about it. But," he said, "I'm perfectly certain that even in the middle of a reorganization you can run this thing, which isn't going to amount to anything, either."

For the next ten months life just really was not worth living. I had gotten a chief assistant librarian, who was my successor as Librarian, Luther Evans. He was a man that I chose with one purpose only in mind, that he was a Texan, he had very close associations with the Texas delegation. He was an open, confident, useful man, but he was not a man I would have thought of to complete the reorganization. Well, actually, he completed it wonderfully. That just shows that you shouldn't trust your judgment. Almost all that time I spent out of the Library. I'd get back there at the end of the afternoon and make a nuisance of myself and finally I gave up even doing that, and spent my Sundays at the Library. I put full time into Facts and Figures.

There were many different offices created at the same time, too, weren't there? Didn't the Office of War Information bring together the whole group of offices and try to put them under one roof, so to speak? Bill Donovan, for example, was coordinator of information.

Bill Donovan, as coordinator of information, held the office that was oss in its first beginnings. It was as coordinator of information that he came around and asked for space in the annex and asked us to help him set up his research and analysis. It had three names. I've forgotten what the second one was. It shortly changed, this second form, and in that form it still had its connection with the Library of Congress. owi took over from the Donovan organization (I better refer to it in those terms because I've forgotten what the initials later became). It was run by Robert Sherwood and renamed the Office of Foreign Information. Sherwood ran that, and the people that came with him came out of the old Donovan operation, Jimmy Warburg[22] and quite a lot of others. They were sort of small empires themselves. But this is later, late summer and autumn of '42, that that amalgamation began.

To stay with off for just a minute, I quite soon discovered and, in fact, if I had been a little more adroit in listening I would have learned this from the president himself, that off was not his idea; that it was Mrs. Roosevelt's idea. That he wasn't in favor of it, and that the reason it was called the Office of Facts and Figures, which was his name, was that it was not to be the very thing that Mrs. Roosevelt wanted it to be. The Office of Facts and Figures meant, as the president explained to me, that it would be the place in Washington where you could, if you were a newspaper reporter, go and get your government-wide facts and figures; anything you wanted to know about the government, the Office of Facts and Figures would tell you. Well, of course, that was an ironic remark, because no reporter would go to such an organization for anything; it sounded too much like a feed trough where you would get prepared information. So, we were in trouble from the very beginning. The last thing Mr. Roosevelt wanted was a repetition of the Government Information Service,[23] whatever it was called under Wilson in the First World War, which had a very bad reputation for very good reasons, but he did want to have a central check-out point where you could find out whether things were right or wrong and he wanted that to be central for the whole government and not to be like the departmental intelligence offices, which were all attorney operations. They pleaded for their clients. They didn't give you a straight business.[24]

We were in trouble from the very beginning because of that and, as a result of that, we got a very poor executive order. All the new organizations set up at the time of the war, and I guess at earlier times, were set up under executive orders. This one was drawn by Sammy Rosenman,[25] speech writer and lawyer, and gave me no power at all, a lot of aspirations and no power. We didn't have money. We had to scratch and fight to get any money at all; we finally got a fairly considerable sum, but it didn't come willingly. This was every sign that Mr. Roosevelt wasn't in the least interested. We finally got ourselves some offices in an apartment house, somewhere off as if in Passy, the remote parts of Paris—Washington, of course, being Paris!

What was the reaction of the press and the people?

I was what they were looking for; they were just waiting for me! First of all, they wanted a scapegoat. Everybody wanted a scapegoat at that period because there were a lot of things that needed to be loaded on a goat! There's no other way of describing it! And also, in my one-man battle against the America First influence, I'd accepted several invitations to speak in New York and Chicago and roundabout. One of these was a speech to the Organization of American Editors and the Associated Press. These organizations had meetings together and when you were invited to address one you found yourself addressing both. I addressed both these bodies and faced, as I knew I would, a very chilly audience, and went off to Pennsylvania Station to take the train back and bought the early edition of the *Times* and found I'd made the front page.

So I was just a natural-born target for abuse and it began very early. There's a letter from Elmer Davis[26] in which he says in his own inimitable way that most of all he had me to thank for drawing upon myself a lot of the lightning that would otherwise have hit him! Which is not true! He got plenty! There was that, and then we also had an opponent, a man I enormously admire, who later became president of the United States, Mr. Harry Truman. One of the first things we did at OFF was to put out a pamphlet on the American preparation effort. Harry Truman accused us of everything under the sun. He was a very outspoken man, as you may have heard. We were accused of lying, and faking the books, and we hadn't done any of those things but we'd been pretty wrong on a lot of things. Some of our material was written by amateurs who could write like angels but they couldn't report like reporters. That didn't get us off to a very good start. And also, there was the fact that our relation to the various departments where the news was actually being made was flimsy at best and only voluntary on the part of the departments. My executive order gave me no authority to go to anybody and ask for anything.

I set up a thing called the Committee on War Information which met once a week, and I asked each of the departments to assign someone to it. In certain instances, this worked like a charm, and in other instances, it just didn't work at all. For example, the attorney general himself, Francis Biddle, came to represent the Justice Department. Now that was pure friendship for me. From the navy, they sent a young assistant of Frank Knox, whose name was Adlai Stevenson, and Adlai turned out to be, of course, enormously helpful. The army would occasionally send Jack McCloy, who was one of the very best men anywhere.[27] So it went. But the State Department would send (I discovered later on how the State Department worked it when I became a member of the State Department) anybody who was able to avoid and evade questioning on the particular subject which was then apt to be up. So this was a most unsatisfactory arrangement. Most of the people who did take part, Wayne Coy from the White House, for example, worked hard over it and were very good and very helpful. But the rest of them just buggered us right down the line. We got very little information.

Then we also had representatives in the various departments, that is, I had deputies. I had a whole table full of deputies whom I sent to the principal departments that were concerned with the war. And some of those people were remarkable. Bob Kintner, who was one of the people who came to see me, covered, I think, the army, and did it extremely well. Then we had Chris Herter, who was later secretary of state and also governor of this commonwealth, who was one of my deputies, and Barry Bingham, the editor of the *Louisville Courier Journal*, very skillful newspaper man and good reporter, covered the navy, which he later entered.[28] They were really quite good people but they had to fight for what they got, and they got very, very little. So the situation is one of a brand new organization with no executive order, next to no money, no authority, charged with the responsibility for organizing information, totally unable to do it, and obviously facing defeat from the very beginning.[29]

The only thing we had on our side is that we had the most remarkable group of people in Washington at that time. In retrospect it's very clear about that. The list of poetic people, the writers, included Andy White (E. B. White); McGeorge Bundy; young Arthur Schlesinger; Henry Pringle of Columbia. He ran it; he was the dean of the faculty.[30] They had around eight or ten magnificent writers, extremely good women writers. We had a devoted lot of researchers organized on the basis of *Fortune*'s researchers. They knew everything; they also knew everybody, one way or another. That part of it was very rewarding and very good. They were loyal and loving people; they were wonderful to work with.[31] And the rest of it was just pure hell. I used to drag myself out of a day of defeat at OFF and go back to the Library of Congress and face the bad news on my desk and wonder if it was worthwhile going through tomorrow.

The OFF was set up for reporters to keep up to date on the current facts and figures that were coming from all the various offices, but it also disseminated material directly to the press and public, through pamphlets or some other medium.

Well, the second part of what you say is true, and the first part isn't. We were supposed to be available. This was Mr. Roosevelt's view: you'll have all the facts and all the figures and the press will come to you. And, of course, they didn't; that was the last place they came. Instead we started a publications division right away, and that's why all these writers came down. We began putting out material quite soon. Some of the material was really extraordinarily good. Later we started our radio division, and we had a poster division.[32] We branched out into all forms of publication. In other words, what we began to do was to try to put out statements which we attempted, I think with considerable success, to keep calm and quiet and down rather than up. We had to state the American cause; the American cause was our cause, and by God we weren't ashamed of it. Fortunately, as I said, Harry Truman burned our fingers very early. If he'd done it later, I don't think it would have been as effective, but he did it early enough so that we could begin to see that taking a factual matter like the state of American preparedness, which was pretty precarious, naturally it always is, and printing the good facts and not the bad ones was not a good idea. So we became a great deal more even-handed about that sort of thing. But when it came to the question of what fascism was and what democracy should mean, what the Republic was, what it had been, we never hesitated to take a very strong position—*the* position.

It's said that you, yourself, wanted to stick pretty much to facts and figures, but that there were people within the department who felt very differently from you, and that this did cause some internal disagreements.

Well, I suppose so. You put together as many men of letters as we had and you've got that many different positions. I imagine that was true. I don't myself remember any open ructions between me and the writing staff. They had ructions among themselves, and Henry Pringle had difficulties with particular people. Henry was a marvelous, even-handed, very intelligent man.

You mentioned that Harry Truman came down very heavily on you at one point. Did President Roosevelt ever respond directly to some of the information coming up from that office?

I just don't remember, and I think I would if he had. I think it would be fair to say that by this time my relation to him was such that if he had anything to say he would have said it to me. On one occasion before OFF, for example, he did. In the election in 1940, a very close friend of mine named Russell Davenport, Mitch Davenport, whom I'd known at *Fortune* and known also at Yale, had joined Willkie and I'd seen a good deal of him during the campaign.[33] I liked Willkie; I admired him but was, of course, against him politically. Mitch and I talked about the destroyer deal.[34] As I told you, Sherwood and I had gone to see the president long before either of us got into the government to see whether anything could possibly be done to change the American policy of complete neutrality toward Spain. We'd set up sort of an informal organization which had strong views about the destroyers, and I had kept on with this on my own, saying nothing to the president about it because I had already said my say and I knew what he could do and what he couldn't do and I didn't know what the final decision about the destroyers would be. I think that the decision to give the destroyers to Britain was in September of 1940. In any event, I called up Davenport out in Colorado Springs. Willkie had gone out there for a rest, and I said, "Look, Mitch, this is far too serious for anything but the frankest speaking in the world. I'm not speaking for the president. The president doesn't know I'm calling you and he probably would cut me if he did. Will you find out from Mr. Willkie if he thinks the right decision was made about the destroyers? (Britain was then just on the verge of going under.) Would Mr. Willkie, if he didn't support it, at least not use it as a club to attack?" Well, Arthur Krock[35] got hold of this. Arthur Krock was my imaginary model of a son-of-a-bitch in flight. All his life he was. And he had a piece on the front page of the *Times* the next morning reporting this conversation. I don't know how he got hold of it and I really don't care. I just sat in my office waiting for the telephone to ring. I'd called up Ada and said "Begin to pack." About eleven o'clock the telephone rang, and it was Missy Lehand, and Missy said, "The boss says to tell you, 'That's the boy'!" So if he had wanted to come down on me about anything that O F F or O W I did, he would have done it; I would have heard directly in no uncertain terms.

Were you then doing any speech writing for the president?

At that time, I wasn't writing speeches for him. I had enough to do! But I did see him from time to time. For example, I saw him in connection with Alexis Léger in the Library of Congress. This is what I was told and what I believe: Mr. Churchill and the president had been talking about a situation in North Africa at that time. The president knew from me that Alexis Léger, the former head of the Quai d'Orsay and also the poet St.-John Perse, was in the Library of Congress. They wanted to persuade Alexis to do something, say something, go to North Africa, in some way see what he could do to get French aid, not French opposition, to our forthcoming invasion of North Africa. (Again, I think I've got this in the right order.)

So I was called down to talk to him about that. They, for some reason, didn't want to talk to Alexis directly. I wanted them to do so, partly because it would have been so delightful to have the president of the United States and the prime minister of Great Britain inviting a $3,000-a-year clerk from the Library of Congress to come down to advise them! 'Cause that's all we could get for poor Alexis. That's what he lived on for a couple of years. I tried to work this out. I had a word with Alexis, and Alexis wouldn't even talk to me about it. So the president asked me to come down and I saw him and I said, "Mr. President, if you'll let me say so, Alexis Léger is a very, very distinguished man. He's way above my heights in this political world, and instead of being an intermediary in this I'd like to send him down in my car so that you could talk to him." The president said, all right he would.

And Alexis went down, and apparently it was a very stormy meeting. Alexis came back to see me. Although we were dear friends, he was furious with me for not warning him of what he was going to run into. And I said, "Didn't you have an opportunity to state your own views?" And he said (all his conversation was in French; it was going by me like bullets), "I did have an opportunity to state my own view, and I stated that I am a French citizen, loyal to France, and that I will never take part in any conversation or discussion of French policy until I am again in my old position, and then I will speak, as I should speak, through my superiors." That's just what he told Churchill and the president. And they gave up. I had expected it; they hadn't. I did want them to hear it from him.

OFF was a huge office apparently. There was a letter to the editor in the New York Times *that said something like, "We're sick and tired of being spoon-fed information about the war by 34,000 press agents of Archibald MacLeish."*

I have forgotten how many we had at any one point. Anyway it couldn't have been 34,000! It was not 1,000; it might have been 100.[36] But there never has been a history of OFF, and I don't believe now it will ever be written. It would have been—if it had been done fifteen to twenty years ago—a very valuable thing because a lot of OFF, in its brief period of time, became a sort of nexus for all sorts of problems around the country. They all came in to us. They were extremely difficult to deal with; we didn't deal with them very well, but at least we tried. It was the only place you could get air into them.

My escape from OFF was facilitated by the fact that Bob Sherwood agreed with me (once Pearl Harbor had happened this all became serious; no one was playing anymore) that there had to be an effective and powerful information service, and that neither of us ought to head it, and that it ought to have Elmer Davis, who was to both of us the ideal man. The fact that we both agreed about it and the fact that we both had access to the president made it possible for us to begin to plead that cause, I think as early as March. The president, who had some other things to think about, turned it over to Sam Rosenman, who eventually agreed with us, and OWI was set up with all the necessary executive orders and all the necessary money and everything else and with Elmer, but I don't think it ever really took fire. It was too big.

As far as my part goes, I then became assistant director of OWI for domestic affairs in June 1942, which meant that I could go back to the Library and do my job with OWI part-time. I think the rest of the information story from my point of view is simply that in OWI I was *supposed* to be assistant director for domestic affairs and I became Elmer's deputy for foreign affairs. That's what it was in practice. For example, we had to work out our relationships with the British government because we proposed to broadcast to American troops in Britain and you can see what that situation would have been and what problems it raised. We also had, through Sherwood, a concern for political warfare, which was no part of OWI's task but which got dumped on us. We had to work out our relation, in regard to this, with the British political warfare people. They had to be coordinated above the army level. So I went to England to talk to Anthony Eden[37] and to talk to the various British political warfare people. I ended as a sort of an ambassador of home instead of a domestic director! OWI had a London office, but we weren't in Paris, of course, until after the Liberation. England was the only place where OWI was operating. But that was because we had American troops in England in such numbers, and because we had these constant problems.

One thing I want to say personally about that: in many ways that experience was one of the best of my life because the British we had to deal with (Jimmy Warburg and I were the people who most often went; we went together) were extraordinary human beings and there was no national rivalry of any kind; there were no difficulties about prestige or rank or who went in the door first. It was a common cause, a common commitment, a common devotion, and we became very, very close friends. Two of the closest friends I ever met in my life were David Bowes-Lyon, the dowager queen's brother, who's dead now, and Lord Ritchie Calder, who at that time was Ritchie Calder, a science journalist, a Scot who came from gamekeeping origins in the eastern Highlands. I can remember one occasion (Ritchie and David were very close but were constantly kidding each other) when we were sitting at a table and David said something slightly uppity to Ritchie, and Ritchie said, "Glamis thou art; Cawdor wilt be" from *Macbeth*. Well, Cawdor is Calder and Glamis is the castle in eastern Scotland where the royal family have been going for a couple of hundred years! It was beautiful! Just went like that!

You didn't stay very long in the Office of War Information.

I went from June '42 to January '43. I want to read that letter of Elmer Davis. It's barely legible but I think I can make it out. This is dated January 1943.

May I not, as Woodrow Wilson was fond of saying, supplement my published regrets with some further acknowledgment of all you have done to get this organization going. You not only did a great deal of the spade work in OFF on which we were later able to build, or try to build. I would not say that we have yet got a completely satisfactory structure, but you interposed yourself as target for many bricks that, once thrown, are not likely to be thrown again. [That was the phrase that I misremembered.] No doubt you noted this morning that even the *Times Herald* seems to feel it something of a loss now that you have gone, and will have to look around to find a new objective among the prose writers. [I hadn't noticed that about "the prose writers."] But you did far more than that of course, in helping me to get acclimated when I came down in relation with Congress, in information as backgrounds around town, and not least in representing O W I in relations social and diplomatic with our foreign brethren and with other agencies of the government far more effectively than I could ever do it. For all of a fairly good job (I'm not visionary enough to hope for much more), you will deserve a large share of the credit.

As ever,
E.D.

Did you resign because you had to devote full time to the Library, or were there other reasons?

I hated information work. I did it because I was asked to do it, and I always detested it. I suppose in times of peace, so-called, you could probably devote yourself to information, trying to help a self-governing people to govern themselves by seeing that they got the information they had to have. But in war you were always on the verge of propaganda and, as we were saying a little while ago, although some of the propaganda you could give your whole heart to, some you couldn't. I just detested it. I loved the human relations; I was surrounded by friends. I didn't really give a damn about enemies; they're fly-by-night enemies; they are gone by tomorrow morning. As soon as I felt that I could honorably get out of it, I did, after I'd finished this work in England. I told Elmer that I just couldn't go on pretending to be Librarian of Congress and not be Librarian of Congress and that the Library of Congress would be there long after he and I left. And he agreed.

We read a little story about you in Newsweek *that is hard to believe: that you were so tense and under such great stress during your time in the OWI that at one point you had to be held back by aides from a physical assault upon a person who was running an air hammer.*

Haven't you ever wanted to kill a man? But I don't remember it.

In your essay entitled "The Classified Minds" you discuss the Pentagon Papers. You must have been required to do the kind of thing, in a way at least, that the attorney general did with the Pentagon Papers—to keep information from the American people. It must have been very difficult for you.

This whole nauseating business of secrecy—even during a war—it didn't make any sense.

You commented that when you were in the OFF you were not writing any of Mr. Roosevelt's speeches. Yet several people have suggested that one of the reasons that President Roosevelt really wanted you down there was so that you could write for him.

I don't think so. I think I better talk about something else first and then I'll answer your question. I said that I wasn't writing any speeches for him, but in 1940 the Library had a big do about Thomas Jefferson. It was during the summer of the campaign in which Mr. Roosevelt was opposed by Mr. Willkie; the Library of Congress undertook a Jefferson celebration which included a great many things. For example, we got together all the outstanding copies of the Declaration of Independence. We got them all but one. The copy, the most important copy of all, John Adams's copy, was loaned to us by the Adams family and came down wrapped up in an old newspaper, with a label on the outside of it. It wasn't really old newspaper, but it was sort of that kind of wrapping material. And when we inquired as to how it happened to come that way, we were told that that really ensured its safety because nobody would think that the Declaration was inside that, which may very well be true. In any event, we had that exhibition, which was a stunning thing, and we had various activities. It included a seminar which I asked Willkie to attend, and he did, together with scholars from around the country. Willkie was a very good Jefferson scholar. On the day of this seminar discussion, which took place around a little round table in my office, the Jefferson Memorial was dedicated, and Mr. Roosevelt had asked me to write a speech for that event. I got word from him, in which he said, "You're doing a lot about Jefferson up there; you must have a lot of ideas about Jefferson. Why don't you write that dedication for me?" Which was, of course, the last thing I needed at that point. But I wrote it, and we went down in cars, including Mr. Willkie, and occupied seats in the very front row where the president couldn't help but see us. The president proceeded to deliver his speech of dedication. And it was the speech I had written, every word of it. He didn't change a word. It was the only time in my association with him that this ever happened. He just delivered the speech as it was. Usually when you worked for him, your "input" was "inputted" into the furnace and boiled up with a lot of others. Later, toward the end of the day, I got another call (I think it was from Grace). Grace never really quite wholly understood what was going on but she was a very faithful reporter. She said, "The president didn't like your producing his opponent in the front row of the Jefferson dedication." I said, "Oh my God, that never crossed my mind. He was a very devoted Jefferson man, and he was very happy to go." I said, "What can I do about it?" "Well," she said, "I don't think you have to do anything about it because he said to tell you that he liked the speech he gave."

I think that that is really the beginning of the idea that I might do some work for him in that connection. But that was very sporadic. Sometimes I was working down there night after night after night. Sometimes I wouldn't go to the White House for a month. It wasn't like Sherwood, who was there all the time. I was never shown anything to go over; but when he had something going on, he wanted a number of different points of view. He would get Bobby Sherwood and Sam Rosenman and Harry Hopkins, who kept a close eye on them, and then sometimes I would be in on that. But you couldn't quite tell when it was going to happen.

During those years in government, you were also writing the series The American Story, *which seems to overlap the periods at the Library and the State Department. This series of ten plays was part of NBC's University of the Air. Can you discuss how this series came about?*[38]

It was before I left the Library of Congress and moved to the State Department as assistant secretary. They were produced in the spring of '44. Muna Lee, a Mississippi-born poet who was at that time married to Muñoz Marin, who was the governor of Puerto Rico, came to see me. (Later they were divorced. She never ceased nor desisted to be very much in love with him and the fact that he shunted her off and married again didn't make any difference to her feelings. She was simply devoted to him. She was a remarkable woman.) She was working in the State Department. I can't seem to remember what she was doing, except it had to do with Latin America. She spoke very fluent Spanish and was a very cultivated woman in terms of Spanish literature.

Some way or the other I got started on the early discoveries along the American coasts, all the American coasts, and Muna said to me about that, "You know, this would make a marvelous theme to hold together some radio broadcasts which could be used for the entire continent, both continents. Every one of the American states went through the same sort of thing. The discoveries were different—and the extreme southern tip of Cape Horn is Magellan and it's a story by itself, but the discoveries in the North were largely English and Dutch and Scandinavian, but it's all the same sort of thing and the relation with the tribes in the interior came about in much the same way. The struggles were the same, the battles! You had a high degree of civilization in Central America, very primitive people in the far North and the far South."

This stayed with me, and I finally agreed to do it and I did do it. And I remember getting up at five in the morning, and working at it there.

There was obviously a great deal of work involved in research for these.

Here again Muna is the heroine. I did absolutely none of the research. By this time I'd known her quite well over a long period of time. I knew the way her mind worked. I knew I could trust anything that she told me; anything that she said was to be found in such and such a book was to be found in that book. She went back to the original records. I remember asking her for some English sea chanties or sailor songs of one kind or another and she came up with marvelous ones that are in number two, I think. "Wouldn't a wallet do well," and so forth. Beautiful songs. So that I could not possibly have done it in two years, even if I had nothing else to do, if somebody hadn't done the research for me. She gave me this stuff in a form in which I could use it. She didn't try to put it together. She just gave it to me in piles of sheets and organized so that Peruvian stuff was together, Mexican stuff together, and the relations between them were suggested.

Let's take "The Admiral," the first one, as an example. What would she have presented to you and how did you transform it into the play that we see?

Almost impossible for me now to recall this. This was the one period in my life in which I can forgive myself for forgetting as I do. I was the assistant secretary in charge of the San Francisco Conference, which was coming up in '45. I had all the cultural and also news relations outside this country of the State Department. The things that are now separate things, "The Voice of America" and so forth, were something that we sort of did with our left hands, insofar as we could do it at all! I was also engaged in things that I'd started in owi. It was a terribly crowded time and I just simply don't remember. It's a blank to me. I just know that those plays came out of it and I was astonished last year reading through them and finding that they're as good as they are.

Were most of the materials used in the preparation of the scripts in the Library of Congress, or did she have to use outside sources, or do you know? There's obviously an abundance of material. How did you decide on the subjects of the ten plays? How did you narrow down the material? Do those questions ring a bell at all?

I can just answer them in general terms. Muna knew the Library of Congress extremely well, knew how to handle it. The State Department also has a remarkable library and where she did her work I don't know. We didn't meet as often as I would have imagined we would, but we were very closely in touch on what we were, what I was doing. One thing suggested the next one, suggested the next one, and so forth. I'd hesitate to make any statements about it because I'd almost certainly be wrong.

Do you remember anything at all about the preparation involved for the broadcast? Did they assemble a repertory company of players, or do you know?

No, this was done by NBC. I was trying to remember the name of the man who had charge of it. I grew to dislike him very earnestly. But they did it quite well, I think.

Two of the plays, "Nat Bacon's Bones" and "Socorro: When Your Sons Forget," used poems that were written much earlier, published in 1933, in fact. Obviously you wrote the poems long before you wrote the plays. How did you decide to use them?

I think these are two brief balladlike poems which are to me quite successful. They came out of readings in early Spanish American and North American history. Nat Bacon, as we mentioned before, is a figure way back in the early eighteenth century in Virginia. The Socorro is part of the terrible struggle in Venezuela and what is now Venezuela and what is now Columbia.

"The Admiral" was the play included in The Best One-Act Plays of 1944. *Of the ten plays in the series, because you've read them, you said, fairly recently, would you have selected that play or would you have picked one of the others as perhaps the best of the series?*

That's the kind of question I can throw a little light on right now. I think "Between the Silence and the Surf" is one of my favorites. That's the one in which we have "Cleav let my tongue to my palat, / If I doo not in mind thee bear. / If I Jerusalem doo not / Above my chiefest joy prefer." The one I like the best of them all, however, is the Montezuma one, "The Discovery." I remember that we got out of one of the museums in New York some Aztec musical instruments made of stone, which we used in the broadcast.

How did the opportunity as assistant secretary of state come about? Was that in December '44, when President Roosevelt swept out the State Department?

I was in the State Department for almost a year. I went in December of '44. I resigned when Mr. Roosevelt died and my resignation was finally accepted in July. But it was August 1945 when I officially left.

You must have been tired of government and all government work. Why were you induced to accept a position in the State Department?

This relates to something that I can't explain. I know that what I'm about to say is true, but I have no memory of it. No memory at all. It appears that once free of O W I and once back in the Library of Congress, I had told Mr. Roosevelt that I thought I could be (this was while the war was still going on, of course) very much more useful as myself with a typewriter than I could in information; I knew that that was so. I couldn't be any use there anymore. So far as the Library was concerned, the Library reorganization was in a state where I thought it would carry on. Luther had it well in hand. Apparently I told him that I wanted to be relieved. I honestly felt a revulsion against all information work and I wanted, for Christ's sake, to get back and do some writing. I had been away from writing by that time for five or six years, except for public papers. All I remember is that I got home to Alexandria, where we lived, on a hot summer night, and the telephone rang and it was Ed Stettinius,[39] who didn't sound very happy and didn't sound very welcoming, but he said, "Mr. Roosevelt wants you to be one of my assistant secretaries of state." No great suggestions about when we would do what where, and he didn't even say, "Do you accept!" That's the first thing I remember.

Didn't you feel that the appointment as assistant secretary of state would delay your return to poetry even longer?

It obviously would, but Mr. Roosevelt apparently was going to be his own secretary of state. Ed Stettinius's appointment is thinkable only under those circumstances. He wanted to have help from a few people whose minds he knew and whose minds worked more or less as his did on certain points in the department. I think this was an idea that came to him, not in response to my request to be relieved because he certainly didn't relieve me; he put me into a much more difficult job than any I'd ever held before. I think that was probably how his mind worked.

Wasn't there some difficulty over your nomination at the Senate hearings?

The hearings were going very nicely, very pleasantly. This was before the Committee on Foreign Relations of the Senate, which handled all nominations for the State Department. That was a pretty good committee with Tom Connolly as the chairman of it. The Spanish issue had been thrashed out and I had simply taken the position that this country could not view a fascist takeover of Spain as something that was supportable or acceptable. We must all of us, naturally, support democratic institutions; democratic institutions had been set up and, of course, I was against the Franco forces. So was every other writer I knew, and most other decent people, I think. That was fairly heated, but there was no strength back of the criticism. They wanted my views on various other things. I didn't have any views.

And finally, after the thing had lasted all morning and well into the afternoon, Senator Bennett Champ Clark turned up. And he had in his hand this small volume, the size, shape, and color of which identified it to me. It was a volume of poems of mine, one of the first volumes I wrote. And Connolly saw him and said, "The senator have something to say?" And Senator Bennett Champ Clark said, "Well, since you asked me, yes. A simple inquiry. I would be interested to know whether this committee feels that a man who wrote a poem, which I am about to read you, is qualified to be assistant secretary of state of the United States of America." And he read a poem of mine, an undergraduate poem, a sonnet to my wife, Ada, not then my wife, and he gave it all the emphasis he could, and then he repeated his rhetorical question at the end. There was silence in the room and then Happy Chandler, who was the senator from Kentucky, a friend of mine in my days as Librarian, said, "Ah, Mr. Chairman, may I ask the witness a question?" (I don't know if he called me the witness or not.) And Connolly said yes, and he said, "Mr. MacLeish, was it left halfback or end you played on the famous Yale football team?" And I said, "Well, Senator, it was both; I was the universal substitute." And the senator said, "Thank you, thank you; I thought so." And that was the end of the whole thing!

Bennett Champ Clark retired and, one little additional note, David Chambers Mearns, who was the chief of the manuscript division of the Library of Congress and a remarkably well-read man, was at the hearing, and out of the tail of my eye I saw him skedaddle out of the room when Bennett Champ Clark opened the little volume and began to read. By the time I got back to the Library, he met me at the door. He said, "I thought so, that son of a bitch, I thought so. He, too, was an undergraduate poet! There's his volume!" That was beautiful!

*Did some of the issues that came up at the hearing involve J. Parnell Thomas
and his attack, which was based on your involvement in the Second Writers'
Congress?*

That's right. There was that meeting at Carnegie Hall we talked about before.
I remember it well because it's the only meeting I ever attended at which
Hemingway made a political speech. We got him to come up from Key West.
This was on the Spanish war. It was called by a Communist-backed and Com-
munist-dominated group of writers. I was chairman of the Writers' Congress
and at that meeting my remarks as chairman opening the meeting were to the
effect that I was perfectly aware of the political orientation of the people who
called the meeting, but that when it came to a thing like the Spanish war, with
its implications for another world war, I didn't care who I was with. It was the
people I was against who were important. And I repeated that position, more
or less, at the hearing. I don't think from the way the committee acted that the
suggestion that I was a Communist ever struck them as being in any way
serious. It would have been hard in view of the fact that I spent some years of
my life fighting the Communists on the *New Masses* with everything I had
except the ink bottle.

The Senate investigation is usually a routine procedure, in any case, is it not?

Oh, yes. All the candidates, if that's the right word for it, nominees, for
assistant secretaryships were called before the Foreign Relations Committee;
but the rest of them—Acheson, for example, who had already been in as assistant secretary of state before, Jimmy Dunn, a foreign service officer, and Will
Clayton, the darling of Texas, a very rich Texas multimillionaire, a very
capable man incidentally—they kept for about three minutes. They kept me
for a day. With Nelson Rockefeller they took a little time, too, but that was
just for the fun of asking him embarrassing questions.

Why was the job with the State Department so difficult?

First of all, it was in the State Department in wartime, with major decisions
to make every morning at 9:00, the kind of decision that doesn't come up
once in four years in the State Department in peace time. Second, my office
was, as I said, a new invention; it never existed before. The State Department's having an ambassador to the American people was an odd conception,
and one had to work that out, and that took some doing.

Your friendship with your colleague Dean Acheson preceded this whole period, didn't it?

Well, it did, except that during this period it became really a very close friendship. He was in my class at Yale and he was in my class at the law school except that I went off to the war and didn't graduate until the year after he did. Although we were good friends as people use that phrase, very satisfactory good friends, it wasn't until those Washington years that we began working together with each other and against each other, because we disagreed about almost everything, under conditions of stress and with a great deal at stake and with heavy responsibilities. We had almost a year there together in the State Department. The marvelous friendship which came out of that was also something for which I have to thank those years.

And you were working on the same issues.

In the State Department we were, most of the time. The one time we were ever thrown together, really, on an important issue, was the time we were both wrong, and both had to come round to acknowledging it. And it was a very important issue. It was the issue of what to do about the emperor of Japan. Dean and I both felt, which was remarkable to me because our opinions about such matters would naturally have been almost 180 degrees apart, we both felt that the emperor was demonstrably responsible for the war, demonstrably responsible for the Japanese actions at Pearl Harbor, and that we could not, in common decency, agree to terms of peace which did not bring the responsibility home to him. Well, we were wrong, as history proved. Even General MacArthur, who was wrong about almost everything, was righter than we were about that. One of the last letters Dean ever wrote me was about that, about our wrongness and our responsibility for being wrong.

What other decisions do you remember as being very difficult?

That reminds me of Scotty Reston's question of me when I finally got free of the State Department.[40] He came around and said, "Mr. Secretary, have you ever seen a policy made?" That's a hard question to answer: Did I ever see a policy made? Before I became assistant secretary of state, for a number of years I belonged to a committee on the terms of the peace, to which Mr. Roosevelt appointed me, which met in the State Department with Sumner Welles, the under secretary, as chairman, and representatives of five or six other departments, a rather small group, about twelve people, which took up, one after the other, questions of our policy toward the peace in geographical terms around the world and sounded just like the situation probably at the end of the Crimean War and the end of every other war with decisions in terms of geography instead of decisions in terms of the human spirit.

When you were in the State Department, didn't you direct a series of broadcasts? Wasn't Alger Hiss on one of them?

Oh, the broadcasts, yes! Someone suggested it; it was not my suggestion. I remember Dean Acheson laughing his head off over the thought of doing what we eventually did: a series of broadcasts from the State Department explaining the State Department to the American people. This was in '44–'45. There was one famous occasion. John Dickey, who later was the president of Dartmouth,[41] was the head of an office under me which made him in effect my deputy and right-hand man and everything else during all the time that I was there. He's a wonderful man with the most infectious laugh I've ever heard from anybody in the world and one of the wisest men I know, perhaps the wisest. John Dickey tells a story about our first broadcast. Ed Stettinius, who was excessively dumb, was in Mexico and somebody had come up with the brilliant idea that we would put on the secretary of state in Mexico and he would talk to the American people about whatever it was he was thinking about down in Mexico. I've forgotten it myself, but John tells the story about it. Dean and he and I were together in the control room in Washington, and the announcer for the show announced it, described what it was going to be and said, "And we now take you to Mexico City where the secretary of state of the United States, the Honorable Edward S. Stettinius, will address you," and the usual palaver. Then a long silence, and then Ed Stettinius's voice saying, "Where in the hell did I put those papers!" I think we got about three programs out before it exploded of its own power! I don't remember that Alger Hiss was on it or had anything to do with it, but maybe he did.

He was on one broadcast according to one of the New York Times *articles of that period.*

He probably would have been because he, of course, represented the State Department at the Dumbarton Oaks conversations[42] which preceded the San Francisco Conference and prepared the American position for it and also prepared a lot of other positions. This would have been a natural thing to do at that time; I don't remember it, but it just seems to be very probable. If the *Times* said it happened, it happened.

Did you have any reaction to the Hiss incident—to what happened or what was discovered?

Hiss at the time was pure as the driven snow.[43] To me he was the most complete reactionary I ever saw in my life. He was obdurately opposed to anything that he hadn't himself thought up. He was not an easy man to work with, in other words. The mere thought of Alger's being a revolutionary used to give me hysterics and it still does. There's something very, very funny about that whole story. I mean first of all, the information that was supposed to be in that bloody pumpkin was the kind of information that any postman in the State Department had. It was of no interest to anybody. Why didn't somebody at some point read it? If you've ever read it, you'd know what I mean. But nobody did, not during the trial; they were so poisoned by McCarthy they thought that anything that had been marked secret must be secret for some reason, not realizing that every bureaucrat in Washington uses that little stamp to protect his own hide!

You were also writing various reports and pamphlets during the war. For example, an article in Newsweek *during the forties concerns a report you had made about the mistreatment of Negroes in the army, with recommendations for changes in regulations. There was quite a reaction to that report. Do you recall it?*

I remember it very vividly. While I was assistant secretary of state, there was a great deal of indignation among blacks about the treatment of black soldiers in army camps. It turned out that the army had some very unpalatable regulations, and the blacks were deeply concerned. General Marshall wasn't able to talk to them. I think it was his suggestion that one way to take the heat off a bit was to divert it to somebody else, namely me, in my famous role as a goat. This scene I remember very vividly; I'm in my office. The trouble is, it doesn't look like my State Department office—that's why I was puzzling about dates. I'm in my office and the delegation is led in and the leader is a black woman of fifty or sixty years of age with extremely long arms and almost the ugliest face I've ever seen in my life, but articulate as an angel, who began with some very cool, careful, and objective readings of army regulations. She then went through the reassurances she'd had from various officers and named them all the way up. She stated, "Nothing whatever has happened; there has been nothing but talk. Black men are dying in this war; we want some kind of responsible consideration." Then she proceeded to blast the administration; she didn't blast Mr. Roosevelt but she blasted the army personnel right to the top, right to the untouchable great man Mr. Marshall, and then she turned on me. She knew quite a lot about me, she informed me, as a matter of fact, and she said, "That is all, sir, unless you have something to say." I said, "Well I don't quite see what I can say." So she moved her delegation out of the room and then she closed the door and she came back, and her face had the most beautiful expression on it that you can imagine, and she said, "Mr. MacLeish, your mother opened the door for me." She said, "I am Mary McLeod Bethune,[44] and your mother opened the door for me at Hull House in Chicago many years ago. I owe her everything I am." And she said, "I just wanted to say that," and she walked out.

Once you got into the State Department you became active in the formation of UNESCO in the UN. That idea had been going on for quite some time, hadn't it?

That had been going on. There was a man with a curious German name and a passionate addiction to the idea of a world educational body. He'd been pounding away at it for quite a while with the State Department, and a lot of preliminary spade work had been done. I got excited about the old dream of a republic of learning, a republic of the mind, a republic of the heart; and as we approached the end of the war, as it became apparent that the war was going to be won, it did seem that there must be some way of having a peace that would be more than a nonbelligerent legal situation which would simply be the end of something and the beginning of nothing. So why not be something. I was Johnny-come-lately, but when I resigned—which I did immediately after Roosevelt's death. At that point everybody hands in his resignation. All political appointees do—when Mr. Truman accepted my resignation as assistant secretary of state he immediately made me chairman of the American delegation to the London Conference, which took place at the end of that summer, the end of '45.[45] So I was deep in UNESCO from the end of my service in the State Department through to the next spring. Most of that time I was out of the country, either in London or Paris. Then I went on as American representative on the council of UNESCO for another couple of years and then got free altogether.

How were you involved in setting up the San Francisco Conference?[46]

My office was the State Department area that ran it—all the janitor work. We lined up hotels, we got all the facilities. I hired a man who turned out to be an absolute genius; I've forgotten his name but not my debt of gratitude to him. He did the whole thing; he went out there and within a month he had more real estate in San Francisco under lease to the United States government than you could count. I was out there and I had an assistant with me. His name was Adlai Stevenson. Adlai and I lived in the Mark Hopkins. Thank God for the foggy climate of San Francisco because it enabled us to eat breakfast at 6:30 in the morning and feel good, instead of feeling awful!

A very formal picture of the San Francisco delegation shows Edward Stettinius and a number of other people—but you weren't there.

No, I wasn't part of the delegation. I was assistant secretary of state, and I sat in on all the delegation meetings and had the great pleasure of watching a character named John Foster Dulles[47] do his spade work out there. My God, how I disliked that man!

There was some discussion apparently during that meeting about having somebody like Archie MacLeish write the preamble to the United Nations constitution.

Well, there may have been some talk about that, but what I did write at Mrs. Roosevelt's request was the Declaration of Human Rights. Not the whole thing, not the legal part, but the preamble to that. That was supposed to be a dead secret; I never mentioned it to anybody—but Mrs. Roosevelt, before she died, in one of those columns she used to write, told that story. So I felt that I was thereby released.

At a luncheon in about 1945, as you were talking about the future of the world after the war, you said that a group of men had been working on a charter for something like the United Nations for several years.

I guess that's the Dumbarton Oaks conversations. I can't tell you how far back those meetings went. I don't know about before Pearl Harbor. Mr. Roosevelt was very clear in his mind from the beginning of the "phony war"[48] that there would be war. A great deal of very long distance preparation was going on but whether the discussion of the United Nations goes back that far I couldn't say; I would doubt it.[49]

At a Theta Sigma Phi[50] luncheon, you were quoted to the effect that various consultants had joined together since Pearl Harbor to draft a charter for an organization like the UN. The work done by these people enabled the Senate to proceed as speedily as it did because so much of the work had been done.

I knew much more about it then than I do now. I remember after the adoption of the United Nations was a reality, I was addressing an organization of women reporters. They have quite an active organization in Washington, or did have then. They wanted to know what the UN was or was going to be. Partly I suppose it was the fatigue and partly the enormous relief as a result of the adoption of the plan, but whatever it was, midway through what was a business article account of what had been going on in San Francisco, I broke down. Suddenly my eyes filled with tears, I couldn't talk, and they were surprised; what was it in those statistics that so moved me? I said to them I can't go on talking about this; I have to talk to you about what really happened. For the first time, we have a positive result of victory in a war. We are going to impose something that will make war very much more difficult and more unlikely. And you're women, and I just feel I have to talk about that. I don't want to talk about the rest of it! I'll write you a letter about the rest of it. I remember that. And that's the way a lot of us felt; Adlai felt that way too. Adlai used to say to me, "You and I were just suckers, weren't we?" Well, we weren't quite suckers, and he didn't think we were.

Do you still feel the United Nations holds promise?

It's hard to feel that now. It's become a political football used largely by the third world for propaganda purposes. But if you stopped its activities, the minor organizations of the UN, not the UN itself, but the World Health Organization, for example. If you stopped the World Health, if you stopped UNESCO, if you stopped any one of the principal active agencies of the UN, there would be disaster. It would be unbearable. It has become essential.

How did Truman respond to your resignation?

When I resigned, I put in with my resignation to Mr. Truman a letter giving him personal reasons why I really wanted to be relieved. And I have a letter from him out there which sounds as though he might have wanted to keep me on. I don't think so because he never quite got over his feelings about me at the time when he was a senator attacking O F F. He held me personally responsible for that.

Was he really the way he's being presented on stage now?[51]

Oh, he's just like that. Harry Truman didn't have any other persona; he just had Harry Truman! Totally himself all the time. And Bess was totally herself. Dean Acheson—two men could never in the history of the world have been so unlike each other!—Dean absolutely adored him.

Thinking back over the various people that you worked with and knew during that period, are there some that you feel have not been given the kind of attention that they should have been, who maybe had a greater impact upon what's followed since the war, the movements of the country since then?

I don't know about impact, but there's no question whatever in my mind— and several of my friends who went through the same experience I think would say exactly the same thing—that the great man of that period, not the most influential man, not the most powerful man, not the man that one would most like to be with, but the honorable man and honorable Roman was Marshall.[52] Marshall was a very, very great man. He was sort of a model for a great man. His influence, of course, was nothing like Mr. Roosevelt's. Mr. Roosevelt was the president if a man ever was, and he was a man I dearly loved. But Marshall was just a remarkable man, a man of total integrity, total responsibility, and great intellectual power. The one thing he wanted to be was commander of the Allied forces at the end; he wanted to command that vast army in the field. It was he who made the decision that it should be Eisenhower[53] and he knew perfectly well that Eisenhower was not a great general. But all the aspects of the situation worked out that way; the man who commanded had to be an American; he had to be an American who would get along with the Allied commander, even Monty, even Montgomery.[54] The only man who could do that was Eisenhower. He knew it, so he made the decision. The president thanked him.

Where do you feel that we've come to as a nation since the war?

A Boston radio station is coming tomorrow to talk about Mr. Carter's first hundred days. They want to talk to me because I'm almost the only man alive who was around in Roosevelt's first hundred days! There's a very obvious comparison, and there is a very radical and dramatic difference, of course. Both men took the presidency at the time of great public danger with a potential disaster facing the nation, but the differences are remarkable. In Roosevelt's case, everybody, even at the end Hoover himself, recognized that it was a disaster, that it was a danger; you couldn't live in the Depression without knowing what the Depression was; you could smell it, you could feel it, you could see it. It was the horrible moment in the history of the country. Whereas in Mr. Carter's case, according to the polls, half the country is just totally unwilling to face the fact that we may be in an even deeper disaster, eight, ten, twenty, thirty years from now.

The second great difference is that in Mr. Roosevelt's case, the danger was man-made as a result of human stupidity, human greed, human irresponsibility of an extraordinary nature. In Mr. Carter's case, it is in large part human, but nature gets also involved, so that there is that old struggle with nature. Insofar as Mr. Roosevelt was concerned, Mr. Roosevelt was exactly what the doctor had ordered. What he called for in that acceptance speech in Chicago, you may remember, the speech in which he talked about the New Deal for the American people, was a new order of competence and courage; and that's what he got. The phrase which really won the battle the moment it was spoken was the phrase in his inaugural: "We have nothing to fear but fear itself." What had to be done, he did; he put an end to fear; he acted, he took action. He was able to deal in terms of understanding with the kind of people, the arrogant rich, who are going to be a difficulty for Mr. Carter.

In Carter's case, you also need, as in Roosevelt's case, somebody who can act. Carter has acted; he will act. You also need a new order of competence and courage and Carter's got that and he will do it. But you need something more; you need somebody who can lead the country in making a deliberate change in this industrial organization which will require scientific and technological knowledge of the highest order, and Carter is the first American president in history who can speak the scientific and engineering vocabulary effectively. The thing that is lacking is the thing that you just referred to.

There was a horrible television incident a couple of days ago: a rich Texan, saying that he wasn't going to give up his Cadillac and his wife wasn't going to give up hers and his daughter wouldn't give up hers. That he liked to drive Cadillacs, that he liked the prestige of being seen driving a Cadillac. Just think what Mr. Roosevelt would have done with that man! He would have crucified him so high that shame would have filled the hearts of his friends. Mr. Carter can't do that. That's the reason we're going to pray that FDR might return.

Perhaps what you're saying is that you feel a lot more optimistic right now than you did two years ago, three years ago?

Yes, I feel a lot more optimistic. I really think that Carter is capable of action, and by God he has already assumed and exercised leadership. He is the leader of our country without any question and he also is the world leader; he has no competitor. All these mediocrities—from the Soviets to Japan and back!

Was it all worth it? Those years in government?

The Library of Congress experience down to the outbreak of war certainly was for me. I'm assuming, because the evidence seems so to indicate, that it was of some value to the Library of Congress as well. I don't think that it is too vain to say that, because I think it did work out and some things were accomplished. But I think that even for me, it was a very valuable thing because the Library of Congress is Jefferson's library. If you are at all vulnerable to Mr. Jefferson (I am profoundly vulnerable to him), you feel his influence there all the time and I learned things about the government of the United States which I never would have learned if I hadn't been in it, in it in a very special sense.

I was not in the executive branch. I didn't have responsibility of any kind, but I was in a position in the government from which the operations of the government became very visible and very clear and in some ways very disturbing and in some ways, given the war and given the character of the people who were involved in the government, very exhilarating, filling one with pride and admiration and love. I think that my passion for the Republic, which is very real with me and realer as I grow older, would never have been inspired if I hadn't been in the government for a period of six years. Or at least if it had been, it would have been for reasons of ignorance, not for reasons of knowledge.

I did have a great deal of knowledge of what was going on. And then again as a human experience, to be in touch with men whose greatness you could feel and who, even at the age I then was, let's see, I was forty-seven when I became Librarian, and even at that age, which is an age at which you don't think much about human greatness or much of it, the figures in Washington—the president, Colonel Stimson, General Marshall, the people on the Court, Felix and Hugo Black, some of the people even in the information community, particularly Elmer Davis—these were associations which were demonstrations of what it was possible for men to do.

The realization, which is as clear in my mind now as it was on the morning after the Battle of the Coral Sea, that we could have lost that war and were within inches of losing it, never left me in Washington. And what I watched going on—particularly Marshall, of whom I saw a good deal, and Stimson, and in the White House—has left me with a conviction that even this vast hetero-geneous, largely cynical, unbelieving society in which we live is capable, really, of governing itself and can find the men to do it. So all that was the kind of enrichment that you don't hope for from most experiences. And the dis-illusionment, the frustrations, the moments of defeat and so forth, were nothing compared to that. I think what I'm trying to say is this. What would have been a kind of wishful optimism, a hopeful optimism that Jefferson was right, the hope that Lincoln was right, became in the crucible, because it was the crucible, the experience of conviction. I know it works!

As a man and as an American, certainly, you feel that it had a very positive effect on you. How about as a poet, if you can separate those things at all? You didn't write much poetry during that period.

I wrote only one poem while I was in Washington and that was "The Young Dead Soldiers."

The Young Dead Soldiers
for Lieutenant Richard Myers

The young dead soldiers do not speak.
Nevertheless, they are heard in the still houses: who has not heard them?
They have a silence that speaks for them at night and when the clock
  counts.
They say: We were young. We have died. Remember us.
They say: We have done what we could but until it is finished it is not
  done.
They say: We have given our lives but until it is finished no one can know
  what our lives gave.
They say: Our deaths are not ours; they are yours; they will mean what
  you make them.
They say: Whether our lives and our deaths were for peace and a new
  hope or for nothing we cannot say; it is you who must say this.
They say: We leave you our deaths. Give them their meaning.
We were young, they say. We have died. Remember us.

I wrote that in seven minutes at my desk at about five minutes of eight one morning when I was called up to the Treasury and asked for something that they could use. They were running a pure propaganda operation, for propaganda reasons. I thought I had to respond to this request because it came from Secretary Morgenthau.[55] So I sat down and wrote it and then looked at it in the afternoon and discovered it was a poem. And never sent it to him. That was the only poem I wrote there. It wasn't until two years after I left Washington when Mr. Roosevelt died that I was able to begin again with *Actfive* which was a conscious attempt to try to turn that whole Washington experience into its meaning, but an attempt which I think failed because I didn't realize then as I do now what the meaning really was, so I somewhat flubbed it.

But I think that whatever happens to a man committed to his art in his life, provided it really happens to him, can only be grist to his mill because poetry does involve, must involve, the whole of human experience, not simply certain aspects of human life, certain emotional situations, love or grief. It must involve the whole of life to be itself whole. And this means even something like the experience of working as an editor of *Fortune* for six or seven years, the knowledge it involved of the continent, the way the Republic works, the way the economy works—things that I never would have thought of, left to myself. That became enormously fruitful to me. What little I know about the continent, which is more than quite a lot of people know, I owe to *Fortune*. And what I know about the Republic and what I know about the innards of American history, I owe to those years in Washington. So that although I was, in effect, silenced as a poet for almost a decade at a time which should have been the most productive time in my life, I think it was useful and well done and a proper loss. If it was a loss. A proper preparation. I really do believe that if the art of poetry is, as I deeply believe it to be, the art of making sense of the chaos of human experience, it's not a bad thing to see a lot of chaos.

The Harvard Years

1946	Chairman of the American delegation to the First General Conference of UNESCO, Paris. First American member of the executive council of UNESCO. Decorated commander in the French Legion of Honor. Elected to the American Academy of Arts and Letters.
1947	Awarded Encomienda Order el Sol del Peru.
1948	*Actfive and Other Poems* (poetry). Random House.
1949–62	Boylston Professor of Rhetoric and Oratory at Harvard University.
1950	*Poetry and Opinion: The Pisan Cantos of Ezra Pound* (prose). University of Illinois Press.
1951	*Freedom Is the Right to Choose* (prose). Beacon Press.
1952	*Collected Poems, 1917–1952*. Houghton Mifflin Co. *The Trojan Horse* (verse play). Houghton Mifflin Co.
1953–56	President, American Academy of Arts and Letters.
1953	Pulitzer Prize for *Collected Poems*. Bollingen Prize for Poetry. National Book Award in Poetry. *This Music Crept by Me upon the Waters* (verse play). Harvard University Press.
1954	*Songs for Eve* (poetry). Houghton Mifflin Co.
1958	*J.B.* (verse play). Houghton Mifflin Co.
1959	Antoinette Perry ("Tony") Award in Drama for *J.B.* Pulitzer Prize in Drama for *J.B.*
1961	*Poetry and Experience* (prose). Houghton Mifflin Co.

What were those first years like after you retired from government service?

When Mr. Roosevelt died, I submitted my resignation, which Mr. Truman accepted with, I think, a great deal of pleasure 'though he wrote me a beautiful letter about it when he was sure! We then came up here to Conway, and I went through something—like what happens to deep-sea divers after rising from the depths with the bends ahead of them! They have to walk or be carried into a compression chamber and decompress themselves. Well, that's what I was doing. I didn't realize it at the time, but I'd been living for almost five years at absolutely top pressure. The Library of Congress was one long crisis while I was in it because we were reorganizing the whole thing. And then I had the Office of Facts and Figures to add to that; then I was also working in the White House; then I was working at the White House and the Library of Congress and OWI. And then finally I was assistant secretary of state in the worst years of the war. And when I got back up here, having thought that I was looking forward eagerly to release, I found myself in the state that the deep-sea diver does. I can remember fall 1945 (about this season), going out and chopping down saplings and building fires in the woods and anything I could think of to have a purpose—a nearby purpose. That lasted for close to a year, and it was a pretty bad year.

I've since discovered that a great many of my colleagues in the government at that time, though loath to confess it, would admit under pressure that exactly the same thing had happened to a great many of them! Coming out of public office and trying to rediscover yourself for your own purposes is an experience that nobody has ever written about because it's so personal and so dull. You're bored stiff! You were in the middle of a crisis which could go either way. You could hardly get to the White House telephone early enough in the morning to find out what had happened overnight. And suddenly you're up here and the telephone never rings! But that passed in '46, and we then spent our winters in New York. We had an apartment in the Dakota Hotel across Central Park, and Ada started doing some work again and I began writing *Actfive*. Once I got really into *Actfive* I was all right. But it was one, actually two, very, very bad years!

So the call from Harvard really was something that was a good thing when it came?

Yes. That's a very just remark. It was a very good thing when it came. Although actually it was better than I knew. I had no way of knowing how valuable it was.

It was in 1949 that you accepted the position of Professor of Rhetoric and Oratory at Harvard.

It's *Boylston* Professor of Rhetoric and Oratory. Rhetoric was the standard term for what we would refer to as literature, the old Puritan tradition, centering of course on preachers, and therefore on the art of bringing people together through the Word. Rhetoric was very useful, as useful as it was to the Jesuits! The term was simply a normal and natural term. The first incumbent, John Quincy Adams, had no awkwardness about it—read his speech upon installing himself as Professor of Rhetoric and Oratory.

How did the appointment come about?

I have no idea! You know how Harvard appointments go. The departments are aware of their needs and report to the dean of the Faculty of the Arts and Sciences that they need a professor in such and such an area. Then there's sort of a preliminary inquiry to make sure that there's money and that they really do need him, and then they make a proposal, and at that point, the president (and this was one of Jim Conant's[1] great contributions) calls together an ad hoc committee, which is a committee to spend an entire day going over this poor devil's qualifications. And those people include one or two people in Harvard (while I was Boylston Professor, I sat on three or four ad hoc committees; everybody does), but most of them come from outside and it's those people outside who are really savage. They're earning their keep, asking nasty questions. There's no personal confrontation, but there is a tremendous amount of examination. And if the ad hoc committee approves, then there's a serious proposal, which goes to the Board of Overseers, and it's at that point that they call the candidate—he's not really a candidate! he doesn't know anything about it! I didn't know anything about it—the proposed incumbent, to find out whether he'd accept.

And the first I knew about it was a call from Harry Levin,[2] broaching the general subject. He was commissioned by the department to approach me. So I came up to Boston. I was then just four years out of government service and the last thing I wanted to do was to tie myself up in something else. But I respected Harry Levin very much and I had a very, very deep feeling about Harvard and I was suitably flattered by this when Harry told me about it. We spent an evening talking to each other about it and I went off and beat my head against various walls and finally decided that I would do it. There were various other reasons for this, too, that I don't need to go into—some of them financial. And the Board of Overseers acted suitably and with deliberation and appointed me. And then that summer (this all happened in the spring of the year) I went down to Harvard to "find out" what I was going to do, which is the way I would have put it at that time. I turned up in Cambridge in the middle of summer and went first to the then-chairman of the English department (I'd never met him before), and he was very busy and rather short with me. And I told him what I'd come down for and he said, "Well, don't come to me. You don't know what a chairman of a department is at Harvard, apparently. He's just the fellow who pushes around the mimeograph sheets! I don't know what you ought to do! Good-bye."

Then I went to see Matty Matthiessen,[3] who's a Yale man, and a "Bones" man at that, and I thought he'd be friendly. Turned out later that he'd been violently opposed to my appointment! Matty was polite, but he said, "I have no suggestions. How would you like to teach my Shakespeare course?" Well, I had just sense enough to know that I'd have to cut his arms off at the elbows to do that!

So I went to see a number of people I knew and I ended finally with the provost, Paul Buck, who was a wonderful character! Jim was in Washington almost all the time, even as late as that. Well, he was in Germany and Washington. He was all over the lot! But he wasn't at Harvard! And Paul was the real president at Harvard. And I waited outside his office for quite a long time, having spoken to his secretary, who said she'd see if he could talk to me, and, finally, after waiting out there in the hallway for about an hour, he came out and he was obviously busy and I apologized for interrupting him and told him why I'd come down and he heard me out, just barely heard me out. When I got to a breathing space, Paul said, "When Harvard appoints a man a full professor, let alone Boylston Professor, it expects him to know what he's going to do!" Turned around and disappeared!

By this time I really had the wind out. I hadn't the faintest idea what to do! So I got hold of two Harvard professors whom I'd gotten to know very well during the Nieman years. One was Harry Levin, and the other was Perry

Miller, historian and professor of English, and I got them and their wives to come up here one weekend. And we sat under the apple tree out there on the west terrace and talked about various things, Perry Miller making a lot of noise, Harry saying virtually nothing. Finally, feeling even more desperate than ever, I leaned back in my chair and closed my eyes, and Harry said, "Archie, I don't think you understand Harvard. You are talking as though you thought Harvard was run by somebody called 'they' or 'them,' who are going to tell you what to do. There aren't any such people! Harvard is an institution," he said, "and I'll tell you what kind of institution it is. And I'll tell you how to answer your question. When you get up tomorrow morning, polish up the mirror on your bathroom cabinet; get it good and bright and take a good long look into the mirror. That's who runs Harvard, so far as you're concerned." It's completely true! I mean, it's a ridiculous statement which would be denied by anybody, but it's really true.

So I then began to think, "All right; if that's the situation, and nobody will guide me, what do I want to do?" And I came to the conclusion that what I really wanted to do was put together everything I'd ever wondered, or guessed, or hoped, or imagined about the art of poetry, and try it out on young minds and see what I could learn. The hell with them! They could get to be Boylston professors later! I was going to find out! And that's just what I did and it turned out to be the richest experience of my life. By university statute, I *had* to do the final creative writing course, so-called (I hate that name)—but for myself, I did what I would have called, if somebody hadn't previously hooked the name, "The Name and Nature of Poetry." I wanted to do that course and I changed it every year.[4]

How did you organize that class? What kinds of assignments did you give?

I started out, stupidly, by lecturing and trying to get in touch with members of my class by seeing them briefly at the close of the class or having them come 'round to the office. There was a lot of resistance and hostility, let me tell you. It never worked! And after a year or two, I developed a system which worked marvelously for me, and a number of my former students in that course went on to teach themselves and told me that they had used it. It came down to this: each student was told to buy himself a moderate supply of 6"×8" cards and confine his use of those cards to one a week. I think the course was meeting on Tuesdays and Thursdays, and on Saturdays only when there was some good reason why we should. The requirement was that they should accomplish their assignment before the first meeting of the course for that week. The assignment was a single poem. It could be, and it was on one occasion each year that I did this course, "The Rime of the Ancient Mariner," which takes some reading, but also it could be "O, Western Wind," which is maybe twenty-five words long. And what they were supposed to do was to get down onto a 6" × 8" card, preferably one side of it, a reading—their reading—of the poem, and get it to me the day before the meeting of the course.

Then I used their cards to teach the course. It was a dialogue that had already taken place on their side. They had already committed themselves. I had the unfair advantage of the last word. But nevertheless they were involved. I didn't read a card in class unless it had something to say that was different from what other cards had to say. I would start out with the poem and read the poem and then read it again and then read it again. Not the "Rime"— that would have taken too much time, but the usual ones—and then go at the reading of it, interpretation of it (interpretation's not the right word), and compose, out of the cards, which I'd already been through and marked up and put in order, a position which I felt was theirs. "If you don't all agree to this, at least some of you do because this is where you are." And this would start a discussion going that would take your hair off because they were committed. Their names were never mentioned—I never abused that privilege—but they knew what they thought and even when the course was as big as 200, I'd include enough of their opinions so they all felt involved.

One example will throw a lot of light on the course. Anne Morrow Lindbergh[5] had a daughter named Anne Lindbergh, who was in Radcliffe and she came there after I'd been teaching for about two or three years. That particular year, we devoted a lot of time to Emily Dickinson. Largely due to Anne, the discussions were so rewarding that I couldn't bear to stop them. We took about half a year on Dickinson, whereas I expected to spend no more than a month! She had a natural affinity for and comprehension of Emily Dickinson! They just felt alike. She looked a little like Emily, although she was much prettier than Emily ever was. But she had the same sort of quality. I learned more about Emily Dickinson from Anne than from any Amherst professor or world critic I've ever read and much more than I'd ever learned from myself. This, also, incidentally, changed her writing. She found herself committed to something that deeply meant everything to her.

And I think there's a great deal to be said for it as a very simple teaching method. It's a teaching method which involves every man and woman in front of you in that room and involves them permanently. They stay involved. I've had letters about that course as recently as last week. The author of the letter said, "The only two people I remember teaching at Harvard are (somebody I never heard of) and you. This is a confession on my part because obviously I should remember a great many others but you two I remember, and not only do I remember you but I also remember what happened in your course." I said, "That's the important thing! Not what I said, but what it meant to the student."

You would assign a poem to everybody, say on Thursday. By next Monday, they had to have in to you, on a 6"×8" card, their reading of the poem. Just that. You would have to take all those cards, read them through, sort them out. That must have been a very difficult thing to do.

You couldn't sleep that night.[6] But it was worth it. You read them. You would always discard a certain number of dead cards, either because the student was feeling dull that day or because he wasn't any good ever, anyway, or something. But you didn't get rid of many. And it would leave quite a lot. Then you would consider what it was in each card that was usable to your purposes. And you would underline and then the underlinings would suggest how you were going to approach the analysis of the experience rather than the poem. And then you would arrange them in order so that you would move from one to the other without taking a long time to explain in between. And you got to be pretty good at it because it's not a complicated operation. It's simply a rather laborious one. It was a very hard course to teach—much harder than lecturing. But it was tremendously rewarding! There are two former students of mine, who, incidentally, married each other after leaving Harvard, teaching at Brown, who have been using the device for their entire teaching lives. And when I went down there to read over a year ago, they descended on me and said, "If you ever want testimony that the thing goes on working, we'll give it to you!"

What kind of a preparation did the student have to have in order to get into that course?

He just had to put down his name. He didn't have to be a senior, but he couldn't be a freshman, except I did have some freshmen. I'm not very clear in my mind how this worked, but I know there was no requirement in advance. I just took anybody who came along, whereas in the writing course in order to select students I had to do a lot of reading of manuscripts. But in the poetry course there was no requirement like that.

Did you find some poets easier to handle in a classroom than others?

By easy, do you mean certain to attract the attention of the class and to excite them? Yes, there are. Rimbaud is extraordinarily effective. Keats becomes enormously effective. At the beginning, they don't see it. Since his versification and his diction are so out of their experience, they feel that he's stuffy and a bit pedantic, but the cure for that is right at hand. You just say, "Spend Tuesday reading Keats's letters and don't come in here until you've read the last letter." That's the end of that. Then they're mad about him! Rilke[7] is difficult although you can find, even among undergraduates who have no German, men and women who belonged to Rilke's family; they belonged to his life; they belonged to his suffering. I never permitted myself, of course, to attack the great insolvable mountain of Shakespeare, but I'm sure that Shakespeare would respond to this thing if you had an awful lot of time.

Did anybody ever try to tell you, "A poem is a poem. I can read into it anything I want to read into it. It's my interpretation and my interpretation's as good as anybody else's"?

I've run into that, but in this method we're talking about, you've got a man to convey himself through the written word with a reading of a poem which he justifies. He soon gets over talking that way because it's perfectly apparent to him that he cannot take "O, Western Wind" and say it's really a poem about fire danger in Idaho! By the way, that course is the matrix out of which my book *Poetry and Experience* came. That's a sort of a summary of everything I learned. What anybody else may have learned, I don't know.

Were those actual lectures—Poetry and Experience?

They were lectures. I changed my lectures every year. I've never been able to give a lecture twice. I wish to God I could! But I can't. But I saved them so that, at the end of this period, I had twelve years of lectures on the same subject with different poets and different approaches. And in my last year I offered, in addition to the course, thirteen public lectures at Harvard, and those thirteen lectures were made out of this whole body of material. Because the lectures as given year by year, although they weren't completely written out, were, to all intents and purposes, completely written out. That is, the essence of what I was going to deal with was not only indicated by a note or a reminder, it was actually written out on the page.

Now, if you're astonished when I say that I offered it, I'm going to have to remind you that at Harvard a professor can do anything he wants. I just took advantage of Harry Levin's advice to me. I decided I ran Harvard. So I put all that together and announced that I was going to give a series of university lectures in the Poetry Room in the Lamont Library, which the Poetry Room had agreed to let me do, at a certain time. From the first lecture we had to move across to Emerson Hall, where there was an auditorium: there were just too many people who wanted to come. Ada had a seat, but she gave it up to a student and didn't want to stand there in the crowd, so she went outside. She was going by and there were students hanging on the outsides of the windows. Ada heard one student on the ground say to one of the students at the window, "Hey, what's going on in there?" The student up in the window said, "The second coming!" So then we moved it over to Sanders.

When I had gotten halfway through, I had a very serious operation and I had to quit and the book is truncated. It's shorter than I intended to make it, but I just didn't have the strength to go back to it afterward, so I finished the last two chapters, the Rimbaud and Keats, and off they went. *Poetry and Experience* begins with words as sounds; then it goes to words as signs; and then it goes to images and metaphors, and that is the end of the first section. And the second section is "The shape of meaning." First of all, there is "the private world," the poems of Emily Dickinson, and "the public world," which is Yeats. Then chapter seven is the antiworld, that is the poems of Rimbaud, and Keats, the arable world, and that's the end of it. So all the lectures that I gave at Harvard in that course on the name and nature of poetry were here sort of boiled down and the essentials were put together, the essentials I'd been trying to talk about all those years.

In your writing course you screened the students. Were these students who were interested in writing poetry?

Not necessarily poetry. I had a lot of fiction people. But before we get into that, I started to say, when you mentioned rhetoric—one year, sort of in the middle of this thing, I decided that there ought to be a course in exegetical writing at Harvard at a high level, not just the kind of daily themes which turn up in the freshman course on writing. And I offered a course in rhetoric and was dumbfounded when only one Harvard undergraduate applied for it. It was filled with law school students! So I was teaching a law school course before I got through! And I never taught it again. It was not rewarding. At least I got nothing out of it and I don't think you can teach well something you aren't getting something out of.

How did you go about teaching writing?

My theory of what I was doing was that I was providing an audience for fifteen students who didn't have readers, being unknown writers and maybe not writers at all. The only service I could give them was to react totally honestly as an audience, and this meant that I had to give a great deal of time, personally, to students. The course met twice a week in my office, which was up on the top of Widener, at four o'clock in the afternoon and lasted as long as it lasted—sometimes way into the evening and sometimes only a couple of hours, and the method was the only possible one, I think, which was to have the particular student take over with his novel or whatever it was and read—give him plenty of leeway, twenty to twenty-five minutes perhaps, and then stop him and begin to get the class into criticism of it, reaction to it—and then get him to go on and they'd break in sooner and sooner, and finally it becomes a sort of mélange with everybody yelling at the same time. I think that it was based on a sound theory because I really believe that there is no way in the world by which one human being can teach another human being how to practice an art. What you can do is to say at the very personal level, "I remember having had the kind of problem you had getting across from the end of that paragraph to the beginning of the next one. And I remember how I worked that and I'll tell you about it." And then that works out into a conversation. He may learn something from it. He may not.

There *are* a certain number of tricks of the trade that can be told. One of Ernest Hemingway's great contributions to the writing schools of the country was to tell somebody (he also told this to me but I never repeated it to anybody, so he must have told it to somebody else who did) that when he stopped writing for the day, when he felt he was running out of gas, he always stopped at the point where he knew what was going to happen next so that he could begin at once, fresh, without standing or sitting around chewing his pencil, reading back over what he'd written. It is a trick, but it is a useful one.

The only difficulty with it, from my point of view, is that things don't work that way for me. And perhaps this is the difference between working on a poem and working on a short story, although I don't see why there should be this difference. I found that I always had to go back and work straight through from the beginning. Usually rewriting was just throwing away whatever I'd done and redoing it—getting a momentum going so that when I got to the point where I had left off the day before, I had something moving inside me. It wasn't that I knew what I planned to do. It was that I had a momentum which would push me to do what I was going to do next, which is a very different thing. And there are a very few tricks like that. (Scott is full of helpful aphorisms, many of which he didn't practice himself!) Except mostly I don't think there really are tricks about writing.

But I do think you can give a lonely writer in a huge university like Harvard a sense of a little world, a little ambient, of fifteen. Again and again and again in the years after this experience ended, I would get letters from these lads from all around the world, saying, "I can just feel myself in Widener W and the pigeons sitting outside on the window ledge in the late winter afternoon, and I can hear somebody's voice going on, and it helps me. There's strength back there that I can use." I think that's all you can do. You can give him a sense of a much older man who's interested in him, who knows more about what he's doing than he knows—which was frequently the case; I frequently did know more about a novel than the man who was writing it. But that was by listening attentively to him. Things that he forgot he said, I never forgot he said. And I'd remind him of it. Often, he didn't like that.

And by the way, it's amazing the way in which remarks made to students can stick! When Don Hall[8] was a senior at Harvard, he entered my first year of English S, which is the ultimate writing course at Harvard. And he was very cheerful about himself, not satisfied by any means but not unhappy—and good to work with in every way. After some three or four months, I remarked to him one day—without having given the matter any thought beforehand—this was something that occurred to me should be said so I said it—I told him he was lazy, which he was. He talked an awfully good poem but nothing much happened, although it was perfectly apparent then that he was capable of doing excellent work. He has never forgotten that. Every time I've run into him since (and I see him probably at considerable intervals), he tells me how early he gets up in the morning, how early he gets to write. I charged him with this the last time he was down here and he denied that he did that. But he does—every time! In fact, he'd done it just five minutes before I called him on it! So be very careful what you say to students!

Did you find that your involvement with poetry and your familiarity with it made it difficult for you to be helpful in the creative writing course to those who wanted to write fiction?

No, I had no problem there at all. As a matter of fact, the young fiction writer is usually more interesting than the young writer of verse because the young writer of verse is floundering around with all sorts of problems of technique that he's come upon for the first time even though they've been there, and his concern is sort of like a man who's going blind. His concern is to push aside his difficulties and get at the heart of the thing. A fiction writer runs into his technical problems, but later on, and so as beginners they're a little easier to deal with, usually. I had some very good writers as students, not of fiction, but of expository prose. I suppose by common consent the best American prose stylist in the generation now in its fifties is Edward Hoagland[9] who was a member of that course, and who was terribly good at that time.

You said you spent many hours preparing for the poetry course, going over cards and that kind of thing. Did you have to devote a great deal of time to the creative writing course, working over manuscripts?

I spent an awful lot of time in personal, open-ended conversations with the individual. Remember there were fifteen in that course! And that's a lot of people if you're going to give them as many hours as they want. And then, of course, there are the manuscripts to be read, but that isn't a problem once you get going because you can read what they can turn out in a week fairly rapidly.

When you were teaching your writing course, were you ever astonished by a particularly fine piece of work?

Bill Alfred is now professor of Anglo-Saxon at Harvard. When I went in '49, Harvard was full of veterans, second war, and Bill was one. I had him in a general course the first year, and the second year I had him in my writing course, and he wrote, in that course, in that year, a verse *Agamemnon* which still makes my spine crawl! A perfectly magnificent piece of work! Beautiful from every point of view: beautiful control of line. He was a Brooklyn boy—very, very Irish although he's a direct descendant of John Bunyan,[10] which took a little of the curse off that, too. That's the outstanding example, although some very handsome things were done in that course, and done in all my courses.

Did you in that course try to have people who were writing fiction also try to write poetry? Or did they simply do whatever it was they were interested in?

You did what you wanted to do. You did whatever you were doing. I wanted people who were at work at something before they came.

Can we talk a little bit about Eliot House, the time you spent as master?

John Finley, the vastly successful master at Eliot House, went off to Oxford for a year[11] and Mac Bundy, who was dean of the Faculty of Arts and Sciences, asked me to ask Ada whether we would take over, because it very much involved your wife, that job! And we'd just bought a house. We'd just found a house we really liked. We had to buy it to get it. I don't need to tell you that when it came to reselling it, we had no trouble doing so. But we didn't want to leave that house. I didn't like the feel of the thing very much. Neither did Ada. But I also had a feeling about Harvard that if I was asked to do anything, by God I was going to do it. I already owed that institution so much more than I could ever repay it. That was the least I could do. So I took it on, rather reluctantly.

I couldn't rival Finley in his incomparable knowledge of his students. He got to know the whole batch of them—hundreds of them—beginning their sophomore year when they came in. He knew them so well that when it came time, as it did for almost all of them, to write letters of recommendation to graduate schools, he could write a letter that would get the man into Heaven. John is a genius! And a very generous-minded man. I don't think any man ever went through Eliot House who didn't realize what John Finley had done for him.

I couldn't compete with that. I didn't know these people; I wasn't going to be able to know them. And I could only proceed on a sort of public basis. I had the assistance of a superb senior tutor, the present husband of the present president of Smith[12]—not the present husband, the only husband she's ever had, John Conway. A Canadian war veteran, with his right arm gone at the elbow, a very sophisticated and truly educated man with a wonderful sense of youngsters. And with his aid on the undergraduate side, we established a ritual which really worked. It wouldn't have worked for a second year because there aren't enough people on my list of good friends.

All we did was exploit all the friends we had who we thought were exploitable from the point of view of Eliot House. We would invite Oppenheimer,[13] to take one example, to come up and spent one night in the house. We had a guest room—a very comfortable guest room. And the system was to invite four or five faculty members or faculty couples, who were concerned in—since we're talking about Oppenheimer, let's go on with him—Oppenheimer's concerns—physics and elsewhere. And they would come in for a bang-up dinner. We had a small fund which Ada performed miracles with, which recalled the loaves and fishes, but they would all come in and have all the cocktails I could get into them. My idea was to introduce them all "loose." And then we'd go into dinner, a good dinner with good bottles of wine; meantime John Conway and I had picked out about twenty members of the House who were interested in physics, interested in what Oppenheimer was doing—anyway, would like to meet him. There's a separate way in to the master's study which goes through the back of the dining room, and they'd be in there with beer and cheese and crackers, nothing equal to what their betters had been getting at the front of the House, but they were comfortable and cheerful. There was a fire going in the fireplace.

And my job, as I saw it, was to get a conversation going central to Oppenheimer's concerns, which we would carry live into the back room. And we did that at the proper moment—no pause to get to the bathroom; nothing of that kind. We went right straight into the back room, talking about what we were talking about. I introduced nobody to anybody. The guest of the evening, Oppie in this case, took his place on the other side of the fire; students were around the back of the room, and we went ahead with the conversation we had started, which is a great advantage 'cause there's no pausing or embarrassment or hemming or hawing. And gradually the undergraduates—Harvard undergraduates are pretty articulate people and Eliot House undergraduates particularly so—would break in and it would go on and on and on so long as the human spirit could stand it.

The people whom we got up for this were Dean Acheson and his wife, Frost, Marianne Moore, John Crowe Ransom (the very brilliant poet and critic who was active in a small midwestern college in those years and who exerted a tremendous influence on criticism throughout the country), Judge Learned Hand (the greatest judge of his time), Felix Frankfurter from the Supreme Court, Reinhold Niebuhr, a philosopher whose name now runs away from me—we had everything on our smorgasbord table!

And these evenings were memorable for the undergraduates, partly because the guests were famous, but much more so because the conversations were uninhibited. For example—this was '55—Acheson had retired in '52 when the Democrats went out, and was at that point practicing law in Washington, but was bitterly critical of the Eisenhower policies in Korea. And he went on, under the spur of the very few questions from undergraduates, talking about how he would have run the Korean situation. He was not a man to cover his jaw. He exposed himself fully and openly. There were some wildly angry remarks banging around that room, which I thought was all to the good.

The Oppenheimer evening I used as an example because I had this in mind. The Oppenheimer evening was a tragedy! There was a very brilliant young physicist in the House, who was also a beautiful musician, and who was determined on going on into physics. And in the course of the evening, he asked Oppie, who could be very snappy indeed, about Einstein's remark that if he had it all to do over again, he'd be a shoemaker, and Oppie went into a rage, made fun of him, and he came around to see me the next morning, obviously not having slept all night, and told me that he didn't want me to feel that anybody but he himself and Oppenheimer were involved in their difficulty, but he had made up his mind to change his course commitments at once, give up physics, take premedical courses, and go into medicine, which is exactly what he did, too. And the general opinion at Harvard was that Oppie had cost the science of physics one of its most promising people. Well, that's the black mark against this sort of operation. But generally speaking, it was very effective.

Its high point for men in the House was the evening Robert Frost was there. Robert was deaf and the way he dealt with his deafness was to talk himself. Everything he remembered, he called up, and he talked and he talked and he talked! Very well, very well, indeed! And it got to be half past ten and I was quite tired, which Robert, one who saw everything, had seen. And I said, "Gentlemen, Mr. Frost has been extraordinarily generous and kind to us. I think we should thank him and give him an opportunity to go to bed." And they began to rise from their chairs and clap a bit. Robert said, "Archie, if you are tired, why don't you go to bed?" That made the evening! Everybody clapped, and he stayed and I had to drive him home around twelve o'clock!

You did a lot of writing during the period that you were at Harvard: three volumes of poetry, essays, and several plays. . . .

Yes, I seem to be able to get more writing done the busier I am! I don't know why that's so.

Do you remember the kind of schedule you might have set for yourself in terms of your own writing?

I couldn't do that because the preparation for the classes, not the writing course, really drew upon the sources that you draw upon to do your own writing. What I was doing all those years, I discovered when I came out this side of them, was using that experience to find out what I really know about the art of poetry. It was a very illuminating experience—a very sobering experience, too, and I got to writing again. I did the *Songs for Eve* [1954], all at Harvard, and I will never forget going into the elevator at the back of Widener one morning and having Perry Miller, who rarely said a kind word—great man but he didn't believe in wasting kindness on some professor—say, "That's a great book." *Boy!*—I could have pushed the elevator right up myself!

At Harvard did you ever have to get involved in department considerations?

A certain amount, but not very much. The thing that took my time mostly was the Charles Eliot Norton Professorship. I was chairman of the committee that runs that for most of the time I was there. T. S. Eliot came back, not for the professorship, but for reading. And I had him very much on my hands and very much to myself for quite a while, which was a great reward. Edwin Muir was Charles Eliot Norton Professor for one year; Hindemith for one year (who became a great friend of ours);[14] Cummings for another, which was a delight because I hadn't seen him since Paris.

Is this appointment a visiting professorship for a year's time?

It was set up for Charles Eliot Norton who was a culture hero at Harvard. He was a contemporary of William James, a personal friend of his but not as close as all that. But Norton was much admired by his contemporaries and by undergraduates during the period he was there. And when he died a group of—this is as I understand it and I think I am right—Bostonian-Cambridge people, with a considerable amount of money, set up a fund which was to be used to bring to Harvard writers to talk about the fields of Norton's interests, but primarily poetry; hence the title, "Charles Eliot Norton Professorship of Poetry" or "Chair of Poetry"—to bring somebody from outside who would give only six lectures, but would have to be in residence. And one of the provisions was that the Charles Eliot Norton Professor of Poetry must be paid the same salary as the highest paid professor at the university. So Edwin and Willa Muir, who'd been on the verge of poverty all their lives, suddenly had a bang-up salary and only six lectures to do. They had a marvelous time, thank God! Wonderful people! Ben Shahn was Charles Eliot Norton Professor and he accomplished his great work, not by his lectures, which were perfectly good but not too striking, but by taking over a studio at the top of the Fogg Museum, nailing the door open, and starting to work. You know how winter undergraduates smell? I've been up there on winter days when you could smell them two floors down, they were so thick in that room! It's a great tool, that professorship! It has now become really a very distinguished appointment. It's been held by almost anybody you can think of that's really famous in the world of the arts.

During the Harvard period, in 1952, you wrote Trojan Horse. *Did you have any specific reason for composing for the BBC?*

No, they did it first, but it wasn't written for them. It was written as a verse play for radio and the occasion, I need to add, was Senator McCarthy and his foul ways. Well, they talk about people wrapping themselves in the flag! He really wrapped himself in the wooden horse of patriotism. The first time I read it was at Groton School where I went because my friend Acheson had gone there. He wanted me to come up, so I went and I read this right after it was written, and to my astonishment about half the boys at Groton recognized at once what it was about and who it was after. They were furious about it because they were all pro-McCarthy, all these little reactionaries up there, you know. Not that all Groton people are reactionaries, by any manner of means. They've turned out some of the country's best liberals. But that particular batch—the batter had never risen with them! As a play for radio, it has turned out to be a great success on the stage. Molly Howe produced it at the Poets Theatre in Cambridge when that first started in business. It went well and I think it accomplished its purposes. Houghton Mifflin also sent it out as sort of a Christmas present to all their authors in that year.[15]

Did you make any changes in the manuscript so that it would be able to be done on stage?

Just took it as it was. It works the other way around. The blind man is a device which enables one to see what's going on, on the not-there stage of radio. His questions and the little girl's answers set the scene and give you the whole picture. That is not at all a drawback on the stage either because on the stage you just take him as a blind man. Naturally he's asking because he's blind. On radio he's serving a useful purpose.

Was it ever aired in the United States or only at BBC?

I don't remember that it's ever been done on the air in this country. At the time it was written, everybody was afraid of McCarthy, including the people who ran radio and television. Remember the United States Senate has a shameful record of fear. Very brave men just didn't dare pipe up! It took Nathan Pusey[16] at Harvard to first stand up to him and tell him what he could do and then it began to slide very rapidly. One of my great admirations in the generation ahead of me in this country was Colonel Stimson, who was secretary of war during the Second World War. Stimson was the great leading Republican conservative, not a Bill Buckley but a real conservative. Even Stimson said nothing. It's the conservatives who ought to have protested against McCarthy. He was hurting them. He wasn't hurting the country as much as he was hurting them. Stimson was awful slow about it. They were all slow about it, and I was on the receiving end from McCarthy a good deal so I can see why they were. He attacked me in a coast-to-coast broadcast along with other people who were working for Adlai Stevenson in '52.[17] The reaction was "Oh my!" Just came pouring in from all over the country, telling me what a beastly man I was to have offended that great statesman, McCarthy. It's hard to reconstruct a time like that, but you have to remember that Mr. Nixon, who got his start as McCarthy's ball boy, carrying his bags around, was a very popular figure at one time.

The next year you published This Music Crept by Me upon the Waters—*1953. The Harvard University Press put out their edition—the Poets Theatre Series.*

And that was written for the Poets Theatre. It was the first of the series that the press did. The Harvard University Press very kindly agreed to publish the plays that were written for the Poets Theatre.

It had been printed before, however, in Rome.

Yes, it was published in *Botteghe Oscure,* the editor of which was the Princess Caetani, as a verse play.

That was in April of '53, and then it was put on the BBC in June of '53 under the direction of Molly Howe. Then BBC did it again later in 1953. Was it ever done on the stage?

Yes, apparently it was.

That script contains a setting and stage directions.

They're not stage directions, really. There are a few directions—such as when they go in and out of the gate—but they were intended to be read as part of the play. If you read it, you'll notice that it's not at all like the usual description of a setting. It's a cliff above the sea, with a wall at the top of the cliff.

There are very few sound effects if you compare this play with any of the earlier radio plays. The only sound is a phonograph in the background.

Also, voices that come out when the door opens, cars coming. But that's adverted to in the dialogue.

The play is very dissimilar to the earlier radio plays in a number of ways. For one thing, this play is not a warning of any kind to the American public. It seems to be much more private and subjective, more, in a sense, deeply human.

I want to take grave exception to your statement of "warning to the American public." I don't think I've ever written one in my life! The other earlier plays differed primarily in that they had to do with situations almost on a world scene. *The Fall of the City* is a universal play about a universal phenomenon, something that that decade was full of. *This Music Crept by Me upon the Waters*, however, is not simply an inward play. It is a play about an inward subject, but it is on a much larger scale of significance than it seems to be. The significance I would put this way: this was in the fifties. At that time, the airplane was twenty-odd years old as a commercial carrier. I traveled three-motored Ford planes, which were among the earliest, in the early thirties when I was working for *Fortune*, and there hadn't been much carriage of that kind before that time so that we're now only about twenty-five years after the first use of commercial aviation and we're much less than that, only a matter of perhaps fifteen years, after the establishment of really effective air travel.

The effect of air travel was to make it possible for the affluent to migrate like the birds, follow the sun as the birds do, avoid the winter; and it led to the very rapid invasion of the tropical areas, which had before been avoided because they were difficult to get to and bloody uncomfortable when you did get there and not very safe in terms of health and so forth. All this changed with air travel. You began to get big hotels. Hospitals were built; doctors became more numerous, and the result was that the habits of the affluent changed radically. The effect of this was to bring American businessmen, who are the heads of the affluent families, face-to-face with the tropical moon and, more explicitly, face-to-face with their own souls.

This Music Crept by Me upon the Waters is not a romance, as I think anybody reading "and Ann's potatoes"[18] at the end of the play can make out. It is a satiric and sardonic play and what it's about is precisely that experience, the experience of the confrontation with overwhelming beauty and stillness and the sense of *now*, now and forever. Therefore, it is a play which has, in its way, as broad a significance as any of the others. The others have political significance. This is even more important; it's total human significance, but only for the class capable of doing this thing, who, nevertheless, are people.

Don't you think that problem of not living in the present is more than simply a class problem? That happens, it would seem, among a great many people who live for tomorrow or the day after tomorrow.

But it's the affluent who were confronted with this dramatic realization of it. That is, the American business community lives looking forward to the end of the month, or, at the worst, to the end of the year. The men much more than the women are always looking toward the future. Women can live *now*, naturally do. And they have to, in many, many ways. But men, particularly the American male, are incapable of it. A Provençal peasant can live in the present because that's where his crops are, and his temperament is like that, but the American man who lives by making profits is necessarily faced toward the future. And he is always looking for more money. He's looking for more satisfaction of that kind. Suddenly he finds himself face-to-face with everything he thought he might be moving toward. The defeated hero of that little play has lived his entire life looking forward toward self-aggrandizement.

But Peter, who achieves that moment of awareness of the now *with Elizabeth, is called back into the house by a real (what seems to him to be real) emergency there.*

He's called back by something you have to do something about. And the whole thing had fallen away from him and the opportunity to escape them, and they found they weren't living in *now* at all and couldn't stay there. He was living either in the immediate past, the "dead body in the sea," sixty feet below, or the immediate future, finding her, which also was a form of conclusion. It's a fairly complicated psychological plot, but I don't think it's too complicated myself.

Obviously you're familiar with people who don't live this way. Is your own life now *centered? Are you able to do what the play seems to suggest people should do?*

Or was I? That's a very difficult question to answer. I think probably not, but you have to bear in mind that for twenty years we lived on Antigua and although nothing like this ever happened, the kind of people that some of these people were, Halsey for example, horse's asses of the highest derivative, were frequent in the Mill Reef Club.[19] Oliver, the Englishman, is drawn on someone I knew who was one of the wittiest, most cynical of men, and also very much stomach centered, as was Oliver in the play. All this provided a fallow ground. Also the moon is a presence in the West Indies, such as it is not here. It's really an event, tremendous event! You can't avoid it. Sometimes you are brought face-to-face with it and I suppose I was. In fact, I must have been or I couldn't have written the play. The problem that it deals with is a universal American problem, the search for happiness which has become an American attribute since the airplane started going. That also is a present phenomenon that we all are familiar with.

The play works very well; it's a lovely play. Seymour Rudin,[20] whom you know, said of all your plays it's his favorite.

Dick Wilbur[21] told me that too once. That was by way of taking a swipe at *J.B.*, which he doesn't like! Dick is a darling, yes. Whatever he said, he believed.

J.B. *was the next play you wrote. Did you have its performance by the Yale Drama School in mind when you worked on it?*

I wrote the play with no thought of production whatever. It never crossed my mind anybody would produce it. I mean that very seriously. I never thought about it. The contract for it says nothing about dramatic rights. This was just a verse play that you publish. And Houghton Mifflin, who has always been very loyal, very devoted, published it.[22]

Curt Canfield,[23] who was originally the head of the drama department of Amherst, had moved to Yale. Curt saw a copy of the book and read it, and came up here to see me while he was at Yale, not living at Amherst, and asked me if he could produce it. This was in 1957–58. I was very skeptical about it. It was a very long play to produce and I didn't want to cut it, since it was written as a poem more than as a play. Curt said, "All right. We'll play the whole thing," and he did. It was played with student actors. At that time, Yale Drama School hadn't been turned into a professional waiting joint, the way it is now. Brustein[24] turned it into sort of an antechamber of Broadway. Anyway, Curt put it on with student actors and actresses, some of whom were quite good; but none of them, and I'm sure they would forgive me for saying so, none of them really good yet. They were all really young. Curt's direction was good and there was a beautiful setting by a man who died about two years ago.[25] It was put on at New Haven and after the first night, there was to be a party at Curt's house afterward.

On the evening of the production I saw Brooks Atkinson[26] in the audience and I couldn't believe my ears, eyes, whatever I was seeing him with. Then in the excitement I sort of forgot that he was there and I had all the author's doubts and worries watching it go through. At the end of it I was looking for some actor I wanted to talk to. Brooks Atkinson, with his steel-rimmed glasses, stopped me and said, "I want to introduce myself," and I said, "I know. You're Brooks Atkinson." "Well," he said, "I just wanted to tell you that's a great play." So it was in the *Times* the next morning, with the result that I had nine producers on the telephone in the course of that day. We finally ended up with Alfred de Liagre (Delly),[27] who obviously really wanted to do it, whereas the others were primarily influenced by Brooks. In other words, what brought *J. B.* (I think this is a good little morality play) onto the stage was Curt Canfield's producing it at Yale, which took a lot of courage. Elliot Norton[28] was there too and was very much excited about it but didn't review it. That's the difference between Brooks Atkinson and Elliot Norton. It was a combination of Curt's courage in putting it on and Brooks Atkinson's sense of mission. He had a sense that something had to be done about the New York theater, which was getting worse and worse and worse and he would go to try-outs farther away even than New Haven.

Do you know a poem of mine about Brooks? Brooks Atkinson came to the end of, I suppose, the most distinguished career as a theater reviewer in the whole history of New York State. The *Times* wanted to do something about it; lots of people wanted to do something about it. (This is all hearsay to me. I don't know this, but I've been told it.) Brooks wouldn't hear of it. He said, "I'm going to go to my last performance this Tuesday. I get through when the play closes, which will be probably about 9:45 and I'm going home, write my review, and that will be it. That's the end of it." So there was a lot of strong feeling about this and they had a party for him of the drama critics and everybody else, sort of got them together, big party in the theater in New York. I would have given my eye teeth to be there but I couldn't. So I wrote this poem for him, which they read.

> Brooks Atkinson, that quiet man
> who kept the torches of Parnassus
> steady as New England can
> (or could) behind his steel-rimmed glasses,
>
> Brooks Atkinson who loved the tongue
> well consonanted and well voweled
> (Actors who mouthed it should be hung,
> writers who blurred it, disemboweled),
>
> Brooks Atkinson who hated hue
> and cry and mode and art-in-fashion,
> and never wrote a wrong review
> to show his wit or wave his passion
> [something that Clive Barnes spent his whole life doing!]
> or imitate the *dernier cri*

or scratch for academic plaudit
but saw the plays there were to see
and searched his soul and made his audit

and kept alive for thirty years
of Venus in a pouting sweater,
Ares in skirts and art in tears,
the taste for good, the hope for better,

Brooks Atkinson, the role complete,
the task performed, the judgment certain,
prepared to vanish from his seat
unnoticed at the final curtain

Wrong for once. The faithful man
who guards the honor of the muses
never vanishes, never can:
they keep his fame for their sweet uses.

Was J.B. produced overseas?

After the New York production, it had a brilliant production in Italy, marvelous! It ran in Germany for years, a German edition translated by Eva Hesse. It ran in all the Scandinavian countries, in Israel (great success in Israel), Spain, never in France; England—the English performance was a disaster. It just flopped at the end of two weeks. The extraordinary thing was that the play lasted quite well. It was in New York for three-quarters of a year and on the road in the United States for another year or two; but now, twenty years after, it is still running, not in professional theater but in amateur theater. And it's not in colleges but in schools. It seems to work at high-school level, just like a breeze. They go on and on and on.

You wrote, of course, two different endings: the original published version—

Don't say two! At least two hundred! It came over us in Washington that something was very, very wrong with the play. It was indeed! We had two weeks in Washington. We had very good audiences all the way through and none of us liked it. And the great question was what in the world to do with it. Gadg[29] finally came up with a conception which seemed to me to be sound. In fact, I stopped thinking about it after I heard this, and began to work at it. Gadg said, "This is a play about J.B. but the conclusion of the play, as you have it now, is not J.B.'s—it's Sarah's." And I said, "Isn't that true of the lives of most men?" And Gadg said, "Well, it may be true of the lives of most men outside the theater, but in the theater you've got to end the play you began, not some other play." So I worked away at that thing, and came very close to breaking down over it. I just became numb from the task.

I don't like the conclusion that came into New York. I like the conclusion in the originally published play much better, and whenever I have a choice I always go back to it. But you're quite right. There were at least two published ends. There must be somewhere between thirty and forty more floating around in notes and pieces of paper. Gadg and I published in *Esquire* our notes to each other about the play and that little sad story is there.[30]

That's a very interesting article, by the way, especially to anybody who's interested in theater and wants to see how something gets worked over. Is that how you felt during the whole thing—worked over? Did you feel bruised by the experience?

Oh, yes! Tremendously so! There's one anecdote about the performances which belongs perhaps in what we're doing now. When we came into New York, we came in from a battering experience in Washington and we found the New York newspapers were on strike, and the publicity man sent word he wanted to talk to Gadg and de Liagre and me. This was before we opened. And he said, "This is no time to talk in the polite way. We've just got to get down to brass tacks. We are opening in New York day after tomorrow. We're opening a verse play on a Bible theme in a city in which the newspapers are on strike. There will be no reviews in the newspapers. We haven't got a prayer unless we make a special appeal to an audience which would be interested. That special audience is clergymen and churchmen, and there are lots of them around New York. I am not proposing to you, gentlemen; I'm delivering an ultimatum. Unless you will support me in this, I'm quitting as of right now." Delly said, "What do you propose to do?" and he said, "I want to invite every Jewish, Protestant, Catholic, Hindu, whatever, clergyman in New York City, New Jersey, Connecticut, upstate New York, to come to the theater at a period which will put us two weeks beyond opening to keep it going at least that long, and I am assuring them that Mr. MacLeish will be available on the stage for them to throw anything they want at." Delly and Gadg looked at me and I said, "Of course I'll be on the stage and they can throw anything they want." So we parted. We had no hope. We just thought we were finished. We had been working on this thing for three-quarters of a year.

The next morning Delly called me up and said, "Well, there's a line two times around the block." There wasn't, but there was a line around the block, and Delly said, "I guess we can say we're in." So I forgot all about this conversation and the publicity man forgot to remind me and just by luck I walked into the theater that night (I was teaching in Harvard all this time, you see, coming down on the train to look at it). I came in and thought, "What's the matter with this theater? Isn't there anybody in the orchestra?" The whole thing was black. It was black because the whole thing was filled with clergy! That didn't mean anything to me. I was in a state of euphoria! We had been doing the kind of business that they only do in short stories! So I went up to the first gallery, whatever they call that, got a seat in the back, well, not a seat—standing room, and suddenly it came over me the reason all those clergymen were there! After the audience went out, I took my seat and what followed would have been a nightmare if the play hadn't been a success.

It wasn't a nightmare and I could take it a little bit lightly. But I sat there watching, looking at, these people who were assorting themselves. There must have been a number of hundred of clergymen. I thought to myself, "Now, who are going to be my friends and who are going to be after me?" And I got it absolutely wrong! I said *J.B.* is a Protestant play in its theological ambivalence, probably more Protestant than anything else, and for that and other reasons (probably because my mother was one of the most active Baptists of her time and a daughter of a Congregational minister) the Protestants will be for me. The Jews will be violently against me because J.B. is their boy, Job. The Catholics won't approve. They certainly won't approve because there is a spoiled priest in the play and they don't like spoiled priests. The Catholics are against me; the Jews are against me; the Protestants are probably for me.

I was wrong on every score! The Catholics felt there was the Bible on the stage and we were actually standing there talking about questions of theology and religion and that's fine, so the Catholics were warm friends. The Jews, far from being against me (the Jewish scholars, all the great rabbis were in that audience and they made their presence felt from the very start), not only liked the fact that Job was getting a hearing on Broadway, but they liked my view of Job, which is amazing! What is the answer to the injustice of the universe? What is the answer of Job to his comforters? They were against the comforters; they were for Job. Who hated me were the Protestants! We were there well over two hours and the last remark came from a man who was one of the darling white-haired boys of Union Theological Seminary in New York, which is the sacred place of Protestant orthodoxy. His last question was this, delivered with a voice the sarcasm of which I can't reproduce at all. The reason for the sarcasm wasn't me. It was because his head was bloodied; the rabbis had made a fool of him. He just couldn't bear it. So he said, "Are we to understand, Mr.

MacLeish, that your answer to the great problem of the injustice of the universe, to which you have devoted your talents, is love and sexual intercourse between a man and a woman?'' And I just laughed and got up and left the theater. And the rabbis cheered. It was a wonderful evening! But I didn't sleep on the way home.

Was that the only such evening that took place during the course of the run of the play?

You don't think it's enough?

Oh, that was enough! From the way the publicist was talking, it seemed there would be several such events.

There was no newspaper account of it. Nobody ever reported it.

That's the second time that you were up on the stage after a performance of one of your plays.

Once when the Communists were giving me the go-over and the second time the clergy!

One critic says that one of the play's difficulties is that it begins with a theological kind of subject that moves to a humanistic one. Isn't that an oversimplification, really, of what the play is?

Everything in the production of that play, and this bears out what you were saying, depends on who Sarah is; who plays Sarah. If Sarah is played by a woman who gives an impression of herself as a woman, truly woman, so that you don't think she's a symbol of women or a symbol of beauty or anything of that kind but that she is a woman, then it works. If the actress lacks that, she can be just as good as she wants in every other way. If she doesn't have that feeling, the play doesn't work.

By the way, was Ada involved at all in the agonies of preparing the play?

Oh, yes. She was in Washington with me all the time. She didn't get much sleep because we only had one room and the light had to be on. I spent my nights rewriting that damned end.

You were lucky, though, that act one worked as well as it did and it was just the end you had to redo.

In theater, the usual problem is, how is your second act? That is, what is the play itself?

You told us that when you won the Pulitzer Prize for Conquistador, *you were over in Paris and you read it in the morning newspaper. How did you hear about the Pulitzer Prize that you won for* J.B.?

The *J.B.* prize was very, very different! I was in New York two or three days before. At that time I knew the president of Columbia very well. In fact, I was working on something with him and had gone up to Columbia to talk about that and he drew me aside and said something which if I dared to interpret it in the best possible terms meant that *J.B.* had the Pulitzer Prize. The alternative was *Raisin in the Sun*, a play by a black woman who died shortly afterward.[31] That would have been a very good choice. But I didn't dare to believe that he'd said what he said so I was back here the following Monday and my ear was just constantly waiting for the telephone. There was no sound. I certainly wasn't going to call anybody up and ask. I was outside, going to Ada's garden, when I was called in and it was Gadg. And Gadg said, "I've been wanting that so badly for three days that I could taste it, retaste it, and retaste it, but now, I don't have to do that anymore. We have it!" So then I took a deep breath, but that was much less exciting than the first one; the first one was the big one.

Did the play win any Tony awards?

Oh, yes. It got the Tony Award. The Antoinette Perry ("Tony") award. And Gadg Kazan got "best director." [*Reading*] "The American Theater Wing presents to Archibald MacLeish this award for the play *J.B.*, 1958."

J.B. *was not your first play to use a biblical subject. That was* Nobodaddy, *in 1926. And of course you used a similar theme in* Songs for Eve *in 1954. Could you talk about circumstances that led to the writing of* Nobodaddy? *After all, it was your first attempt at drama.*

This is an obvious question to ask, but I don't remember a thing about it. I can't dredge that up but what I can dredge up is something you've already noticed, that the theme is related to the theme in *Songs for Eve*. The weakness of *Nobodaddy* is that it goes on, picks up, and tries to deal with Cain and Abel too, and that was a combination that was obviously beyond me at that time and probably now too. This is the kind of thing that only Milton could have dealt with. But what it suggests to me is that back in my (it was written probably in '20, '21) late twenties I was assailed by the implications of Genesis, the great myth of Genesis which to my mind, with all reservations allowed for it, is the greatest of all the myths. There is nothing that quite does what that does. What it says, and says loud and clear, in tones which subsequent generations have neglected and paid no attention to, is that the beginning of human life, the beginning of humanity, is the beginning of consciousness When we ate of the tree of knowledge it is not—in Genesis—what the fundamentalist preachers make it out to be, a mere knowledge of sex, though down to then Adam and Eve were totally sexless in relation to each other. The beginning of humanity is the beginning of the consciousness of self as human, of the conscious, and it was for that you were going to die if you ate of the tree. It is a tremendous myth. It hasn't even begun to be explored yet.

In that play you talk about not just consciousness itself, which is the awakening that Adam has, but a consciousness of "other" too. Apparently he's aware of Eve in a different way.

That is what consciousness of self is: consciousness in that mirror.

Is Abel meant to be, in the third act, a throwback to that earth consciousness?

Don't ask me. I just can't talk about that third act. I don't understand it! The beginning of it, the first act of the play, seems to me to be not only true but better than true. I think it really perceives something. I think it just wanders off into areas where it doesn't know its way toward the end.

R. P. Blackmur says that "act three is drama at its best."[32]

For God's sake! I better reread it!

It's Cain's cry against God. It's certainly the first voicing of something that comes back again and again in your plays. Has the play ever been performed?

It's never been played, so far as I know, never by anybody.

It really couldn't have been done until after nudity was accepted on stage

because Adam and Eve are naked. Do you remember anything about its
publication?

In 1926 when that was published, we'd been in Paris for two years. I had left it
with my friend Maurice Firuski, who ran the Dunster House Book Shop in
Cambridge. Maurice Firuski was one of the most extraordinary people of his
time. He was a Yale man, like me, and had no right to be in Cambridge at all.
His father, unless I'm mixing two people up and I don't think I am, had made
a very considerable success out of renting furniture to Yale students for years,
that sort of situation. Maurice (and this happens very frequently with Jews)
had, way back in the genes somewhere, a real attachment to—a most fundamental conception of—what literature is. He was left with an amount of
money which gave him a certain amount of freedom, enough to stock a bookstore. At that time, this is the middle twenties—a great boom period—there
was not one good bookshop in Cambridge. And Maurice started the Dunster
House, which really changed Cambridge almost about as much as Harvard
College did. He had marvelous things! He had an instinct for what was going
on, particularly in England. Huxley was all there; nobody else had it but he
did! Maurice and I became very good friends and when I wrote *Nobodaddy*
I had no plans for it. I knew nobody would publish it; so Maurice said, "We'll
publish it," and he did. Very handsomely, indeed.

Your next play was written for television—The Secret of Freedom, *in 1960. It*
was produced by NBC on February 28. In your foreword to it you talk about
how this play could be adapted for presentation in the theater. You also
comment on one of the actors who appeared in the production, Tom
Mitchell, who played the librarian. Could you tell us how this play came to
be written?

It came about through somebody at NBC. The particular issue involving education and teachers with which the play deals was pretty active at the
time. NBC had been interested in the subject and they wanted a treatment of it
which would bring it closer to people than it had been. I remember very, very
little about it except going down to the town in southern New Jersey where it
was shot and wasting a lot of time down there. I haven't read it since it was
done. I haven't any feeling about it at all.

Were you pleased with it? You must have been pleased with Mitchell be-
cause you did comment on him.

Yes, I remember him, and Tony Randall was very good. It was absolutely all right, but it was a pure piece of propaganda on the side of the angels and if it ever had any effect, I don't know. You can't tell.

That was your only experience in writing a television play, is that right?

Yes, but not my only experience in writing for television because I have done other television things. One was *Dialogues with Mark Van Doren,* which we mentioned before. It was a CBS operation that same year.

Dialogues with Mark Van Doren *wasn't writing so much, was it, as simply talking?*

It wasn't actually pen-in-hand writing, but Mark and I spent an awful lot of time preparing. We were told we could talk about anything. But that meant really that we had to spend a lot of time deciding what we were going to talk about. We knew each other so well that it wasn't as difficult as it would have been if we'd started from scratch.

How did someone come up with the idea of doing a dialogue between you and Mark Van Doren for commercial television?

Warren Bush came around to see me and asked if I would do this—if I would engage in a protracted conversation—and I said that depended on with whom. So he asked me for various suggestions and I put first Dean Acheson because, first of all, he's my oldest friend although it was not as easy talking with him as with Mark; nevertheless we'd been fighting for forty or fifty years and I knew we'd go on fighting and I thought it might be quite interesting. But Dean happened to be busy with something and he couldn't do it. Then I said, "Well, there's only one person. If you can persuade Mark Van Doren to do it." So they went and talked to Mark and Mark said sure, to my astonishment. We got small fees of some kind but we never asked for more or bothered about it. We sort of took it as a lark.

But they literally followed you everywhere you went for a couple of days, didn't they, in the process of filming?

Yes, they were out here in Conway for two or three days, and they had a great deal of tape. Bush, the director, edited it and published a book, which is quite a good book. He did a very good job.

And there's a lot more in the book than there was actually on the television.

That's right. Because he was going at it from a different point of view.

Were you involved in editing down all of the conversations they had taped prior to the television broadcast? In selecting, in other words, what would be used?

Oh, no. I told them so far as I was concerned I didn't want anything to do with it. That was going to be his baby and I think Mark said the same thing.

You were apparently satisfied with the editing they did.

I liked the book. The actual television business—I was deeply fond of Mark and I just like to watch Mark, listen to what he says, and so forth. So I have no really artistic reactions to it at all.

In 1962 you did American Bell.

The *American Bell*, first of all, is a *son et lumière*, a French device which has now apparently disappeared even in France. No actors, but lights, a building, music, and voices. The French used it for the great chateaus. They would take one of the chateaus where somebody had died, focus on a little balcony outside a window, turn on the lights and do it.

T. Edward Hambleton was the head of the Phoenix Theatre and I'd had to do with him because Phoenix had done something of mine; I've forgotten what it was. He came to see me in the early sixties to say that the city of Philadelphia wanted to do a *son et lumière* for Independence Hall on May 4, 1962, to commemorate the hanging of the liberty bell. T. Edward asked me if I would like to work on this, and I was very much interested in it because that's holy ground for me, not so much for the reasons celebrated in *American Bell* as for Lincoln's speech the night before he went down through Baltimore to Washington for his first inauguration, when he made that marvelous statement about what the Declaration of Independence was. But I couldn't use that here. Nevertheless, I said I would take it on. There isn't an awful lot to be said about it aside from the device. The difficulty is that Independence Hall is a small building. We think of it as big because it looms historically big, but it's small. And there's very little you can do with lights. My characters were the great figures of Independence Hall—and I got to the point of lighting up a tree to fix your mind on Jefferson, which is not a very good idea.

Whether the play was going to work or wasn't going to work depended largely on the music. The music had to carry it; it had to be dramatic music; it had to be agreeable. And we got David Amram,[33] a man who was gifted but whose music is essentially intellectual. The large part of the city of Philadelphia had to listen to it on loud speakers night after night for months and got to hate that music with a fierce hatred. There were actually physical revolts against it. This was one of our principal difficulties! But it did work. It worked quite well. The city of Philadelphia liked it. I haven't any particular feelings about it at all. It's not the piece I would have liked to do if I was going to do something about Independence Hall.

That was the year you left Harvard. Why did you leave?

I was retired! Senility! They retire you at sixty-five except in certain special cases. And I proudly say I was one! I started to teach at Harvard at the age of fifty-eight, which is the age at which most people retire, or begin to think about it! And when 1962 came along, I was seventy. That's the compulsory age for retirement, for presidents and everybody else.

You were at Harvard twelve years. During that time you published many books and received numerous awards—among them two Pulitzer prizes, the Bollingen Prize, the National Book Award, and a number of honorary doctoral degrees. Obviously, those accomplishments produced their own satisfaction and provided, as you said, stimulus to your growth as a poet. But, as you look back on it, did you enjoy those years of teaching—of working with students in the classroom?

Oh, yes. Enormously enjoyed it! You both know about the mishaps and unpleasantnesses of teaching! I had my fair share of those! But once I'd begun to take those easily and also to avoid them to some extent, the whole thing became very interesting and very exciting.

The Later Years

1963–67 Simpson Lecturer at Amherst College.
1965 *The Eleanor Roosevelt Story* (prose). Houghton Mifflin Co.
1966 Academy Award for *The Eleanor Roosevelt Story* (film).
1967 *Herakles* (verse play). Houghton Mifflin Co.
The Magic Prison (libretto).
An Evening's Journey to Conway, Massachusetts (verse play). Gehenna Press.
1968 *A Continuing Journey* (prose). Houghton Mifflin Co.
"The Wild Old Wicked Man" and Other Poems. Houghton Mifflin Co.
1971 *Scratch* (prose play). Houghton Mifflin Co.
Champion of a Cause (essays). American Library Association.
1972 *The Human Season: Selected Poems 1926–1972.* Houghton Mifflin Co.
1975 *The Great American Fourth of July Parade* (radio verse play). University of Pittsburgh Press.
1976 *New and Collected Poems, 1917–1976.* Houghton Mifflin Co.
1977 Presidential Medal of Freedom.
Cosmos Club Award.
1978 National Medal for Literature.
Riders on the Earth: Essays and Recollections. Houghton Mifflin Co.

Right *after you left Harvard, you taught at Amherst, as a lecturer.*

I never really did teach at Amherst. They had a lectureship (they still have it) called the Simpson Lectureship, which, I believe, was set up for Robert Frost. He held it for years and years and years. They gave him a small income, very small, but one that was helpful to him. And Cal Plimpton, who was president of Amherst when I came back from Harvard, was a good friend of mine, and suggested that I accept this lectureship and see what I could do with it.

What had Robert Frost done with the Simpson Lectureship?

The sort of thing he was always doing! I mean, he lived down there in Amherst, whereas I lived up here thirty miles away. He had students in in the evenings in his rooms at the Lord Jeffrey and went out for walks with them. He was wonderful that way! He could give something that you couldn't put into words very well that was very useful. But I was only doing it for half the year and it just never did catch on. Cal felt it himself after a while and suggested we cease and desist, which was the right thing to do. It really just didn't work out too well. It interfered with me quite a bit and it didn't help anybody else very much.

You held the lectureship from 1963 to 1967. During that time you continued to do a great deal of writing. In 1965, you wrote the film script of The Eleanor Roosevelt Story. *Can you tell us how you happened to write that?*

I don't remember how it started. There was a producer in the background. He probably was there from the very beginning. There was a producer and a photographer.[1] The producer's chief virtue, in my mind, was that he left me a completely free hand. He didn't attempt to even hear anything about it or to control it in any way. It's all mine and not interfered with by him, which is something you can't often say.

The most interesting thing about it photographically was that the first motion picture we could use was of the time of the return of President and Mrs. Roosevelt from the Versailles Treaty, when he was the assistant secretary of the navy, right after the First World War. Prior to that we had to use still pictures, and the amazing thing (perhaps it's peculiar to *The Eleanor Roosevelt Story*) about it is that those still pictures were so much more effective than the motion pictures we used. This poor, miserable, miserable-looking—maybe not unattractive-looking but just miserable-looking—girl was caught in these pretentious photographs. You didn't need to say a word about them. They just were there on the screen for a minute and they said everything that needed to be said. The Roosevelt family liked that film very, very much because it gives her a chance to do for herself. Nothing's being done to her. I think that's fair, and I think that's right. I like it as a film. It's shown on television now. It's been cut down from motion-picture size to television size. I haven't seen it in that form, but it's going around.

Did you have anything to do with the selection of the photographs and the film or was that entrusted to somebody after the script was finished?

Oh, no. I had a chance to be heard on it. The script was done first and then the photographs were selected.

The film won an award that year.

It won the Academy Award for Documentaries, which doesn't amount to anything.

So did you get one of the Oscars?

No! I wrote to the producer (I heard about this about a year afterward) and said, "Haven't you got something for me?" and he never answered. He was a dubious character. Well, I guess not dubious at all!

In the very early part when you're going back to Eleanor Roosevelt's childhood, you describe her as a child who lived in a "magic prison." The use of that term is striking in view of your use of it in connection with Emily Dickinson. What kind of comparison would you make between these two women?

Of course, Emily Dickinson is not the inventor of the phrase, you know. "Magic Prison" goes way back before her. It was probably just coincidence.

In the same year, you also wrote Herakles, *in which you again use the* son et lumière *device you used in* American Bell.

I was in Athens at that time and the Acropolis is lighted at night and there is always a *son et lumière* going on. You don't hear, if you're down in the city, the music. You don't hear words but you do see the Acropolis. It was luminous with a slightly rosy light, quite beautiful. If you had been in the Hotel Grand Bretagne at that time, you couldn't have seen anything else but the Acropolis.

Why was Herakles *dedicated to George Seferis?*[2]

Mr. Seferis is the great Greek poet of this century. He was a very high-ranking diplomat who was very much involved in the history of his country and whose relation with the affairs of his generation was therefore in the public sphere and the private one. He's a fine poet. I would say one of the four, five, six great poets of the century.

The play shows a really tremendous familiarity with things Greek. You have already commented on your being in Greece at that time. Had you gone to Greece often before?

Yes, a good many times, and you know it's home for everybody. As Paris is a contemporary home, Greece, the islands and Athens, not the Peloponnesus, are our sort of eternal homes.

Just as the myth of Herakles is an eternal myth.

I felt very strongly then that the myth of Herakles was *the* great modern myth,[3] but that play was not able to persuade an audience of that fact, nor have I ever been able to persuade anybody of it. I say the great modern myth because the labors of Herakles were all of them labors of delivering the world from its fears, from its monsters, delivering it from evil, creating a world in which people could live simply and humanly, which is very much what the modern myth of science has been. Science fights against cancer. It cures infantile paralysis. It puts an end to yellow fever. It accomplishes miracles in regard to the decency of living. The myth of Herakles ends with his return from his labors and the discovery that in his wars against the monsters he has destroyed his own sons. This is also the myth of science for us. Science has produced the bombs; science has produced the destruction of the young. No one has been able to accept that view, which is a judgment on me; I just wasn't able to write the play I set out to write. I feel a good deal of grief about this because I think *Herakles* has the best dramatic verse I have ever written. I think it should have done much more than it did, but then I have to say that in a performance at Ann Arbor, in which Rosemary Harris played the counter-role to Herakles, Herakles' wife, it, to me, worked like a charm.[4] She's a magnificent actress. She reads verse as almost nobody else does. She and Chris Plummer are, to me, the two great readers of verse on stage now. It was going to be produced by T. Edward Hambleton of the Phoenix Theatre after the experience in Ann Arbor in 1965 in which it had large audiences, but T. Edward didn't feel that he could bring it into New York. He felt it would not, couldn't, possibly succeed. Alfred de Liagre, who had been the great mainstay of *J.B.*, said, "I might as well tell you now frankly, I would not bring it into New York." I don't have a sense of failure about it because the play works for me; therefore I can't say it's a failed play, but I have a very clear sense of not having succeeded in doing what I wanted to do, not writing the play that could have been written.

Do you think that's because there are perhaps two plays in there struggling to get out? The first act focuses on the scientist and the second is an inter-working with the Herakles myth. The commentaries and the relationships that are set up are very interesting, but the tie-in between act one and act two, except for the carry-over of the carriages, isn't clear.

I agree with you about that. Act one was written after Ann Arbor. At Ann Arbor it was perfectly apparent that what I was trying to say wasn't being heard at all. Therefore I concocted, and I think that's the right word for it, act one, which is a perfectly good act and interesting enough but it doesn't make its conjunction with the play itself. I'm still tempted to try to do something with it but I wouldn't know what to do. It doesn't work and I do feel badly about it as well as confused. Practically nobody I know undertakes to play it. There are no amateur productions of it. I have been for years tempted to go back to it again, but I put in so many years on it that I'm afraid that I've exhausted the oxygen around there. I don't know that I could get moving on it again.

Herakles' anguished cry is very similar to Cain's great question at the end of Nobodaddy and there is also a similarity even to J.B. Herakles wants to hear something out there that will at least tell him that he has done well if not support what he's been trying to do.

They couldn't be more different! What J.B. wants is to be shown his fault, his guilt. God admits that the world is unjust. God admits that all these things that Satan has done to him were undeserved, that J.B. was an honest and upright man, a just and upright man. He admits the injustice of the universe and indeed God would be hard put not to since it's so obvious. And what J.B. has to feel to feel himself a man, to feel his life justified, is what he has to know—his fault, which would explain these horrible things which have all happened to him. J.B.—a man in a corner, with death, blood, and feces around him—wants to know why this has to happen. If he felt he knew why, he could bear it but he can't bear it. He learns he can bear it only through love.

Now Herakles is the optimistic opposite of that. He starts out to destroy the monsters. He undertakes the impossible labors, the ten great impossible labors. It's a perfect image of what the whole scientific operation, whether seen or not, has been. Cain's problem is guilt—his own guilt—and that's a different thing altogether. He doesn't belong in this area at all. But in the case of Herakles, the answer given the oracle, the real answer given by the oracle, lies in his realization that he has, totally unintentionally, by complete chance, destroyed his sons, which is the ambiguous answer, I'm afraid, that you have to give to the great advances of science. As we look around the world which science has now made possible, there's very good reason to believe we've killed our sons. I don't find that this is a view that other people share, but that's certainly what that play says.

Herakles becomes an ironic victim in his quest because whatever fulfillment he was hoping to achieve, he cannot achieve. Because of the murder of his sons and because he finally is unanswered and cannot be the god he was hoping or expecting to be, he's a failure; his quest is a failure. Cain is also looking for answers to the unanswerable, as is J.B. They may be opposite questions or different ones, but it is possible to see the futility of asking the large questions posed in each of these plays.

I don't think it illuminates any of these things to put them side-by-side that way. I may be quite wrong about it. It's what people who organize ideas inevitably do and naturally do and properly do. Well, it doesn't seem to throw any light here. I think J.B.'s is, as I said, the last ultimate squeak. "Show me my guilt. At least I can live with that." But the thing that drives him crazy is he thinks God's unjust and he can't live with that. And that has been the human situation as long as we've known anything about human consciousness. You know how the myth of Herakles ends. He puts over his body the skin of the Nemean lion, and it burns into his own skin.

Can you tell us anything about the circumstances of the writing of Herakles?

I have no memory at all of the circumstances of the writing of *Herakles.* I remember where I started it. I started it in New York City, of all places, and the immediate scenes, the scenes that suggested a locus for the play came out of a trip that we had made to Greece to speak for the state department in Athens. We lived in the Grand Bretagne from the front windows of which you can see at night the Acropolis illuminated for *son et lumière,* as I said before, and it was a very striking thing. Also we saw a good deal of Greece. Went up to Delphi, Ada and I alone, just wandering around doing a few things here and a few things there. The scene I had in mind for Delphi, the wellspring of the temple, came from Delphi itself. You're at a very considerable height. You look down. You could look in many directions, but the natural perspective of the village is down toward the southwest, so that you're looking toward the sea, which you see as a glitter infinitely below you and a little degree west of you; and that whole area is covered with an enormous forestation of palms, I suppose date palms, which can give a dark, somber, green, almost long-light cover at that extreme height, and you look back of you at the great mountains and low places ringing with myth, ringing with memory. I wanted the scene at the temple, at the prophetic temple at Delphi, to have that sort of quality. It didn't in the Ann Arbor production, although as I've told you it did have, in Rosemary Harris, the most beautiful woman's voice on the stage today, which was more than a makeup.

There's one other comment about it. As I said, the present first scene of our Nobel laureate was written after the Ann Arbor opening because it was pretty clear that I had assumed the knowledge of Greek myth and in particular of the Heraklean myth which people generally don't have anymore. And I wanted to amplify that. I think perhaps I pointed the finger a little bit too persistently, sort of "Look, look, look!" I shouldn't have done that. I think if we're going to do that as one of the radio plays which WGBH is going to do.[5] I'll just drop him altogether and begin up there with the goat bells.

Can we talk now about Magic Prison, *commissioned by André Kostelanetz and performed first June 12, 1967?*

André wanted something and I had gotten very much involved with all the voluminous material on Emily while I was teaching at Harvard. The thing that interested me most was that scene in the drawing room in Amherst when Colonel Higginson, who had been corresponding with her for eighteen years, came up and met her for the first time. It's a beautiful situation because it exists on various levels. She always addressed him, of course, as "Dear Preceptor" and he's a nice man and quite an intelligent man and well bred, well brought up, and as he was very polite he answered her letters and never guessed at the truth, which was that nobody in her family knew that she was writing poetry (well, they knew, there were two or three things printed, but that was all), including her sister, Lavinia. She simply had to have a reader for them. You can't work and not. There's got to be somebody out there who hears. So what she did was use Colonel Higginson as her audience and particularly for poems which came out of whatever the great love affair of her life was, things which she just couldn't talk to anybody else about. The subject was taboo; the fact that she was writing poetry was taboo. It was all taboo; so she used him. Even when he finally came up and met her, he didn't realize what had been happening. He didn't realize that he had been used. She'd let on to playing the part of a mouse in face of the pussy cat, and he didn't realize the roles were reversed. So the material is wonderfully good. I mean the material all exists in Higginson's marvelous piece in the *Atlantic*. What poems Emily showed him nobody knows, and it was therefore possible for me to choose what I wanted to. So I chose the poems that clearly do relate to a deeply emotional experience in her life and his reaction to it and so forth. There's only about five words of mine in the whole script. It's just an editorial job and I turned that over to André, who professed himself delighted.

We got a composer,[6] who was really quite good. He understood what the whole thing was about. It was produced with a famous television performer, E. G. Marshall, and a girl from Washington who was very good, terribly good.[7] A good voice, a good actress, professional. It all worked fairly well except for the fact that the acoustics in the auditorium where the New York Philharmonic was at that time working were so dreadful that great pieces of it were lost. It was a disastrous experience. Everybody was very much upset about it but nothing could be done. I think André has done it a couple of times since.

Then it was done in Greenfield by the Pioneer Valley Symphony.

I remember the year.

In the little introduction to it in Saturday Review—*"Introduction to the*

Text"[8]—you talk about Kostelanetz's being a friend of yours. Could you tell us how you met him?

Antigua. He's a great world traveler. He's been everywhere on earth and he knows how to travel and how to be in strange places. Antigua was one of the places he liked. He always went there when nobody else was there. We had a house of our own down there for close to twenty years, and we'd go down for Christmas. André always wanted a place to be at Christmas where he wouldn't be alone. And so we got to know him very well. He's a very lovable, charming man.

The premier of this work and the commission by Kostelanetz was for a very important occasion because this work inaugurated the Lincoln Center Festival in June that ran through the summer. The New York Times *printed on July 9 of that year your remarks to or at the festival and I think the remarks were delivered at the opening. (Why they waited three weeks to publish them, it's not clear.) In those remarks you talk about the importance of the festival, the need for art in an age of advanced technological achievement, and therefore your delight at the festival.*

You couldn't astonish me more! I don't remember anything about that. I don't remember. Where would I have spoken?

Would you have spoken at that concert?

No. Can't throw any light on that at all!

What did Ada, as a professional musician, think of the Magic Prison, *the composition?*

It was a question really of my morale. The disastrous performance actually just broke me up. I've never seen anything so sickening! It's nobody's fault. It's just that the whole machinery of the place failed. What she really thought about it I don't know, but she'd tell me that it was great. I'm sure she didn't think that!

Have you heard the recording that was made in 1970?

Yes, I have heard it. It is a very audible and very good recording of the thing not under the conditions of that hall.

Were the words hard to understand in that theater?

Hard to understand! You couldn't hear anything. As I recall it, the whole public address system went off at one time during the performance and then it came on. Everything was distorted. Just a disaster!

They did it again Wednesday and Thursday night that week. Did you go a second time?

I did not. I wouldn't have been seen dead in that place! But they did do it again and I think it went better. André is still apologetic about it.

At about the same time that Magic Prison *was first performed, you resigned from Amherst. In the next few years, you wrote the play,* An Evening's Journey to Conway, Massachusetts,[9] *"The Wild Old Wicked Man," a volume of poems, and* A Continuing Journey, *a collection of essays. Then in 1971 you published* Scratch, *another play. You dedicated that to Peter Hunt and Stuart Ostrow. Who are they?*

Stuart Ostrow is the producer of *Scratch* and Peter Hunt was its director.

So the production was already planned before the book was printed?

It must have been. I just don't remember what the relation was between the book and the production. Ostrow came to me with a suggestion which I thought was so preposterous I didn't even answer his letter which was that I should consider a play made out of Steve Benét's *Devil and Daniel Webster.* My Yale classmate, Douglas Moore the composer, had made an opera out of *The Devil and Daniel Webster,* which was done at Sturbridge and then many other places too, and I had no interest in that at all. Well, Ostrow then finally turned up here with his charming wife and a couple of children and we talked about the thing very late. It occurred to me that *The Devil and Daniel Webster* might be a lot more interesting with the historical Webster than with simply the Webster who's supposed to be the smartest man in New Hampshire, which is what he was for Steve Benét. Steve used him for his ability to out-talk anybody; he could beat the devil. Steve had a great sense of humor, and that was a very humorous story.

I don't quite remember how all that happened except that I finally got very much interested in Daniel Webster's defense of the Union in the Senate during the years before the Civil War, which had the effect of postponing the

Civil War for about ten years. Webster was willing to make compromises. The result was the South missed its golden opportunity and we won the Civil War. And that aspect of the story seemed to me to be interesting—the relation between Webster's feeling about the Union and the real underlying issue— which Lincoln uncovered in that speech of his at Philadelphia on his way down to his first inauguration and again at Gettysburg, turning the issue in the Civil War into what it really was, the great issue of human freedom, and thus winning the war.

It struck me that maybe the famous trial before the jury of the dead and damned might be interesting to work on that way. So I moved it in that direction, and to my surprise, to my continued surprise (my surprise right now), a great many people, including my beloved friend Boylston Adams Tompkins[10] and his sons, all of them, thought the play absolutely came over in those terms, and so did a growing audience in Boston. We were playing to full houses when we came to the end of our three-week run in Boston. We'd had a good review on the front page of the *Boston Herald*. We'd had a dreadful review from Kevin Kelly, who used to write theater reviews for the *Globe*, and a sort of ambiguous one from Elliot Norton.[11] But we were doing very well and then came the murder in New York, and it was a murder, by Clive Barnes. The thing just closed down. It opened, played two nights and then closed. There is a very strange story in back of it, which is sort of irrelevant to what we're interested in here, but making it as brief as I can, it comes to this. Kevin Kelly's review was just a smart aleck, little boy review with wisecracks which I would have simply ignored. It had no merit. But the *Globe* couldn't ignore it or at least so it seemed. The *Globe* published a full column editorial, in effect telling their dramatic critic to read a little American history and to read the play before he began talking about it. I've been told (I've never looked into it—I really don't want to know) that he went and cried to Clive Barnes, who was a brand-new English dance reviewer, who was taking on the theater for the *New York Times*. Barnes apparently felt the call of a wounded comrade. He haunted our rehearsals when we were preparing in New York. And he simply let us have it—killed it cold. And Mr. Adolph Ochs,[12] who had written me a warm, excited letter of enthusiastic congratulations after the opening, wrote me the saddest little note afterward, and Scotty Reston said, "I have nothing to say. I'm just too embarrassed to speak." It was one of those nasty, nasty things that happen in theater and one reason why I think commercial theater is something to leave alone. It's not a free business!

Has Scratch *been done since?*

I think a few times, but it requires actors of the kind that amateur groups can't come up with. *Scratch* has to be played by a man as good as Will Geer and there was only one Will Geer!

Following Scratch, *you were writing essays and* Champion of a Cause, *and you produced another poetry collection,* The Human Season. *Then came the Bicentennial. We counted nine events that you were involved in that had you hopping all across the country. First of all there was the performance of* The Great American Fourth of July Parade *in Pittsburgh. (These are not necessarily in chronological order.) There were the poetry reading in the Library of Congress, the appearance on* CBS *amidst the tall ships, the speech at the American Philosophical Society, the reading of* Songs for Eve *at the Mohawk Trail Concert, the sermon at the United Church in Conway, the reading of* An Evening's Journey to Conway *for the Conway Festival, the Bill Moyers interview, the Boston radio station birthday party, and the opening of Boston's bicentennial year with your new poem "Night Watch in the City of Boston."*

I know, but only a few of those are really bicentennial; the WGBH radio appearance, for example, was in connection with the publication of a new book I have out this year called *New and Collected Poems* and the sermon with the Conway church just happened to be in the year 1976. But you've got the principal ones. It began with *The Great American Fourth of July Parade.* That was proposed to me by my friend Sam Hazo, a remarkable Arab—he asked me to refer to him as an Arab; his father was a Levantine. He started the International Poetry Forum in Pittsburgh and ran it for about ten years. It's an extremely interesting organization. He's built up a good audience. It's quite an achievement. I think I opened it and then I think I read two times more and I really got to know Sam quite well—a very charming man. He called me up, oh heavens, it must be about two years ago in 1974 asking me if I would consider doing a play of some kind for them, that is, something that they could commission and they could put on and publish. I was pretty skeptical about it except that I had been thinking about the same thing, but what I was skeptical about was whether anything would happen, that is whether I would be able to really get it finished.

Was he thinking of it in terms of a verse play for radio?

No, at that time it was just a large idea. I don't think that Sam, when he first thought of it, even said play, but I immediately began thinking about a play because for thirty or forty years I had been fascinated by the correspondence between John Adams and Thomas Jefferson and I have always wanted to do something with it and I knew just what I wanted to do and it seemed to me very appropriate for the Bicentennial, which it actually did turn out to be. And I went out to see Sam and we had various negotiations about it and finally worked it out and I wrote it and it was to be done in the spring of '75. I started working on it the year before that, wrote it through that winter. I made the decision quite early that it would be a radio play. (I have always liked the whole business of the radio verse play. It's very flexible, it can be mounted cheaply, and it's made for a man who writes verse because all you have is the verse, all you have is the word. You can have a few sound effects, but they are always intrusions and this is truly a splendid thing. It's a shame that television was ever invented. We'd still have radio verse plays if it hadn't been.)

And I finished it in the winter of '75, and having made up my mind that it was going to be a radio verse play, I was looking around for somebody who would produce a radio verse play. I had no idea where to turn. Back in the old days, in the thirties when I began writing verse plays for radio, I would simply have gone to CBS and to their experimental theater which was a marvelous thing for verse plays of mine. But there is nothing like that anymore and the big networks aren't interested at all, although I'll have to present an exception to that a little later in this account, as you will see. But I'd been fishing around and I can't remember now who it was that told me about Ear Play out in Madison, Wisconsin. Ear Play is the radio wing of PBS. What they do is to put on productions of radio plays and other radio performances which they distribute free of charge to all the noncommercial radio stations in the country, which means all the college and university stations, like WGBH in Boston. And I got in touch with them. They sent a remarkable woman east to see me, a woman in her late twenties who is directing for them, very attractive, very intelligent, and they agreed that they would do this. So that there were two operations in mind in the beginning and the middle of 1975; one was preparing a proper text for Ear Play and the other was arranging for the production Sam wanted to put on in Pittsburgh. These things went along sort of like two horses with different ideas of speed. The Ear Play thing went fairly well. Their production was really quite good. I can't be more enthusiastic about it because there were some casting problems which Ear Play couldn't solve. They had a very good Jefferson and a very good Adams. Will Geer was Adams and couldn't have been better. He's just wonderful. He's not a character actor at all; he's a good actor who is also a character actor. The contemporary voices—they didn't have money enough—are satisfactory neither to Martha

MacLeish at Harvard.

MacLeish at the time of *J.B.*, c. 1960. *(Sunday
Bulletin*, Philadelphia)

MacLeish with President Kennedy at the
dedication of the Frost Library, Amherst College,
October 26, 1963.

Ada and Archie in Conway, 1970s.

VanCleef, who is the charming young lady director, nor to me. They were just some kids they got in off the street and kids off the street these days do not articulate the English language. They make a noise that is understood by their peers to be words. At any rate, I don't want to be too hard on them because they are a wonderful generation from whom we hope great things.

The Pittsburgh production was a stage production and more difficult to arrange.[13] Sam finally got hold of John Houseman, who had directed *Panic* in the thirties, and they got a cast together. The production was as good as Ear Play's and, from the point of view of casting, better, because they had better people. They had no Will Geer, but I mean right down the line it was better. It was produced then on three separate occasions in Pittsburgh. At the same time the book was published by the University of Pittsburgh Press. Houghton Mifflin very kindly stepped out of the way and University of Pittsburgh Press published it. And the Ear Play production was released in the middle of the year, I think. I heard it on the air from the station over in Amherst. How many radio stations around the country did it, I don't know. It's very difficult to say.

Now so far as the Bicentennial goes, I think this was a bicentennial operation, but it was not done in the bicentennial year, it was done a year earlier, which I think was not a bad idea, really. But the actual bicentennial performance of part of it developed out of the blue in the spring or the late winter of 1976. I was down in the West Indies and I got a letter from the head of CBS News who told me that they had decided to devote sixteen straight hours of time with Walter Cronkite running a marathon on the Fourth of July and they wanted to know if I would do something for them. I wrote back: "I just simply can't do it; I've too much to do and I've rather shot my bolt on this occasion because I've already written a verse play for radio which has been produced and is therefore of no interest to you," and bowed out. And a month later I got a reply saying that the head of CBS News had read the play and could he please do it or do parts of it. They were going to use it in two ways. At some time during the day, they didn't know quite when, church bells were going to ring all over America. My play, *The Great American Fourth of July Parade*, begins in a radio station in New England somewhere, which is going to go on the air at dawn on the fourth day of July as the sun comes up at the easternmost extents of Maine with the sound of church bells going all over New England. The play begins with conversation between the man playing the part of the director and the engineers, who have a hell of a time getting anything that sounds like church bells. But then the bells do come in and the poem names every church in New England where the bells ring and in what order. Well, this crew set off, and they went to every one of the churches named; they photographed the area; they photographed the church or did something that identified it.

There's a line in the play with reference to "Nantucket where the bells are buoys." B-u-o-y-s. They went to Nantucket and there's the most beautiful buoy you ever saw in your life. So, this was one thing, the bells.

Then they taped a long section of the beginning between Adams and Jefferson, with Jefferson's introduction first with his fiddle and then his voice and then Adams. They didn't try to put anything of a bell sound with it, although they did use photographs of paintings and so forth. And these two things were going to appear sometime during the day. Walter Cronkite wrote me. He didn't know quite when they were going to come, but he thought one would be about two o'clock in the afternoon, which is when the bells were supposed to go, which struck me as odd since my play deals with dawn, and the other, the Jefferson-Adams conversation, would be in prime time. But the thing that was supposed to have happened in prime time happened at 11:15 in the morning. I was just turning the television on when I heard my own voice, and the thing that was supposed to be at two in the afternoon was in prime time in the evening: the bells! Aside from that, everything went beautifully.

You were introduced as our poet laureate and you were photographed here in Conway.

They photographed me while I was reading. They sent a crew up here to Conway. CBS has extraordinary roving crews, marvelously competent people and almost always very pleasant to work with and this was about the best I've ever seen. The man they sent up in charge knew exactly what he wanted out of the play and we spent a day recording all this. They photographed me in the chair out there on the lawn, reading both Adams and Jefferson. Then they moved away from me, thank God. But, no, this all worked quite well.

There's an amusing aspect to this. My agent in New York, Jerry Talbert, was very eager to find some company that would record *The Great American Fourth of July Parade,* especially for schools and colleges. He's a graduate of the Harvard Law School, which is unusual for someone in a theatrical agency, and he is a stubborn man who will persist. He was after the head of the Columbia Records business, which is owned by CBS, and he had been turned down for about the fourth time when he just happened to ask me—this was before the broadcast—whether I had any connections with CBS, and I said, "Only Walter Cronkite, who is doing pieces of *The Great American Fourth of July Parade* on July Fourth." Jerry went through the roof, called this man back and said, "You don't keep in touch with your own operations, do you?" So, anyway, Columbia is going to do it. They haven't done it yet [1977] but this means that recordings will be available for schools, and I like that idea, not because it's my play, but because Mr. Jefferson and Mr. Adams speak pretty much the way they really did.[14] So it gives me some pleasure. Well, this was the most extensive and time-consuming part of the entire operation, I mean the most time-consuming part of my relation with the Bicentennial.

Was there any confusion or conflict between your dealings with the Madison place and Pittsburgh?

No, they were doing totally different things. Madison was distributing their recording of the play gratis to radio stations all over the country. Pittsburgh was, one, publishing the book through the University of Pittsburgh Press, and second, putting on a big public production. They never got into each other's hair at all. There is a recording of selected elements of the three nights at Pittsburgh. They chose the best performances of the various parts of the play. And that was produced in very few numbers of recordings; I have forgotten how many. They were financed—incidentally, this is an interesting story, a very touching one to me—they were financed by a gift which totaled something like seven or eight thousand dollars, which was made by Milton Eisenhower, who was General Eisenhower's brother, an old friend of mine, and a Pennsylvania judge named Roy Wilkinson, whom I see every winter and am very fond of, and a third man to me totally unknown. These three got together and financed the number that could be made.

Did you go to Pittsburgh?

Oh yes, indeed, I did and it was very pleasant. I wouldn't have missed seeing Jack Houseman for anything. But to get back to the Bicentennial. The other principal bicentennial operation (there are two or three, but the second perhaps in terms of order) was an address. My old friend Julian Boyd[15] of Princeton, who was editor of the Jefferson Papers, was, down to last year, the president of the American Philosophical Society, with which I had my major row some thirty years before[16] and to which I had never belonged. And Julian asked me if I would write an address for a symposium that they were going to hold as a bicentennial operation of the American Philosophical Society. And the invitation coming from whence it came, there was nothing I could say about it except that I would do it, and I did do it and delivered it in April.

It was sort of a tricky situation because there were enough old timers who remembered back thirty years to make the atmosphere a little chilly, but the thing went like fireworks and the *Times* heard about it and the end result was that it was prepared for (I didn't prepare it much) the Op-Ed page of the *Times* for the Fourth of July; they ran it the day before. They gave it a title: "Now Let US Address the Main Question—Bicentennial of What." And they gave it the whole Op-Ed page except for the two outside corners. That, I think, is probably, I gather from the reaction to it, my principal contribution to the Bicentennial. It produced reactions of a contrary, I was going to say violent, nature only from one segment, but the violence, although it was violent enough, was a little bit hysterical and there weren't many members of the chorus. These were people who regarded the whole thing as an attack on Nixon because Nixon is once mentioned in it. The Nixon defenders are now really paranoid in reverse. The general reaction to it, particularly from the *Times*, was quite the opposite and that's something I take a good deal of satisfaction from, not that I think it's the last word on the subject, but it does get at what I think has always been the real question.

The Bicentennial has been treated by people like our present president and others as a sort of national birthday, with hoopla, congratulations, and so forth. It is nothing of the kind. What it really is is the anniversary of the Declaration of Independence, which is what happened on the fourth of July 1776. And the Declaration of Independence poses, whether you think about it in anniversary terms or not, a tremendous question, which is the question, "Anniversary of what?" What was the Declaration of Independence? Was it what Adams thought it was, just independence from Great Britain, or was it what Jefferson thought it was, the greatest revolutionary concept in all history, the revolution in the individual human being against exploiters of all kinds? Well, I don't think there is any more I can say about that.

There was a third event, which is perhaps more important to me than either *The Great American Fourth of July Parade* or the Op-Ed thing (the American Philosophical address). It had various stages in its development, but I can talk about it best in one specific dramatic situation. There takes place every year at Bread Loaf in Vermont a writers' conference which is usually late in the month of August. It is preceded by the Middlebury School of English, which somehow or other succeeds. The Middlebury School of English gets together, both among people who teach at it and the people who go to it, some of the best people in the whole area of literature in general and American literature in particular. It's a marvelous audience to read to; I've read several times in the past and it is now in the hands of a professor at Middlebury College, Paul Cubeta, who had told me that, although he wanted me to come considerably after the Fourth of July, he was going to make that evening their bicentennial operation.

Now, I didn't like that very much. The Bicentennial seemed to me to be dragged in by its scruff, but it turned out that wasn't his idea at all and so I began seriously to think about what I could do and an idea occurred to me which proved to be workable. I decided that I would take my relationship, so to speak, to the great Republic as a topic and just engage it on a decade basis, decade by decade by decade, because it has changed very, very much, using poems from each period, some of which we've already talked about. That is to say, in the twenties, when I was going on myself from late twenty to middle thirties, I really wasn't very aware of the Republic. I took it entirely for granted. I'd come from a home which was intelligent and orderly. My father was a Scotsman with very deep feelings about Scotland, but even deeper feelings about the United States, which he'd come to at the age of eighteen. And my mother was the daughter of a Congregational clergyman whose ancestry was straight Connecticut, right back to Elder Brewster, who landed somewhere else as you recall. Between the two of them, my mother took Connecticut totally for granted; she took New England for granted. She moved to Illinois and Illinois was a new experience. She went to work in Hull House and thereabouts as soon as her children were old enough to learn. But she had three hundred years of the United States back of her; and she had no serious questions about the Republic at all. Her assumptions were assumptions of total acceptance. She realized its faults. She didn't talk about them much, although she fought them like a tiger when they met her, when they got in the way of what she cared about. A swastika on the church in Glencoe, Illinois, put Mother, at the age of ninety, on a war horse. She had that whole town turned upside down by five o'clock in the afternoon.

With this kind of a background and going to a very establishment preparatory school, Hotchkiss, and going to Yale and Harvard Law School, I was interested in the intellectual world as I began to learn about it, but I was not much concerned about the United States; I simply accepted that situation. And the question didn't really arise for me until, first of all, my year during the war and then my wife's and my return to Paris five or six years later and the six or seven years we stopped there.

I came back from that with a very sharp realization that to be an American was a question, not an answer. And out of that came a poem which I wrote to my friend, Gerald Murphy, shortly after I came here, called "American Letter," which is an examination exactly of those emotions. The question underlying the poem is why, back here on this hill, in my own country, my mother's country, I should feel so drawn by Persia, for an example, the Mediterranean coast, France, Paris, why, why? And this is the beginning and perhaps the first move that is involved. So I first read "American Letter" and then talked a little about it in more or less the way I did just now. And also we had "Years of the Dog," which, as I said, had nothing to do with Americans in Paris, which is now a fashionable and wholly contemptible topic because what was going on in Paris was infinitely more important than the few Americans who were there. It was people from all over the world who were there and they were tremendous figures: Picasso, Stravinsky in full operation, Joyce. Talking about it as "the Scott Fitzgerald in Paris thing," really (although I love Scott) makes me vomit. It's disgusting! There's nothing to do with us, neither of historical, literary, or intellectual interest. It's tripe.

Then the ground shifts a little bit because of the consequences of the world war, the First World War. What happened in the middle of the twenties was that it became pretty apparent, even to people my age and even to the people who had been involved in the war as I had, that the war, the Wilsonian rhetoric, and the British propaganda which my brother bought, was all an enormous fraud and fabrication; the war was nothing but a commercial war. There was no reason for it except reasons of commercial competition. There were no moral reasons, no humanitarian reasons, no humane reasons. Nothing. It killed millions of men. It slaughtered an entire generation. It's the most disgusting thing that has happened really in the history of this planet. Vietnam is just a smear beside it. And as I told you I lost my brother in the war. He was shot down a month before the end of it. He disappeared. I was sent back during, actually in the middle of, the second Battle of the Marne to take a new battery at home and three months after that I had word that he was missing. His body was not found until the next winter and that was all about as bad as it could be. I then began to have an attitude toward the Republic which was anything but loving. I took it hard; I took it personally. And I also took it childishly, which I think you are inclined to do, and at Bread Loaf I read a number of poems which deal with that. The one that deals with it most is "The Silent Slain," which is the first poem in that collection.

The Silent Slain
for Kenneth MacLeish, 1894–1918

We too, we too, descending once again
The hills of our own land, we too have heard
Far off—Ah, que ce cor a longue haleine—
The horn of Roland in the passages of Spain,
The first, the second blast, the failing third,
And with the third turned back and climbed once more
The steep road southward, and heard faint the sound
Of swords, of horses, the disastrous war,

And crossed the dark defile at last, and found
At Roncevaux upon the darkening plain
The dead against the dead and on the silent ground
The silent slain—

I also read "Memorial Rain" and "Lines for an Interment," which is again about my brother fifteen years after, and the whole mood here at home. Nobody would talk about the war, and it was just more than I could bear to see the whole thing just wiped out with a wet sponge. The American Legion started parades, the whole thing became very hard to take.

Then the second shift came home and by the time the thirties came along, the whole situation was different. My feeling toward the country was even more violent because the Depression was so palpably a great deal more than merely an economic disaster; it was a great human disaster. It was the most humiliating period of years I have ever lived through. You were ashamed to have enough to eat as you looked at friends offering you apples for sale! And out of that came a group of poems called *Frescoes for Mr. Rockefeller's City*, which are all Depression poems. Another was a Harvard Phi Beta Kappa poem, which I published as "1933" (it's the "Elpenor" poem), and then some satiric pieces like "Invocation to the Social Muse." And then in the middle of this you get the Spanish war and I read a poem of mine called "The Spanish Lie," which was written about the time of the destruction of Guernica.

And the next decade is the forties. None of these distinctions, of course, are chronological, and the edges are all blurred, but nevertheless, the fact is that once we got into the war, once we were committed to it, everything changed. The country somehow or other pulled itself together. There had been at the beginning of that decade a very severe, very deep split in the American psyche. The America First movement was a reaction to the First World War. "We're never going to be sold again," they said. They didn't realize that what was happening in Germany presented a very different problem, indeed, presented really the question of survival of free societies. And when the war was won, by the end of the war, we'd come into what seems to me to be the noblest period of our history that I know anything about. We fought the war superbly once we got started. We started late; we suffered Pearl Harbor and the Battle of the Coral Sea. We suffered terrible mauling in Africa; we were definitely underdogs; we had a brand new army—people who had never fought before. We pulled ourselves together. We felt that we had been true to ourselves; we felt that we had a real enemy and that we'd destroyed him; we felt that we had achieved ourselves and we had. It was an extraordinary decade. This period of change from the thirties to the forties corresponds to the period when I went to Washington. I was working on *America Was Promises*. And that was a poem about that feeling in the forties, although it was written in '39.

In the poem you call on the brothers to speak, to seize the promise, to grasp hold of it even if it's painful to do so. Apparently, to you the next decade showed that this promise was fulfilled.

Yes, at the time the poem was written, I could feel (and this note is struck again and again in the poem) or thought I could feel, a surge forward in the country under great leadership—the first leadership in twenty-five years, ah, fifty. A sense of achievement, of self realization. And the end of it (it ends with the phrase "Oh believe this") was a wish and hope together because nobody knew it would happen at that time, but it did.

If you were writing that retrospectively, would you have changed the tense of the title?

No, because the point is that by 1945 America was no longer a promise—that promise was realizing itself. The promise ran all the way back to Columbus. Anyway, I resigned, of course, from government in 1945 when Mr. Roosevelt died and I devoted the next five years to a long poem and some short ones— the long one called *Actfive*, which was an attempt to make sense in my terms, that is, in terms of the problem that I was concerned with, of the events of my six years in government. And the conviction that the thing had happened, that it had momentarily happened, is very strong in the end of that poem, at least it is to me. I didn't read all of the *Actfive* to that audience up there because it's too long to read, but I read a little bit from the end of it.

Then the fifties became a strange sort of loss of interest almost as though we'd had something in our hands and broke it and were letting it drop and the name for that is McCarthy. And I read some of the poems from that mood. There's the "Two Priests," and "The Black Day," which is a poem about the suicide of a lad whom McCarthy denounced on the floor of the Senate as being, doubtless, a traitor—not one iota of proof that he was anything but the most devoted, as he was one of the most charming, of men. And the "Corn Cob and the Lie," which was again McCarthy, and ending with "The Ship of Fools."

And then I finally ended the whole thing with a poem among the new poems in this book, which is called "National Security," which is about the mess that Nixon was a subscriber to. I have gone into this at great length, but

I'll give you this list of titles because if you can't read them, you can at least look up the pages and you'll see it. This was, in retrospect to me and from the point of view of things I cared about most deeply . . . this was the most important involvement with the Bicentennial. That is, it was trying to make sense of my what is now a love affair with the Republic, very strongly so, but which has been very many different things in the past.

So you would really see the late forties as being a time at which we came closest to achieving the promise of America, as you described it.

We began losing it very fast though, too, and in that same period for me there is a poem called "Brave New World" about Thomas Jefferson's grave, which is a protest against our failure to seize the moment of triumph, to reassert our commitment to the things we really believe in, to the American Revolution. We let the retrogressive reactionary Russian Revolution step in and take the east of Europe. I am not suggesting that I agree with Churchill that we should immediately have declared war on the Russians; this is something that I couldn't accept for a moment. I hated the idea at the time and did everything I could to belittle it, but we just lost all interest in the cause. I mean we lost all public interest in the cause for which we had been fighting. I feel sure that if Mr. Roosevelt had lived and kept his strength, it would have been very different in the late forties.

In The Great American Fourth of July Parade, *you say the same thing about the need for people to know what that revolution meant for the Republic to be saved, for the Republic to endure. Now the play ends . . . optimistically?*

It ends with a phrase that Jefferson uses in that letter of June 24, 1826, to the people of Washington, in which he declines the invitation to come down, and which has that wonderful phrase about the mass of mankind which has not been born, saddled, and bridled for a chosen few to ride by the grace of God. It picks up "the grace of God, the grace of God." It works dramatically. It doesn't read dramatically. I mean to say that, in the book, it doesn't work as it worked on the stage in Pittsburgh or as it works in the recording.

Do you feel optimistic now about America's promises?

It's awfully hard to be optimistic with the kind of leadership we have at this moment, which is flagrantly political and self-serving. That the convictions of the country at large are the kind of convictions that Mr. Jefferson would have applauded, I think it's very probable; I don't know how you talk about things of this kind. I don't go out and take private polls and I see very few people, but judging as well as one can judge reactions as they are reported in the press and so forth, I think the country is set, ready, eager, and waiting for the kind of leadership that it ought to have. We are a self-governing people and what a self-governing people must do is find the agency by which they will govern themselves.

In 1976, you also wrote a commemorative poem for Yale University's 275th anniversary.[17]

Yes. That is the proper phrase to use, but that's not what the poem is. I'm afraid the poem is a sort of declaration of war. But I like it now; I think it's a pretty good poem. And Kingman Brewster, the president of Yale, likes it very much.

In 1976 you had published the New and Collected Poems. *In connection with that, could you tell us how a book of poetry evolves—how it is generated, and the process of putting poems together. Do they come in cycles, for example?*

The *New and Collected Poems* took several years, and I can deal with the principal part of your question easily, in a very few sentences. You never think in terms of a book until you've got enough poems together to make one. Then you consider whether they will make a book, and you try to get your friends to advise you about it, get your publisher to talk to you about it; then you decide how you are going to put these things together, in what order. Above all, what's going to be the first poem and what's going to be the last? Those are tricky questions. But the book of poetry differs from books of another kind. You could set out, of course, to write, and I have so done, a prose book—on a single theme or a combination of themes—and do all your writing with the book in mind. In the art of poetry, you're always concerned with the poem and not with the book at all. You never think of the book until you're ready to go ahead—that is to say, even with *Conquistador*, which I knew was going to be a book, a book which was going to be concerned solely with *Conquistador*, nevertheless, I thought of it only as the poem, and the form of the poem. I've never had very close relationships with a publisher although I've always liked my publisher. I like my present publisher very, very much and Bob Linscott, who was the occasion by which I got into Houghton Mifflin in the first place, fifty years ago, was a very good personal friend; but I've never sat down with a publisher as Scott Fitzgerald used to do with Max Perkins[18] and talk about what I was going to do next and how I was going to do it. So that my experience of the book as such isn't very active.

You've always done a good deal of public reading of your work, especially in recent years. You read at the Carnegie Library in Pittsburgh several times, for example.

I read there four times. It's the International Poetry Forum I mentioned before—at the Carnegie Library in Pittsburgh, financed by the Mellon Foundation and really international. This time, in 1977, the audience completely filled the auditorium of the Carnegie Library, which is a huge auditorium. They were just hanging from the straps! I don't know why. For them, I did what I did at Smith a year ago, which really did work. It was another chronological approach. I took a considerable number of poems dealing with the same experience from very early poems down to very late ones. I raised specifically the question with the audience before I started and as I was reading as to whether there was any progression among them, whether you could say of a given poem that it was new in comparison to what preceded it or whether you couldn't. I never asked for a vote, perhaps cowardly on my part, but it would have terminated the evening if I had. There would have been a lot of debate! I did that, but with fewer poems and with a longer preparation at Pittsburgh and it, too, worked extraordinarily well! In both cases I took off from Saul Bellow's[19] statement and his quotation at Stockholm of Proust's statement that without art we would know neither ourselves nor anybody else, and used that as a point of departure. This is a true statement; at least, it's true to me and I can't imagine its being untrue to anybody who knew what art is.

Let's take the theme of love, which is probably the most common theme in poetry. Poetry has dealt with that theme since the beginning of time and is always dealing with it and will always so continue to do. Do we really know more about that experience as the result of the poems we have read, the poems that have been written, or don't we? In other words, what is the justification for the art of poetry? One can be quite positive about all these things; at least I'm very positive about them. I haven't any doubt at all in my own mind that Proust is dead right. Proof of that is that when the psychiatrists come right down to informative communications of their own, they almost always quote poems or use poetry in one form or another. Freud was constantly doing it, God knows.

At Pittsburgh a very, very strange thing happened. I had this carefully worked out. I wanted to give Sam Hazo his money's worth. I was going to read for fifty-five minutes. Reading and talking got to be about forty-eight minutes, forty-nine, and then I had gotten down toward the end, about five or six poems I wanted to read, but I was reading a sequence of these, the new poems in my collected volume. I read "The Old Gray Couple" and at the end of it the whole room came up. Whoosh! They were on their feet! There was a tremendous amount of noise! I could just see out of the corner of my eye, on my watch, that I had about five minutes to go and I finally got them silenced and then fumbled around for something to read and put my hand on a poem that was right next page to "The Old Gray Couple"—"Definitions of Old Age."

Definitions of Old Age

Your eyes change.
Your handwriting changes.
You can't read what you once wrote.
Even your own thoughts sound wrong to you,
something some old idiot has misquoted.

When apple trees are old as you are,
over-aged and crooked grown,
something happens to their occupation.
What's the use, this late, of bearing apples?
Let the apples find a father of their own.

Or put it in contemporary terms: the time
when men resign from their committees,
cancel their memberships, decline
the chairmanship of the United Fund,
buy a farm in Dorset or New Fane
and still get up at seven every morning
right on time for nothing left to do but
sit and age
and look up "dying" in the yellow pages.

old age
level light
evening in the afternoon
love without the bitterness and so
good-night

I started to read it without realizing what the last one (the last definition in "Definitions of Old Age") is—what the last two lines are. So I read "love without the bitterness and so / good-night" and walked off the stage! It looked as though I'd planned that whole thing! I was ashamed of myself; too slick for words! I woke up that night and felt myself blushing in bed.

Did you happen to see the article on Hemingway in the Sunday Times?[20] *Did you have any response to it?*

Yes. It just infuriates me! Disgusts and infuriates me! What is principally irritating is that there isn't even the faintest pretense, in that piece, of dealing with Hemingway's work. It is a gossip piece. It is a particularly nasty kind of gossip piece. The idea that in some mysterious way, because Hemingway's idiot of a mother, one of the biggest fools who ever lived, kept him in girls' clothes for the first two or three years, there had to be something wrong with him sexually! And because he liked to shoot and really liked warfare, liked to have a gun in his hands, he had to be in some way compensating for some sexual defect! This is so obvious, so boring, so tiresome, and has so little to do with anything, that it infuriates me. I read it because I felt I had to. What did you think of it?

It appeared to be an attempt to update the Hemingway image, which has suffered somewhat from being so macho.

I know, but the way to go at that, if one is interested in Hemingway as a writer, is to talk about his writing and get rid of some of the manure that has been spread on his name. By the way, he wrote me very shortly before he died and told me that he had three novels in the safe deposit vault in New York, and I apologize to him now because I didn't believe him at the time. I thought that this was one of those delusions that he was under at that time. Well, obviously one of them was *A Moveable Feast*, the Paris thing, and another was *Islands in the Stream.*[21]

You obviously feel very strongly about what writers can be subject to in print. How are you handling the matter of your own biography? Have you chosen someone to do your life story?

The whole thing's very distasteful to me. The whole idea of the biography makes me sick, but Roy Winnick[22] had been after me for some time to see if he could get my permission to do a biography of me. And at first I told him what

I told everybody else: that I don't want a biography if it can possibly be helped. But if that's an unrealistic view of it, I certainly don't want one while either of us, my wife and myself, are around. The one thing I detest more than anything in the world is reading about myself!

But it became pretty plain, a year or two ago, that if I didn't take some action, such as saying, "All right; you're the man. Go ahead," then I would spend a great deal of my time talking to people who had plans of their own. And this has dealt with that. I must say that's all quieted down. Roy Winnick (he has a degree from Princeton—Ph.D.)—was a graduate student at Princeton and working with Lawrance Thompson, under what terms I don't know— maybe just for his own education—on the Frost biography when Thompson became ill and died. And he had to take over—pretty difficult job. There was research left to be completed, a lot of it; and then there was the entire writing, and the writing had to be an adaptation of Thompson's style so that there wouldn't be a complete, shocking break for the reader. This meant that he had to imitate Thompson. He also had to adopt all of Thompson's major feelings about Frost, which were just impressions in Thompson's mind. He couldn't suddenly start a new biography when Frost was sixty-two or whatever age he was at the end of the second volume. The reviews were not particularly ex- citing, but you would hardly expect them to be. Thompson was dead and from the point of view of most reviewers the whole thing was over and the third volume was just a sort of necessary addendum. Well, it turned out to be a lot better than that! How in the world Robert Frost stood having a man around as his assigned official biographer for about thirty years is more than I can see! I think Thompson saw too much of him—learned to dislike him very heartily! Which ought to be a warning to anybody!

But we've been working. I've been busy over the last two or three weekends with him, and I have to let him up in the attic and he finds letters. I have to look at them before I can let him look at them. He's an extremely inventive youngster. (I think he's just under thirty.) On the way up here, for example, he stopped off at the Hotchkiss School, which I attended, and with which I've had no connections since I left. I left in quite a huff. I think a mutual huff. Huff all around! And he stopped and was warmly greeted by the present administration who told him he could Xerox anything out of my file, which he proceeded to do. The file included a number of letters from my beloved mother, who was concerned about what I was turning into. And Winnick brought them along and read me one which has views about myself which I never felt my mother held. What a hell of a time to learn! As a matter of fact, at this point he knows more about me than I do. A great deal more. And he can quote chapter and verse. He silences me at once!

Was biography the reason for Riders on the Earth—*or at least the second part of it?*[23]

A while ago I embarked on what was going to be a rather small book, not more than 150 pages perhaps, dealing with the years we were in Paris and the question which that relates to in our lives: my wife and myself. That is to say, the really crucial question of breaking off from a standard means of livelihood like the law, and committing yourself to the most risky and unremunerative of all activities: the writing of verse, singing of songs. And that's the theme: the growing certainty that I had to do what I had started out some eight or ten years before as a boy to do, in spite of the fact that I hadn't done it, I hadn't written one line I thought much of. I had a very deep conviction that I had to give up the practice of law—and do it.

It's almost a reverse of the attitude you think of as "doing your own thing"—because I could have been perfectly happy going on and practicing law. I probably would have made quite a lot of money and everything would have been cozy, except that we would have had to live on the North Shore somewhere. All that would have been fine. But it would have left out one compulsion under which I live; I had to write the kind of poem I wanted to write and I didn't even then know what it was. I tried doing it while I was practicing law. I tried that very hard. My theory was that I could have Sundays anyway and maybe some hours on Saturday, forgetting entirely that if you have a case going on and have a witness on the stand at the time the court adjourns, all you can think about all week long and all weekend long is what you're going to ask him when you face him again on Monday. And as for having a mind sort of free to move on its own—no. It's that situation and its gradual resolution in Paris that I attacked in this thing.

So always we return to the beginnings, and your dealing with demands from outside and inside—the outside ones trying to take you away from your work. For instance, the next reading. How is the preparation coming?

Not very well. I haven't started it yet.

Isn't that next week?

Yes, I've got two days now to do it.

Do you work well under pressure?

Why not? The pressure's here!

A F T E R W O R D

1979	Gold Medal for Poetry from the American Academy of Arts and Letters.
1980	*Six Plays.* Houghton Mifflin Co.
1982	Died April 20 at Massachusetts General Hospital in Boston.

After the series of interviews was completed, updates were conducted. The conversation was more wide ranging than before because there was no chronology to observe. The first of these was June 12, 1980, when MacLeish was eighty-eight.

*

I've been reading a book called *Three Farms*, by Mark Kramer,[1] which is an examination of the agribusiness farm out on the coast, another commerical farm in mid-America, and then a farm farmed by a single farmer which has developed extraordinary techniques for production of milk. And that single farm is here in Conway, owned by my friend Ray Totman, and is now run by his son Lee, whom Mark defines as the best dairy farmer in the United States. Up against agribusiness, he's made a tremendous success of that farm. But the great thing about the book is not the judgment it comes up with but the way it's written. Kramer is not a farmer. Everything he knows about farming he learned on the job as it were—just watching the thing in operation. But he's just a hell of a good journalist. Instead of working from the newspaper to the novel, which has been happening now, he reverses it. He works from the novel into the industry. And the portrait of Ray Totman which emerges is one of the great portraits of a Yankee ever gotten on paper. And Kramer has just now shifted from the university[2] to Smith College, which is going to produce results. One knoweth not what—but results of some kind!

You said you aged eight years in the last six months. How come?

I was not being very serious about it although I am fairly serious about it. There's a great difference between eighty-eight and eighty-seven, I'll tell you!

Was it a stressful year, last year, in any way?

No. The principal difficulty has been I let myself in for the job of rewriting a number of the plays I wrote for radio in light of the new developments in radio. And in two weeks time I'm going to hear the results. WGBH is going to send out a crew and let me hear two of the plays and having agreed to do that (I started to do it about a year and a half ago) I have really been working at nothing else since.[3] I didn't foresee the demands on time would be so great and I didn't at all foresee I wouldn't be able to do anything else. That makes me very mad. I hate myself for getting into a snare like that. Actually, I've totally rewritten *Nobodaddy,* my first play, based on the book of Genesis. That had to be really reconstructed. Robert Monteigel, who's producing it, has by this time finished his production. (You finish your play before you begin it in that trade, you know. It's all on tape, now.) His excitement is that he succeeded in finding some absolutely superb actors: a woman who plays Eve in *Nobodaddy,* who he says is just an experience coming over the air, and a couple of very good men. I'm fascinated by all that, but I do resent the time put in on it. I'll never get that back again!

But what kind of changes in radio called for changes in the plays?

They get the sound onto tape and then they go through a rite which they refer to, I think, as mixing. And they mix. They produce not what used to be called sound effects, but sound quality: distance and nearness. For instance, the footstep of God when he comes upon Adam and Eve and observes well enough to know that they now know. I gather—I haven't heard this—you can do things with that sound. It can approach not just somebody walking into a room, but it can approach in a discovering sort of way so that you have the sense of God's reaction to what he sees. Isn't it amazing that they can do all that with sound!

Are you reprinting the plays in a volume as well?

It came out today. And I've had a copy for several days.

What's the title of the work?

Six Plays. It begins with *Nobodaddy,* and then *Panic,* which was a stage play and is now a radio play—rather longer than most. I mean there is no half-hour or hour limit. I don't know quite how long *Panic* will play. Then there's the first radio play I ever wrote, *Fall of the City;* then *Air Raid;* then *The Trojan Horse;* and then *This Music Crept by Me upon the Waters,* which is also quite long.

Which required the most revision, as you worked on them?

They varied very much. Almost nothing had to be done to *The Fall of the City*. That continues to work, to my ear, as a radio play, and the same thing is more or less true of *Air Raid*. *Nobodaddy*, as I said, had to be just completely re-handled. It begins in a different form—a prelude—and is radically changed. *The Trojan Horse* is very much as it was, and *This Music Crept by Me upon the Waters* is largely rewritten, but I don't think anybody would know it who didn't compare the two plays: the old form and the new form. Each play also has a little foreword by me as of now. That may be of some interest.

You're speaking soon at the dedication of the Hemingway Papers,[4] *aren't you?*

No. I told them I didn't want to come down. The trip to Boston is just too much for me. I do not like to leave Ada. I hate leaving her overnight, and most of the places that want you are in Kansas! But a few things have already happened. I read at Harvard two months ago, on the Morris Gray Fund, the thing I used to run when I was Boylston Professor. And it was a tremendous success. It was a young Harvard audience: actual students, you know, not just members of the faculty minding a target. It worked extremely well. It was one of the nicest things that's ever happened to me. And I may go out to Brockport in New York where the University of the State of New York has one of its university colleges and where a number of very good young poets have gathered. They're all great friends of mine.[5] I may go out there once, and I may go back to Bread Loaf once more. But I think that's got to be just about all. Bread Loaf isn't a problem because somebody will drive me up there and if I really want them to, they'll drive me back that night, so that I can handle that.

You were speaking about Panic *earlier. Have you been meeting with the people from ABIA*[6] *who are going to do the* Panic *production in Greenfield in July?*

The woman who is directing it has been over here a couple of times. And she wrote to me about it. I said I wanted very much to talk to her. I told her the history of the play as a stage play—from the point of view of the theater business, a very disgraceful history because it only lasted three days. It should have closed at the end of two, but it lasted three, for reasons I told you about. I told her that also I didn't like it very much as it was, that I was working on a complete rewriting of it which I liked very much better. But her heart was given to the old form. So I said, "I can only wish you well if you want to go ahead with it, but I think it's only fair for me to tell you that I, in your place, wouldn't do it." She said that she, in her place, would, and she's going to. I haven't seen her since. I take it, from what she told me on that occasion, that the city fathers agreed to help; they'll close off a street, some street somewhere.

They're going to do it on Bank Row right in front of the big bank that faces the common in Greenfield. They're closing off that whole area. Are you going to see it?

I certainly will go to see it, yes! And if I were asked to go over to a rehearsal (if there are going to be rehearsals) I would certainly go over at that point. I think what she missed was the importance to the play of the blind man, whose conception of economic development and change is the belief—the Marxist belief—which at that time and among the New York Marxists was very strong—that economic necessity ruled everything as the Fates did. Necessity is the word the Greeks used to use, you know. The mother of the Fates was Necessity; that is, the word, the name, translates out "necessity." And as the now revised play goes, McGafferty stumbles onto the Blind Man, who does not come along with a gang of leather-coated types into his office as in the original, but he finds him in the subway, as he's going down to work. We hear the Blind Man's cane moving down the subway train, stamping on the iron floor. He's touching people as he goes by—he finds McGafferty and he enunciates disaster—he tells McGafferty that he and his kind are finished, are done for; they have no future, that the whole country, the whole economy is damned, finished. And McGafferty is enormously affected by the way this happens: a man's fingers on his face, the blind face, the blind eyes, and the words of total disaster! And this was what the young Marxists in New York were saying at the time: that the Great Depression was the end of the Republic, the end of individual freedom, the acceptance of the rule of economic law.

The play, then, is a struggle between McGafferty and economic necessity in which events conspire to present him with a situation in which he increasingly feels he has to believe. First of all, the whole banking community refuses to make advances of funds which would carry through the bank closings, which were then going on in New York; and then his closest friend, the man he most admired in New York and Wall Street—in his community—commits suicide in front of a mirror in a public bathroom. And the key to this whole thing on the personal side is his sense of his old age, of his failure, of his inability to lead as he had led, his loss of belief in his own love for Ione, and above all, of Ione's love for him. He's too old to be loved as she would love him—had loved him. And the play is an inward and outward play about man's struggle with the Fates, the Law, the Necessity. It is the fundamental struggle which underlies the attempt to create a society in which men can govern themselves, which is what we are in this country. I think she thought the bankers were all villains and that the message of the play was a propaganda message. If she's read it carefully, I don't see how she can think that, and I may be quite wrong. Maybe I ought to get her to come over and talk to me.

How will you feel if they totally misinterpret the play in the production?

It depends on how they totally misinterpret it! I won't be able to do anything about it! She has every right to put the play on; but I think I'd better get her to come over here; ask if there's any way I can help!

What you say about the dilemma that freedom presents to the individual trying to live with it is reminiscent of the recent article, "The Conquest of America," in the Atlantic.[7] *Apparently they called you before they reprinted it.*

Bob Manning called me about it and they presented it in quite a visible way, as you can see! And they sent me all the letters that came in. They're going to publish an enormous letter column about it at some point. They asked me to reply to any letters I wanted to. The last thing I wanted to do was reply to letters at my age. Let somebody else answer the letters!

In his brief headnote, Manning mentions some parallels between the two decades—containment of Russia in the forties and Carter's hoping to do the same thing today.

Carter, or more specifically, Kissinger, who, as we now realize looking back, was having directly or indirectly a great deal of influence on Carter right from the very beginning. I don't know whether they've ever met and really talked or not!

What is your response to a dilemma like the Iranian crisis,[8] which serves to create an object of resistance (the Iranians or somebody or something) for political purposes? As a matter of fact, you mention in the article United

States support of alternative but repressive governmental systems like the shah's as an indication of how illogical and immoral the goal of containment is.

It's a perfect example. There's no question at all that the Nixon line, which is what that line really ought to be called although we've been doing it before Nixon and went on doing it afterward, put us "in bed," is the phrase I think I used here, with every enemy of human freedom there was in the world! We were "in bed" with all of them because they were against the Russians! The prize example is leaning backward in Iran, the way we've been doing. That much of it is true, but here we also have the monstrous illogic of the Iranian assay into terrorism—the state was practicing terrorism! The ayatollah was practicing terrorism! They all were! And it wasn't a question of who was doing the worst thing; it was a question of our doing the worst on both sides! We had lined up with the Pahlavis earlier and they were a monstrous repressive force in Iran; but when this came up, instead of taking the position that we had to take, we were, of course, so concerned about the hostages, and understandably so, that we never made a clear confirmation of the fact (because it was a fact) that we found ourselves opposed, for the first time in the history of the world so far as I know, by terrorism in office! And the terrorists in the United States embassy were supported and may very well have been invented by the ayatollah. Who knows? I think we've just made a complete mess of the whole thing from beginning to end!

Have you been writing any poetry?

That's what I was complaining about! I've been writing these goddamn plays! But I think it's over and I hope very much I can get started again. You know, you do come to the end of things! And the sort of feeling which you get to recognize and get to know almost like a physical feeling like the beginning of hunger, for example, that feeling which you not only associate with the attempt to make a poem but which you regard as a sort of announcement of a poem—that can leave you! It can just stop! And that's what one worries about. Everybody has periods of it, but there's a limit to the time! Picasso said a marvelous thing in one of the statements quoted in "The Diary."[9] Did you see it on television? He was talking about his old age, his prolific production, and he said, "If you work hard enough all your life, and if you work long enough, there's no problem about the pictures. The pictures come to you. They come to you all the time. They come to you already done. You don't have to do anything about them. In other words, you just paint them." Well, the opposite's true! You do count on the poem's coming to you—but if it doesn't, after a while you feel despair and that's not too strong a word.

Are you going to try to get to see the Picasso exhibit while it's in New York?

I wanted to so much! We were invited to go down to the opening before the opening. Bill Rubin, who is the director of the Museum of Modern Art, asked us specially to come. It's heartbreaking not to be able to go. But how do you get to New York from here? In your youth you get into a car and next thing you know you're in New York. Not now.

What is the status of your biography?

Roy Winnick's been working on this for about two or three years and we must be getting well along toward the end. He comes up about once a month and puts in a weekend, and the last time he was here it sounded to me as though we were approaching the cliff after which—nothing! He's sympathetic, not in the unpleasant way but in the pleasant way; that is, he's on my side, sort of, which is a comfort. But he's completely in control. I'm not telling him what to do and he wouldn't do it if I did. The only agreement we had was that the book won't appear until after I'm dead. Or after Ada's dead, too! And I don't know of any other restriction of any kind.

What does the process of biography involve? Was this a learning experience for you, too?

I've never had anything to do with one before and it can involve pretty much whatever is of interest. This book is bound to be, to some extent, a critical biography. It should be, I think, a critical biography of my verse and plays. But as we meet and talk, we find ourselves spending a couple of days on one aspect of the Library of Congress only—and there's an awful lot in these various areas—teaching experience at Harvard and the Washington experience in various ways, relations with Mr. Roosevelt. It just goes on and on forever, and I think he has got to begin to do some editing *before* my demise, rather than afterward, if we're ever going to finish! He's also seen all my family, all my friends. Fortunately my most candid friends, like Dean Acheson, are not within his reach! They would have had a picnic with that!

How do you feel now about having a biography done, because I know at one time you were very set against it?

I was very set against it and I finally agreed to it because the alternatives were much worse. I had a communication from a man in Alexandria who told me that he was doing a biography of me. He had never talked to me about it and he was well along in it!

You are in many ways a very private person even though you've been involved in a lot of public activities. You must have had some feelings about Mr. Winnick's talking to your friends and family and all the rest of it.

I have reserved the right to express my opinion about that. There are certain people he wanted to talk to who, for one reason or another, I thought would add nothing and would actually confuse him and readers, simply because they didn't know what they were talking about! Everybody has friends like that, you know. Helpful friends who've got everything wrong—always have had!

A biography could be very difficult to deal with because as you live your life, you have a certain idea of yourself and your life and the way you want it to be. And to have somebody come from the outside and start digging and poking and constructing what may be a totally different picture from the way you see it—

It's a very disturbing thing; he knows more about my life now than I do! And I really mean that because my memory has never been very good and is now quite bad. Among other things, he invented five poems of mine! He didn't invent them; he found them! They're five poems I published in an avant-garde magazine in France in '27, I think: *Transition*. Why I never included them in a book I don't know. One of them is really very good. Roy found them and copied them off and turned them over to me and I've now sent them off to John Nims, the editor and publisher of *Poetry* in Chicago, and said, "I know you have a policy of never republishing anything, but these are a peculiar case. They've never been published in the United States. They are not in the public domain because France has the same copyright protections that we now have but didn't have then. This is a rather special case. How about publishing them under the title 'Five Poems from the Twenties'?" But to all intents and purposes Roy just invented these. Pulled them out of the air!

How did he ever find them?

He went through all of *Transition*. It only lasted about three or four years. It was published by Jolas[10] and his wife, and it's quite an important avant-garde magazine of the period. I wasn't very sympathetic with its publishers, which is perhaps why I never went back and looked at the poems!

*

The second update took place on September 28, 1981, when MacLeish was eighty-nine.

*

What have you been doing since we saw you last?

I haven't, very much. This has been a pretty bad year. Mrs. MacLeish had a difficult summer. I've really just plain had to put working out of my head, but I hope that's not final by any manner of means because I still haven't finished what I wanted to do. No, I've been just sort of taking life as it comes along.

You didn't get to Bread Loaf, then?

No, I was up to Bread Loaf last year. The man who runs it tells me I've been there longer even than Frost. I can't believe that but he says that's true. Frost was an absolute fixture there for something like forty years. I began very shortly after we came back from France.

We're talking about having a symposium next May at the college, centered around your ninetieth birthday. People from all over the country would be coming. Papers in the afternoon; then at night maybe a performance of Songs for Eve *or a reading of* This Music Crept by Me upon the Waters. *Then some further papers on Saturday. And we thought it would be wonderful if you'd come and say hello.*

Yes, I think I'd like to—of course I'd like to! I can't say exactly what my condition is going to be like at that time, but I think probably all right. One thing has been bothering me a great deal, which is that I have some sort of ear difficulty which even a good ear man can't locate. They keep offering a hearing aid when that's the last thing I think I need. What happens is like the feeling you get when you dive too deeply and water penetrates your ear—you know the feeling; you also know how it goes away. You shake your head one side to the other; it seems to bust out the bubble. Well, I have that without any diving into the water. It just sort of overcomes me. Very difficult to get rid of it! And while that is going on, I can't hear my own voice. I can't pick words apart. And that makes it impossible to read poems! You can't do it! And I've therefore recently just been avoiding the embarrassment, which is one reason I haven't been going around very much. What I keep hoping for is that I can find someone who will explain this and, better still, do something about it. I think it may have to do with the fact that I was, ridiculously, the captain of the Yale water-polo team, and I had both ear drums burst at one time or another, and that probably is what's coming back to bother me now. When that condition's away, I can hear about as well as I ever did, but you never can tell when it's going to go away. So I'll have to be very cautious now about accepting any invitation. I'd love to do it! I love reading! But I just don't dare unless something happens so my hearing is all right.

What do you think about doing the Songs for Eve *for them?*

You mean simply a reading of the sequence?

A vocal performance too—the setting by Alice Parker.

I thought her work on that was extremely good. And it's desirable to do something of that kind because—for example, when Roy Winnick comes up here, he stays at that motel in South Deerfield. And he came up the second morning in a state of excitement and said that he, for the first time, really read *Songs for Eve* the night before. He'd read it, with a small "r," but this time he *read* it and he was carried away. And I feel that way about it. I think it's certainly as good as anything I ever did and maybe better. And some of my Harvard colleagues, like Perry Miller, as I once told you, felt very strongly about *Songs for Eve.* I think it's easy to listen to. It may not be very easy to understand, but the music helps. Anyway, I think I would love to help with what happens. I would love to read *Songs for Eve.* I have to be awful cautious on something that far ahead because, after all, I will be ninety! Houghton Mifflin may at that time publish a selection of letters which Roy Winnick has put together. He now has an enormous number of letters! And he brought up with him this time a selection of about thirty letters. They impress me a great deal because he chose them by subject; that is, there are a number of letters to Ernest that deal with our relation to one another, and other areas of choice. I had a letter today from Dick McAdoo,[11] saying that their company jury has not met on them but that he likes them and he knows I do and the jury may be affirmative. If the jury is affirmative, the question is whether they can get it done by May. Such is the crawling of the gods when it comes to publishing.

How did you find the experience of having a biographer trail you around?

Largely because he is a very tactful young man, it didn't bother me at all. I thought it was going to. I was really worried about it. I think if we had established the practice of his coming here to stay for three or four days at a time, it might have worked out very differently. But he tactfully retired himself to the motel down below, would have lunch with us, and was very considerate in every way. He couldn't get Ada to yield to the blandishments of the camera, but nobody can do anything about that! I can't understand it. Ada just is adamant. I never, as I said, understood this because she hasn't liked to be photographed, oh, since her sixteenth year. And she was absolutely ravishing in those days. It's very curious to me! There are a few photographs of her that one of the various Houghton Mifflin photographers, one of the New York women, took and I have them in the drawer of that desk over there, but they're not good photographs of her. Somehow or other, the photographer succeeded in exorcising the life even in Ada, who has more than almost anybody.

Have you read any of what he's done about you?

No. I told him at the very beginning I didn't want to. He could feel perfectly free about that. I was never going to ask him. I hate reading about myself. It makes me self-conscious for a month afterward. And he understands.

*

Our last interview with Mr. MacLeish was a rather hectic affair. The date was November 30, 1981. We had brought with us two photographers from the college who were taking pictures for a proposed slide-tape on the Conway home.

*

The symposium [the ninetieth birthday tribute set for May] is coming along. We wrote to about thirty people last week asking for papers or reminiscences, in addition to our first mailing to scholars. We have so far decided on six papers discussing various aspects of your work. We have one on a poem. "Into a Poem by MacLeish—'Companions'."

Oh, "Companions"! That's Bill Heyen.

Companions

The flowers with the ragged names,
daffodils and such,
met us on the road we came,
nodded, touched.

Now, the golden day gone by,
we walk the other road:
they throng the evening grass beside,
touch us . . .

nod.

Bill Heyen is one of *the* gifted young poets—he teaches out of the State University of New York in Brockport. That's one of my favorite poems and it's Bill's favorite in the world, he proclaims to large audiences. And I'm delighted that he's going to do that.

Donald Hall is coming, and he's going to talk about his experiences with you and its relation to his own development as a writer. At the conclusion (we were going to make this a surprise but we won't), we are going to have a cake and champagne. We're going to have a number of people make toasts, like Jill and John Conway and Henry Steele Commager. We should have lots of people there to drink a toast to Archibald MacLeish on his ninetieth! So that'll be very exciting!

That's splendid.

You had someone from the electric company here when we arrived. Are you having trouble?

I had to explain to the coordinator of rights-of-way of the Western Massachusetts Electric Company why I couldn't walk two miles with him down the right of way here to find out where our line gets into trouble, as it very frequently does. They are the nicest men, these people! I don't know what their racial origins are. They all seem to be about the same. They're enormous! They have very American faces. They have the least American names you ever saw except for Chinese! And they're amiable, friendly! Anyway, he called because I was moved to put on my bill: "I know this is illegal. I shouldn't communicate with your right-of-way people when I'm sending you

a check, but maybe you would send it along to them for me." I told them that
we've had three outages at intervals of a week in the summer; they all seem to
happen in the same place; there seem to be branches hanging on the wires,
which falls into their domain—their jurisdiction. And they're just as nice
about it as they can be. They'll go along there and pretty soon they'll find dead
trees and they'll have them down within a day or two. Because of the period
that we bought the house—fifty-three, fifty-four years ago—we get our power
from Shelburne Falls. Everybody else gets it from South Deerfield. But we sit
up here in the dark and they all have lights! And the power comes in, crosses
the Deerfield by Bardswell Ferry and follows the Bardswell Ferry Road and
then hits a rough patch of woodland just before it hits the Shelburne Falls
Road and it's in "thar" that all the trouble begins.

*While the photographers are taking pictures, perhaps we could talk about the
house. What can you tell us about this room (the music room) that we're in
now? Was this part of the original house?*

No. This and what's over it is what we built—it is the only thing we built.
Ada was then singing. This turns out, as I think I told you, to have beautiful
acoustics. We had a quartet up at Marlboro at the music festival up there who
one year made a regular habit of coming down just to play here. . . . But I think
the thing to do is to start with the book room up there. I'll talk to Ada about
that. I don't want to bother her. [*Exits and returns*] It would probably be best if
you could do it now. She doesn't want to put you out in any way but I think
that that would really help—if you would get that done before she comes
down for lunch. Then you can do anything you want to outdoors and this
room.

How about the Stone House?[12] *Is it possible for them to go down there?*

Because of the illnesses this summer, I haven't even been in it this year. I've
no idea what it looks like. But why don't you do it from outside? The outside
doesn't change much. Inside the mice take care of it!

[Moving through the hall and up the stairs] *These are your government
pictures, aren't they?*

These are diplomas and honorary degrees. And this is government—Mr.
Roosevelt and John Kennedy; Adlai Stevenson. [*Looking at photograph of
house*] That's the house at the time of the Civil War before anybody touched

it. Of course it had no architect. It had just a carpenter's drawing. It's classic. It
is classic.

What were you doing with Mr. Kennedy?

That was when he came up to Amherst to dedicate the Frost Library.[13] And
I was speaking; therefore I was in that relation to him. And the smile is
because the sheriff of Hampshire County, who is a good deal more Irish than
John Kennedy himself, had just made the appropriate announcement of that.
[*Mounting stairs*] We've got some poets along this wall. Robert Frost and
Ezry! And James Joyce and Yeats himself! And my darling friend, Mark
Van Doren. And that's B. Hand, a very, very dear friend. Judge Learned Hand,
greatest of the federal judges. And that is Felix Frankfurter and that's Dean
Acheson. Gentlemen of the cameras, please don't take any photographs of my
honorary degrees! Every time I go by them I blush! I'm very proud of them and
delighted to have them; as long as they're there on the wall, they're all right!

*James Joyce played the piano as well as having a beautiful tenor voice, it
seems* [looking at picture].

James Joyce, yes. That's just the way he sat at the piano! His back bent, the
backs of his hands sort of down.

*Where are you in the football picture? Oh! There you are. They used to call
you "the dirty little center," didn't they?*[14]

At the time I weighed 165 and I played a kind of center that now, I think, is
just about standard but not then. I played a center who acted exactly like
a defensive back. I was about two yards back of the line and free to move, and
since I could move a little bit faster than the right-size men, I could sometimes get there before they did.

[In upstairs study] *Is this your collection of poetry that you were telling us
about?*

The smaller stack. And that too, which is French, Spanish, etc., etc.; then
there's some novels in here, plays, and books about books.

*Was this always a book room since you've had it or did you bring the panel-
ing in or what did you do?*

We put these shelves in the minute that we moved into the house. When paneling was taken out, as it was, about the middle of General Grant's era, it was never put back. But somebody thoughtfully put it up in the attic and we just put it back again. We spend our time here. But we also have, I'd like you to understand, we also have a parlor. I'll let you look at the parlor. [*Moves to living room*] I think the furniture is all ours. It almost all was collected by Ada's father over a long lifetime of trout fishing all over Connecticut.

Where is the wallpaper from?

We bought it! I suppose it is a replica. I've never seen the original. But it was bought because of that chair. That chair comes with the house—we found it in Ashfield. So the paper goes with that. [*Moves to dining room*]

Do you use this dining room often?

Now that we have that Danish stove, we can use it in any season, even winter.

When are you going to put your bonnet on?

I'm going to put it on if anything takes me outdoors. The usual protection of the male head I don't have!

[The group has moved outdoors] *That view is magnificent.*

Yes, but the strange thing is, which perhaps a photographer would understand but I don't, the Monadnock becomes totally insignificant in any photograph that I've seen of that distant view. You put yourself in the middle of it, you pose, you think there's a mountain back of you, it's a mole hill! Now over here is my wife's garden, which is hewn out by her small hands very largely. She has it arranged now so that there is no season for that garden; it's just a continual change. You wake up one morning and it's altogether different from what it was the day before. There is the picking garden, which has dahlias at the lower end and then everything you can think of in the rest of it.

[Back in the music room] *This looks like an authentic Windsor chair. Is it?*

This is a reproduction by a man named Nutting,[15] who made reproductions which, to me, are really much better than their originals. But *that* is an old highboy, which came from one of Ada's father's fishing expeditions up into

Cornwalls.[16] I've forgotten what he paid. The owner refused to sell it to him and so he said, "Well, I don't want to be a nuisance but there must be something you need or something you'd like." And she said, "Yes. Yes, there is. I never had a set of false teeth." I don't know what they cost back in the 1870s or 1890s. But he bought it and took this away. The drawers were all full of nails.

Is this a Masson poster?

It's a poster used by the Museum of Modern Art when they had their André Masson show. I admired it very much and they sent me a carefully guarded copy of it and I've got it hung where you can't see it. André was a most agreeable man. Ernest Hemingway met him first and then Ernest brought him around and we sort of made a brother of him. We saw a great deal of him in Paris. Small, lively, very French Frenchman. I've really got to shift that poster. That other picture is Japanese. Japanese mulberry-colored. Only one family in Japan in the thirties knew how to do this. Someone who became a friend during our long stay in Japan gave me that when I left. I did not put it in an envelope and forget about it!

Who did the painting of your father?

A journeyman painter and, as that hand indicates, not a very good one. But the head is a remarkable likeness. He was born in 1838 and he came to this country in '56 and I would guess that this was made probably just after the Civil War. It couldn't have been made before. He was having a wretched time, but obviously at that point he'd saved up at least enough money to have a suit. And I can prove the authenticity to you backward. This [*pointing to photograph*] is my oldest son Kenneth, now dead. He died of cancer about five years ago. But there is a likeness between those two that I used to be able to see more clearly—an extraordinary likeness! Ken was more of a Scotsman than his Scottish grandfather! And he cared more about it.

Was your son Kenneth in the army?

Oh, yes. He was, first of all, in "lighter-than-air," which was a very hazardous occupation. This was submarine watch in the Second World War. And he patrolled in the North Atlantic and as far down as through the Bahamas and into the Caribbean. My brother, for whom he was named, was one of the first naval flyers in the First World War. And, as I told you, he was shot down and killed after two years on the front, which is almost unbelievable. People lasted ninety days and thirty days. Kenny lasted for two years and was shot down in October 1918, a month before the armistice. If he'd lived one more month, he'd be here. Now that I'm talking about him, I have to show you a picture of him. He was an extraordinary human being. He was flying with a British squadron when he was shot down and he disappeared and no sign of him. He was shot down over Belgium, and he was found by a very nice Belgian professional man, who was the owner of a farm. His body was in the farmyard. And it was—how would you say it—a very agonizing experience for everybody, but the amazing thing about it was that there was no plane anywhere near him—it would have been a British plane. The first people that went in there made a search for that. His own outfit just turned in their time to see if they could find it. Nobody has ever found it. He disappeared on the 18th of October and the body was found, well, at the end of January or early February.

Could you tell us something about the piano? Has that been in this room since it was built?

There were two pianos at the beginning. They were Ada's. Her father gave them to her. One in this corner and one in that corner. And we gave one of them to our daughter when she married because Ada had about stopped singing at that point. This we can't bear to part with. It makes no pretense to being in tune.

When did you add on this room?

We bought the house in 1927, and it looked like an old Southern plantation house in Mississippi. The pair who bought it at the very end of the last century were both from the South, and they added pillars, porches, and columns. We took them off just as fast as we could. We were both outraged by them! What an awful thing to do to a Yankee house! Then, over the winter we went back to Paris—for the winter of 1927–28. And during that winter this wing was built and the pillar mess was finally cleaned up and the house was in many ways rebuilt. We put two or three more bathrooms in it by squeezing closets. It had a telephone, which came up the side wall, halfway up. And there was electricity. However, that all had to be done over again. And by the time we came back in midsummer of 1928, we came right here with our children and whatever furniture we brought back from Paris and just guessed that the house would probably be ready for furniture. And it was.

When you write, where do you do most of your writing?

I used to do it in the Stone House until this last summer but this last summer I had bursitis, which is a particularly painful form of rheumatism, in both hips. And I simply couldn't make it. So I started trying to work down here, but I couldn't make this either for a while.

Do you find, when you're writing, that there's certain times of the day that you write better, things come together better, than during other times of the day?

I began, at the very beginning of serious writing, writing in the morning and I've done so ever since, moving the morning farther and farther forward, which is just the opposite of most American writers, who seem to write at night, moving it backward and backward 'til finally they're up 'til 4, and then 5. But the morning is, I think, the right time.

What are you working on now?

These are just tasks that I've taken on for various people. I'm going up to Dartmouth in January to celebrate the 100th anniversary of the birth of that great Dartmouth man, Daniel Webster. At Dartmouth they're going to give a reading performance of *Scratch*. And I'm going to talk about Daniel Webster. Daniel Webster is a much underestimated man as regards his achievement for the great Republic. His "liberty and union" is at the heart of what's wrong with us right now. And I'm going to try not to make a political speech but it may turn out to be one, slightly. The second reply to Hayne is really something that ought to be compulsory reading for these kids who say they aren't interested in American history. They'd be interested all right! So I'm still fighting wars of my own. But of course what I want to do is get going on writing again. The experiences last summer just knocked that out. But I'm sure it hasn't knocked it out for good.

When did you last write a poem?

I can't answer that because there are some beginnings which maybe are the beginnings of poems. Who knows? I don't. There's nothing finished for a couple of years.

Do you still approach the writing of poetry as you did before? That is, do you write about something that you might see or that you might feel? What clicks within you to express words? Or is that question about process impossible to answer?

Yes, it is. There are some specific questions, however, which can be answered. I used to try this on the students in my writing class at Harvard. One question is: What comes into your head first? There's various possible alternatives: an idea, an image, a sound, a rhythm, a combination of rhythm and sound and word. Well, if you play around with those things, and if you have just come through the experience, which is always different, you'll find—*I* find—that it all begins with a sound, which is a rhythmic sound which clearly has a meaning but you don't know what—meaning that hasn't even words yet. You hear something that is a beat but it's a beat that could become a phrase, a clause, a sentence, almost any minute. And it's when it begins to do that that you know you're at work. That sort of thing I think you can talk about because I think you can recognize the experience. You can't reproduce it but you can almost reproduce it. And that has been true of me almost all my life. So much so, that I have to say that is the way it happens to me.

Is that true even when you're writing a poem like "Night Watch in the City of Boston"?

"Night Watch" is a very good example really because it was the one and only request to write a specific poem that I've ever accepted. But I did accept that. It seemed to me that if the city of Boston and poor old Kevin,[17] who was always about to lose his pants or his shoes or something, were willing to take a chance, there was no reason I should be snobby about it and say, "I don't do that!" But what I found was that until I moved into a situation where the process I was talking about a minute ago could work itself out, there wasn't any poem. And this becomes pretty clear if we look at the poem. If you'll excuse me for one minute I'll get it. It's right outside the door. [*Gets framed broadside*] Now what actually happened—you'll have to take my word for this— was that, since this was a new operation of mine, I forgot what I've just told you about the process as I thought I knew it. And I moved directly into, not the language but the subject. But after the first break—"I almost saw it once, a law school boy"—it wouldn't move. It didn't budge. It wasn't until I put Perry Miller and the Yankee Admiral of the Ocean Sea[18] into it that it happened. And what I think you will notice as I read these twelve lines is that there is a very strong rhythmic pattern.

Old colleague,
Puritan New England's famous scholar,
half intoxicated with those heady draughts of God,
come walk these cobble-stones John Cotton trod,

and you, our Yankee Admiral of the Ocean Sea,
come too, come walk with me.
You know, none better, how the Bay wind blows
fierce in the soul as in the streets its ocean snows.

Lead me between you in the night, old friends,
one living and one dead, and where the journey ends
show me the city built as on a hill
John Winthrop saw long since and you see still.

Whatever is true of the rest of it—and I don't say that anything's true—is or isn't—whatever is true of the rest of it, that's a poem. It's a poem because its rhythm carries it. And its rhythm and it carry an emotion and the emotion makes possible—whatever. In this appeal to these two, there is as yet no idea at all. There is just the appeal, calling them, one dead, one alive, calling them out of the night. But this is something nobody has the right to talk about much because nobody knows.

There is something else we wanted to discuss with you—which ties in with what you've just been saying. We have a new course coming up at the college—a course on you. It's going to be a MacLeish seminar, limited probably to fifteen students, upper-level undergraduates, our students and juniors and seniors recruited from the other area colleges. The course will center mostly on the tapes we've done with you, and we're most likely going to look at particular poems and plays written in certain periods. We're still thinking about the focus. Now, if you were going to teach a seminar on MacLeish, where would you start? How would you do it?

I never even thought about it. But you're absolutely right that there is a focus from which and there's a focus from which not. If you take even John Keats from the wrong focus, he comes out where I in my childhood thought he was, a mummified creature, a perfection not to be touched or even sought after. And of course that's all nonsense. But one question that really raises this very succinctly is the question of Yeats. Yeats being clearly the great world poet of this century, why has there been no biography that anybody thinks is a biography? At least, I never heard of one. I never read one. There are fact books, but there's no Yeats. Yeats is his own best biography! Nothing else counts. And the reason, I think, is nobody ever got quite the right focus—how to deal with this poet who thought himself a public man. That was a problem never solved! And I think you put your finger perfectly on the nature of the problem.

I wouldn't even dare to guess what the focus in my case would be. It has to be, I suppose, an attitude about life different from any other's. Shakespeare's so complete and so illuminating that it really becomes a key to the world instead of Shakespeare himself. When you get down to our level, it becomes not easier, but harder. The great delight of having Mark Van Doren alive, instead of dead, and up here at least twice a year and sometimes more often, was that the talk was always human talk. I don't think a word of what is called the technique of the writing of verse ever crossed his lips nor was I ever tempted to do that either. He belonged in his time. He wasn't worried about it, but he belonged in it. And then there's another aspect of all this that was true of both Mark and me. We both had families, large families that were insistently present, like his brothers, and particularly Carl, and Dorothy to a very high degree. And you only got Mark when you got him in the light of that family. That was one of my difficulties with him as a friend. Carl was the only one I knew—the great authority on Franklin. Sort of literary historian type—big man, handsome and cheerful, lively, devoted friend to Mark—or they were devoted friends to each other.

I knew something about that because my brother Ken was, I suppose, one of the most loved people in my life. In my case, my mother was the very visible influence. But this is not a fashionable or even an agreeable concept of a poet. You don't think of him as a family man. He's supposed to be something else. He's supposed to be a bit of an Ishmael; he's supposed to be outside, looking in, "God's spies," and so forth. But in both Mark's case and mine, it's very much the opposite. I've been reading quite a bit about my mother these past years, partly because a lot of her letters turned up and also for other reasons. She was a very, very remarkable woman and had she lived a generation later would have been not only a remarkable one but a remarked woman. She was remarked but only in Chicago. There's a book about her, a sort of autobiography. [19]

You told us about her instilling the love of poetry in you, and that was a very important influence in your life.

A very important influence! She was a remarkable woman! I looked a great deal like her. And we had a very close relationship. She had a lot of family to worry about in addition to me, but I was her biggest worry because I was a thoroughly nasty little boy! Always in a scrape. If you could get into a scrape,

I got into it! I was always fighting and choosing the railroad tracks at Glencoe to fight on. That seemed to be the ground where schoolboys would fight in those days! But she once told me, at the end of her life, that she'd made up her mind, when I was about thirteen or fourteen, one day when I'd made her cry by whistling after she'd spanked me (she had to spank me; I was too big to spank but I'd intended to go to school and hadn't gone, and she couldn't take that; so I whistled after she got through and she began to cry), that if she could raise me, I was bound to turn into something! When I got to Hotchkiss—a little bit late at fourteen instead of twelve—I was the victim of agonizing homesickness, as you can well imagine. And mother's response was to struggle, at that period, purely against my homesickness even if I ceased to love her in the process! Only she didn't quite put it that way!

My father's influence was a wholly different one. He was a large, enormous Scot. That picture over the fireplace doesn't look like him but it is him. Large and very impressive man, who, although he never got beyond Glasgow high school, nevertheless had a beautiful articulation of the English language. The Scots did have that, particularly the Gaelic Scots, who had the same language at some point on the way down. A wonderful man!

They were really extraordinary people, both of your parents.

At the time I had no appreciation or even comprehension of what was being given me. At the beginning of the marriage (my mother was his third wife, the first two had died of tuberculosis, as almost everybody did at that time), they bought about twelve acres of high bluff land, clay soil, over the lake, twenty miles north of Chicago in a place which at that time was largely unsettled. It was the edge of the vanishing America because the geese slept on the lake in the day, then flew back into the marshes to feed at night, making that wooden bell sound that they make, and there were foxes everywhere. By now there are suburban bowling alleys. It was a marvelous place to be! My mother had a great feeling for flowers. The house was full of flowers. And my father was remarkably helpful. He was a man who had been very poor himself. His family were poor—small shopkeepers in Glasgow. And he had to count pennies, really count pennies, and then he really established himself as a merchant in Chicago, and more than a merchant. He was one of the people who is really the reason the University of Chicago is there. Not that he had that kind of money to give, but he was willing to devote his time to going anywhere to see John D. Rockefeller. Once he showed me a million dollar check; he said, "Laddie, you'll never see that again!" Later he was able to educate all of us the way he wanted us educated and he also, even in those terrible depressions of the early years of this century, would go on educating his Chinese students at the University of Chicago, whether we had what we wanted or we didn't. He was that kind of person. But I don't know why at the time I didn't realize what was happening to me!

Your children probably didn't realize what a wonderful education they were getting in Paris when they were growing up!

Kenny, I think, gradually came to realize that. Mimi never did.

So if you were teaching a MacLeish seminar, you might begin with that focus of your family, your roots, whence you sprang. It's certainly not New Criticism!

New Criticism was one of the consequences of the discovery of modern science. There must be a science of everything; therefore there had to be a science of the poem; therefore it had to be possible to divorce the poem from the human source out of which it came.[20] All of which is just vulgar misconception.

When you taught at Harvard, New Criticism was at its peak. How did you feel about it when you were teaching poetry?

I never taught criticism. I never taught from the point of view of criticism. It was a course taught for the time being, that is, for that week and maybe the next week, but that week anyway, a course taught out of a poem which, at the beginning of that course, students tended to feel was a very small and unworthy assignment—perhaps a poem of eight or nine or ten lines which of course you could read in a few minutes. But along about Thanksgiving time, I'd be visited by a delegation, saying "Wouldn't it be possible to take a month for that poem?" That was nice to see. That being so, we never got into critical attitudes. We were in the poem.

Your feeling about New Criticism was that it was not helpful?

My poem "Ars Poetica" was acclaimed by the New Critics as a New Criticism poem. It never struck me that way, but I yielded. I yielded to the suggestion as long as it was good natured. But dearly as I love Red Warren, I just can't understand what he's talking about when he's talking about that. Well, we don't talk about it. To me, as I'm afraid I've said too many times, a poem is a means of comprehending humanity, a means of comprehending human life and to a very considerable extent, the only means we have—the only means in which you use the emotions as well as the intellect at the same time—to live understandingly, to live in a considered way the life we live. And to remove the human elements from it is first simply to misconceive the whole operation. John Keats would have said so in the loudest voice in the land.

*

After this interview, we arranged for one more in the spring of 1982 to acquire information on the house in a format that would be more easily utilized in the projected slide-tape for the MacLeish Symposium. That interview was scheduled for March 9, but it never took place. Four days before, we received a call from Mr. MacLeish. He had just been admitted to the Franklin County Public Hospital for a problem which, he said, might require surgery. But he told us not to worry. If need be, we could visit him in the hospital after the operation and have the interview in his room. (He was transferred to the Massachusetts General Hospital in Boston.) We were, nevertheless, worried, and not so much about getting the interview as about him. When we had seen him in November, he was frailer than before, and while he was as alert as ever, physical exertion was obviously trying and tiring to him. We were therefore deeply concerned about any surgery he might have to endure. We wanted him to get over what was ailing him and be with us to enjoy his big birthday party. Unfortunately, he never recuperated. He lingered for a month after the operation and died April 20.

Our birthday party became, then, a memorial tribute. The family insisted that we should go ahead with the symposium, and we notified all the participants about the sad change we had to make.

But everybody came—more than two hundred—and we had papers by Richard Calhoun, Michael Cavanagh, Helen Ellis, Philip Gardner, William Heyen, Judson Jerome, Edward Mullaly, Alice Parker, Richard F. Somer, Barry Wallenstein, and Thomas Walters; reminiscences from Jill and John Conway, Donald Hall, Joseph Langland, William Meredith, and Theodore Morrison. There was a reading of Songs for Eve *by Seymour Rudin and a performance of the Alice Parker setting conducted by the composer. There was a reading of* Air Raid, *directed by Richard Wizansky.[21] There was a series of tributes from friends and colleagues, including Henry Steele Commager, John Kenneth Galbraith, Richard McAdoo, Paul Mariani, Arthur Schlesinger, Jr., and Robert Penn Warren, all of whom had come to pay their respects to "one who lived a long time in this land and with honor."*

N O T E S

I. THE PARIS YEARS

1 Martha Hillard MacLeish (1856–1947). A self-described Connecticut Yankee (*Letters of Archibald MacLeish, 1907 to 1982*, ed. R. H. Winnick [Boston: Houghton Mifflin, 1983], p. 3), she was a descendant of the Pilgrim leader Elder Brewster. Although it is not clear from M's remark, Rockford College and Rockford Female Seminary, where Martha Hillard presided, are the same institution. For an account of her life, see *Martha Hillard MacLeish (1856–1947)* (Geneva, N.Y.: privately printed, 1949), an autobiography with a foreword by M and chapters by Ishbel MacLeish Campbell and Norman Hillard MacLeish.

2 Conway, Massachusetts, where M lived from 1928 until his death.

3 Jane Addams (1860–1935) was the first alumna of Rockford College and the founder of the Hull House social settlement. Julia Lathrop (1858–1932) was a friend of Jane Addams; in 1912 she became chief of the Children's Bureau of the U.S. Department of Labor. Martha Hillard MacLeish was actively involved in Hull House, as she was in several other civic, educational, and religious organizations.

4 Andrew MacLeish (1838–1928). As M later explains, Andrew came to the United States from Scotland at the age of eighteen. In 1858 he married Lilias Young, who died in 1878. The couple had two daughters, Lily and Blanche. In 1881 he married M. Louise Little, who bore him a son, Bruce, in 1882. She died in 1883. He married Martha Hillard in 1888 at the age of fifty. She was thirty-two. Andrew MacLeish was founder and manager of the Chicago retail store of Carson, Pirie, Scott & Company.

5 Norman (d. 1975) was born in 1890 and thus was two years older than M. Kenneth was born in 1894 (d. 1918), and Ishbel (Mrs. Alexander Campbell) was born in 1897.

6 John Aitken Carlyle (1801–79) did indeed write an admired prose translation of the *Inferno*, with editions in 1849, 1867, and 1882. His illustrator was John Flaxman. The Gustave Doré illustrations for the *Inferno*, completed in 1861, accompanied, in several editions, a verse translation by Rev. Henry Francis Carey. Thus there must have been at least two editions of Dante's work in the MacLeish home.

7 M attended Hotchkiss, a boys' school in Lakeville, Connecticut, from 1907 to 1911. It was M's mother's notion to send the "boys East to school" (*Letters*, p. 3). While at Hotchkiss, M was elected Class Poet, as he was later at Yale.

8 M might be referring to his position as editor of the literary magazine. While at Yale, he was also captain of the water polo team and second-string member of the football team. He also belonged to Skull & Bones, the most highly regarded of

Yale's senior societies. Thus he was a "Bones" man, as were Gerald Murphy and Henry Luce.

9 The Fay Diploma is awarded annually to the member of Yale's graduating class who ranks highest in scholarship, conduct, and character, and who gives evidence of greatest promise.

10 M met Ada Taylor Hitchcock (1892–1984) while at Hotchkiss. She was the only child of a hardware merchant in Farmington, Connecticut. M and Ada were married on June 21, 1916.

11 The MacLeishes had three children who survived infancy: Kenneth (1917–77) was originally christened Archibald, Jr., but was renamed after M's brother Kenneth, a navy flier, was killed in World War I; Mary, "Mimi" (1922), later Mrs. Karl Grimm; and William Hitchcock (1928). A fourth child, Brewster Hitchcock, born in 1921, died in infancy.

12 M served in the army from June 1917 to February 1919. He was discharged with the rank of captain.

13 George Grafton Wilson.

14 Charles F. Choate, Jr., who was senior partner in the firm.

15 Claire Croiza (1882–1948), mezzo-soprano, born Claire Conelly, was a highly regarded concert singer of the 1920s and 1930s. Povla Frijsh (1881–1960), born Paula Frisch, was a Danish soprano who introduced Negro spirituals to Paris. Nadia Boulanger (1887–1979) was a world-renowned teacher of composition as well as a conductor.

16 Arthur Waley (1889–1966) was a translator of Chinese poetry and prose. Tu Fu, Li Po, and Po Chu-I were eighth-century Chinese poets. M discusses Waley's virtues as a translator and his rhythmic skills in connection with his own development as a poet later in this chapter.

17 *The New Criterion* and *Commerce* were literary journals. *Commerce* was published by Marguerite Caetani and edited by Paul Valéry, Valéry Larbaud, and Léon-Paul Fargue.

18 *A Moveable Feast* was published in 1964.

19 Hadley Richardson Hemingway was Ernest Hemingway's first wife. They were divorced in January 1927. He married Pauline Pfeiffer in May of the same year.

20 Nicola Sacco and Bartolomeo Vanzetti, Italian aliens and professed anarchists, were accused in 1920 of killing two men and stealing $16,000 in a Massachusetts payroll robbery. Their trial attracted international attention and many believed they were found guilty because of their anarchist philosophy rather than because of the evidence against them. They were executed on August 23, 1927. Porter (1890–1980), an American novelist and short-story writer, and Dos Passos (1896–1970) were actively involved in the protests against the executions of Sacco and Vanzetti. Dos Passos was arrested twice and jailed in Massachusetts in 1927 for demonstrating against the sentence.

21 Felix Frankfurter (1882–1965) was a professor at Harvard Law School (1914–39) and an associate justice of the U.S. Supreme Court from 1939 to 1962.

22 Louis Brandeis (1856–1941) was an American lawyer and jurist; he was an associate justice of the U.S. Supreme Court from 1916 to 1939.

23 Massachusetts Institute of Technology; M first met the Emersons in Cambridge in 1920.

24 Mélisande is the heroine of Debussy's *Pelléas et Mélisande*, completed in 1902.

25 M had asked and Maurice Firuski "had agreed to act as M's agent, without compensation, in the submission of his poems to American periodicals" (*Letters*, p. 155 n. 1). See chapter 4 for M's connection with Firuski and his help in the publication of *Nobodaddy*.

26 The Crosbys' editions of *Einstein* and *New Found Land* were brought out in 1929 and 1930, respectively, after M had left Paris.

27 M wrote to his parents and sister (Nov. 23, 1924) that he had made arrangements to study French poetry "with a chap in Paris named Pierre Garanger who teaches philosophy in the Lyçees and knows French literature in + out" (*Letters*, p. 150). This is likely the person to whom M refers here.

28 "An die Musik" is a setting by Schubert of a poem by Schober.

29 Etienne de Beaumont was a patron of the arts. M mentions him in an ironic message to his brother Norman via his mother as being one of a group of celebrities with whom the MacLeishes purportedly associated (*Letters*, p. 184).

30 The Linscott visit occurred in November 1926. But M's answer does not, finally, address the question. He does not, for instance, discuss his close association with Amy Lowell, whom he regarded as his mentor until her death in 1925, nor his correspondence with literary figures like Louis Untermeyer, Allen Tate, and Marianne Moore. Alexis Saint-Léger Léger, whom he mentions later in his response, was a French poet and diplomat who used the pseudonym of St.-John Perse. He was recognized as an artistic "blood brother" by M as early as 1927, but the two did not become friends until some years later. During the war, Léger was an associate of M's at the Library of Congress (see chap. 3).

31 Robert S. Bridges (1844–1930) was poet laureate of England (1913–30).

32 Sprung rhythm is a poetic meter based on the number of stressed syllables in a verse. Because there is no regard for unstressed syllables, scansion is difficult. The term was coined by Hopkins.

33 "You, Andrew Marvell" was first published in *American Poetry 1927: A Miscellany* (New York: Harcourt, Brace and Co., 1927). It was one of six poems by M in the anthology, which was edited by Louis Untermeyer.

34 Allen Tate (1899–1979), American poet, critic, novelist, and biographer, was active in the formulation of New Criticism in the 1930s. M established correspondence with Tate in 1926. He figures prominently in M's discussion of his work at the Library of Congress in chapter 3.

35 Erik Satie (1866–1925), French composer and pianist, was a spearhead in the musical movement known as Impressionism. Most of his works were for piano.

36 Dean Acheson (1893–1971), a life-long friend of M's, was M's classmate at Yale and Harvard Law School.

37 The Commission of Inquiry on Opium Production in Persia embarked on March 12, 1926, from Trieste. The report of the commission was presented to the Council of the League of Nations on March 11, 1927.

38 F. Scott Fitzgerald (1896–1940) did not publish *Tender Is the Night* until 1934. Thus the reason given for Murphy's renown "during that period" (the twenties) is questionable.

39 M is most likely referring to an exhibit of Murphy's works at the Museum of Modern Art. M wrote the foreword to the exhibition catalog, *The Paintings of Gerald Murphy* (New York: The Museum of Modern Art, 1974) which he reprinted in his collection of essays *Riders on the Earth* (Boston: Houghton Mifflin, 1978).

40 Edward Estlin Cummings (1894–1962) was an American poet who signed his name as e. e. cummings.

41 Sylvia Beach (1887–1962), the proprietor of the bookstore Shakespeare & Co., rue de l'Odéon, was the first publisher of Joyce's *Ulysses*. M elsewhere calls her the prime mover in that endeavor.

42 Mary Welsh Hemingway was Ernest Hemingway's fourth wife.

43 M misremembers here, as he does in his discussion of the Chair of Poetry in chapter 3. Bishop never held that position (also known as the consultantship in poetry, as M calls it here) but was instead Resident Fellow in Comparative Literature. He died in April 1944.

44 On December 10, 1929, Harry Crosby killed his lover and committed suicide. Caresse asked M to keep a death watch on her behalf at Bellevue Hospital in New York. (See Geoffrey Wolff, *Black Sun* [New York: Random House, 1976].) From M's remarks it would seem that Harry's mother was also present.

45 Walter Van Rensselaer Berry was Crosby's cousin.

46 The incident M describes took place in the fall of 1926. It was also in the fall of that year that his son Kenny had been placed, by doctor's orders, "on a Swiss mountain for the winter" (*Letters*, p. 183).

47 Dinah Boyle Hitchcock and William Hitchcock.

48 The legal code composed by a Babylonian king about 1750 B.C. The code contained 300 legal provisions protecting the rights of the individual.

49 The quarrel with M's Aunt Mary continued, in fact, for several years. There was a partial reconciliation in 1927, when the MacLeishes stayed at her farm in Ashfield while they were looking for a house to buy.

50 Cafés in the Montparnasse district of Paris.

51 The same Marguerite Caetani was also, as noted, the publisher of *Commerce*.

52 John McCormack (1884–1945) was a celebrated tenor to whom Joyce once placed in an Irish vocal competition.

53 *The Dialogues of Archibald MacLeish and Mark Van Doren*, ed. Warren Bush (New York: E. P. Dutton and Co., 1964). The book grew out of a series of conversations between M and his friend which had been recorded for a program of the same name on commercial television. M discusses the making of this program in chapter 4.

54 Bra Saunders. Henry "Hank" Strater was usually called Mike. Uncle Gus was Gus Pfeiffer, Pauline Hemingway's uncle.

55 Pound was awarded the Bollingen Prize in 1949. His confinement in St. Elizabeths Hospital lasted thirteen years, from 1945 to 1958. M's interest in Pound's case dates from 1945, but the series of moves that led to Pound's release began in earnest in 1956. As M corresponded with Pound, he continued to negotiate with Frost, Eliot, Hemingway, and various political personages, and he eventually persuaded them to act on Pound's behalf. Pound was released from St. Elizabeths on April 18, 1958, and sailed for Italy on June 30 of that year. For some sense of the scope of M's considerable and determined effort, see *Letters*, particularly those to Hemingway, Frost, and Pound (pp. 397–408).

56 William MacLeish was born August 7, 1928, shortly after the return from Paris. Originally christened Peter Hitchcock, he was rechristened William Hitchcock at the urging of his namesakeless maternal grandfather, William Hitchcock. William (Bill) MacLeish was long known by family and friends as Pete.

57 Henry Robinson Luce (1898–1967) was the founder of *Time, Life, Fortune,* and other magazines.

2. THE 1930S

1   William H. Prescott (1796–1869), American historian, was the author of *History of the Conquest of Mexico* (1843), an account that M called "fine and rhetorical and obviously false as bloody hell" (*Letters*, p. 225). In writing his epic, M used as his principal source A. P. Maudslay's Hakluyt Society translation, published in 1908, of del Castillo's *True History of the Conquest of New Spain* (1632). He wrote to Maurice Firuski in June 1927 requesting a copy of the book.

2   M's trip to Mexico was in February 1929. He worked on the poem, however, for longer than he says. In a January 1931 letter to Maxwell Perkins, Hemingway's editor at Scribners'—with whom M was negotiating for the possible publication of his epic—he speculates that *Conquistador* would be finished in "one year or two" (*Letters*, p. 238). The work was in fact completed that year and submitted finally to Houghton Mifflin, which published it in 1932. So M finished the poem after he joined *Fortune*, not before, as he implies later.

3   In a letter to Hemingway (March 11, 1929), M says he asked the ambassador if the trip was safe *before* he made it. Morrow "didn't know at all" (*Letters*, p. 226).

4   Thornton Wilder (1892–1975), American playwright and novelist, won Pulitzer prizes for *The Bridge of San Luis Rey* (1927), *Our Town* (1938), and *The Skin of Our Teeth* (1942). The dinner took place on May 11, 1966.

5   In his first years at *Fortune*, M was paid at the rate of $10,000 a year, but he received pay only for the half year he was contracted to work. In 1931, he considered working full time for the magazine because of financial needs which became even greater in the spring of 1932 when he learned that there would be no further dividends from his late father's stock in Carson, Pirie, Scott & Company.

6   "He Speaks for America," *Pembroke* (Bicentennial Issue) 7 (1976): 9.

7   Buckminster Fuller (1895–1983), engineer, architect, and inventor, designed the factory-assembled Dymaxion House, a totally autonomous structure, in 1928.

8   Pare Lorentz's film, a twenty-five minute, black-and-white documentary with the same title as M's essay, was produced in 1936.

9   Japan invaded Manchuria on September 18, 1931. The United States responded with the doctrine of nonrecognition, which declared the country would not recognize Japan's conquest.

10 "Ivar Kreuger I," *Fortune* 7, no. 5 (1933), and "Kreuger II: The Accountants," *Fortune* 7, no. 6 (1933).

11 First published in the *New Republic*, October 1932, p. 296. About its reception, M wrote, "Ever since the *Invocation to the Social Muse*, every social-conscience critic in America (& that's the fashionable school) has been after my heart" (*Letters*, p. 264).

12 This was, as M later explains, a "book of photographs illustrated by a poem" (*Land of the Free* [New York: Harcourt, Brace and Co., 1938], p. 89).

13 Arthur Rimbaud (1854–91) and Paul Verlaine (1844–96) were French Symbolist poets.

14 Nicolas Nabokov (1903–78) organized the Russian Broadcast unit of Voice of Amer-

ica in 1947 and served as its first chief. In 1951 he was secretary-general of the Congress for Cultural Freedom.

15 J. P. Morgan (1837–1913) was an American financier.

16 John G. Neihardt (1881–1973) was named poet laureate of Nebraska in 1921. He wrote a five-part poem about white conquest of the Plains Indians.

17 Dorothea Lange (1895–1965) was an American photographer; Ben Shahn (1898–1969) was an American artist, illustrator, and photographer. Both worked for the National Writers' Project in the 1930s. James Agee (1909–55), an American journalist, novelist, and screen writer, wrote *Let Us Now Praise Famous Men* (1941). Walker Evans (1903–75) was an American photographer who worked with Agee and whose photographs illustrate Agee's book.

18 John Steinbeck (1902–68), an American novelist, published *Grapes of Wrath* in 1939. M's *Land of the Free* was published in 1938.

19 The then-new Rockefeller Center in New York City contained a mural by the Mexican painter Diego Rivera (1886–1957). Rivera included a head of Lenin in the mural, which caused a furor. The likeness was subsequently deleted.

20 John Strachey (1901–63) was an English economist and cousin of Lytton Strachey.

21 Wystan Hugh (W. H.) Auden (1907–73) was an English-born poet whose stature as a writer M recognized but whose influence M nevertheless described as "sterilizing and numbing" (*Letters*, p. 321). Stephen Spender (1909–), an English poet and critic, was the subject of M's article "Stephen Spender and the Critics" (*Hound and Horn* 7 [October–December 1933]: 145–47); after it appeared M wrote, "every intellectual has been after my hide" (*Letters*, p. 264).

22 The First American Writers Congress was held in 1935. M also attended the Second American Writers Congress in the summer of 1937. Both were Leftist dominated.

23 M's "The Tradition of the People," *New Masses*, September 1, 1936, pp. 25–27.

24 Edmund Wilson (1895–1972), an American literary critic, was early recognized by M as an extremely influential figure in American letters, but his warfare with him was lifelong.

25 Stephen Becker (1927–), a novelist, was a one-time neighbor of M's in Conway.

26 For an account of the incident at Bread Loaf, see Lawrance Thompson and R. H. Winnick, *Robert Frost: The Later Years* (New York: Holt, Rinehart and Winston, 1981), pp. 385–86.

27 John Houseman (1902–), director, actor, and producer, was, with Nathan Zatkin, a founder of the Phoenix Theatre. M's *Panic* was their first production. The play was performed at New York's Imperial Theatre on March 14, 15, and 16, 1935.

28 James Light (1894–1964) was affiliated with the Provincetown Players, an experimental company first founded in 1916 and later, after a three-year hiatus, reestablished in 1924. Playwright Eugene O'Neill was one of the principals in the company.

29 Harry Hopkins (1890–1946), secretary of commerce (1939–40), was a friend and adviser to President Roosevelt during World War II. As the federal administrator of the Works Progress Administration (1935–38) he was instrumental in creating jobs to employ writers, artists, and actors.

30 In a letter to the Dos Passoses, M names V. (Victor) J. Jerome, John Howard Lawson, and Stanley Burnshaw, three intellectuals of the American Left, as participants in the debate (*Letters*, p. 275). Browder's brother is not mentioned.

31 "Broadway in Review," *Theatre Arts*, May 1935.
32 Wolcott Gibbs, "The Theatre," *New Yorker*, March 30, 1935, p. 28. Contrary to what M remembers, some of the reviews in the New York press were similarly unenthusiastic.
33 *New Masses* was published from 1926 to 1949. It was a Marxist publication to which many major writers of the period contributed.
34 M appears to have forgotten that Lovett was repaid—"the only vital thing is the money to repay Bob & that we have" (*Letters*, p. 274).
35 M's *Fall of the City* was first produced on April 11, 1937. The *Anschluss* (the fall of Austria to the Germans) occurred in March 1938.
36 Merz's call may have come after the rebroadcast in 1938. CBS has no record of a second broadcast.
37 Louis MacNeice (1907–63), Irish poet, journalist, and producer for the British Broadcasting Company.
38 "Air Waves and Sight Lines," *Theatre Arts*, December 1938.
39 M is referring to Picasso's "Guernica" (1937), a painting depicting the horrors of the Spanish civil war.
40 Kenneth MacLeish served as science and medicine editor of *Life* from 1946 to 1955.
41 Mrs. Lucius W. Nieman established the Nieman fellowships at Harvard in 1938 in memory of her husband, owner and editor of the *Milwaukee Journal*.
42 M's tenure at *Fortune* was not easy for him. In 1936 he wrote to Hemingway, "the trouble is moving into and moving out of being a journalist. . . . It takes me a couple of months after I stop journalizing to dissolve the tension in sunlight and get the weight off the gravel so the water can come up through again" (*Letters*, p. 284). In 1937 he suggested to Luce that he resign as an editor and become a contributor instead. In 1938 Luce apparently had asked M to become editor in complete charge of the editorial content of the magazine. When M submitted his resignation to Luce to "go to Harvard on a half-time job, he expressed himself in words which I still vividly recall" (*Letters*, p. 300), which suggests that M's recollection of Luce's response to his departure from Time, Inc. may not be accurate. Subsequent correspondence with Luce is perhaps responsible for M's recollection. In 1943 Luce had apparently invited M to again consider an editorship at *Fortune*. M's reply restated his gratitude for his working arrangement with the magazine, for which Luce had been responsible.

3. THE POET IN GOVERNMENT

1 "Franklin Roosevelt," *Fortune* 8, no. 6 (1933): 24.
2 "Inflation," ibid., p. 31.
3 Robert Sherwood (1896–1955) was a Pulitzer Prize–winning playwright.
4 Keyes Metcalf, Harvard librarian in the 1940s, was a frequent consultant to libraries and later became president of the American Library Association.
5 Nancy Benco, "Archibald MacLeish: The Poet Librarian," *Quarterly Journal of the Library of Congress* 34 (July 1976).
6 Herbert L. Putnam was Librarian of Congress from 1899 to 1939. He was seventy-eight when he resigned.
7 *Roosevelt and Frankfurter: Their Correspondence, 1928–1945*, annotated by Max

Freedman (Boston: Little, Brown and Co., 1967). President Roosevelt had written to Frankfurter on May 3, 1939, asking him what he thought of M as a possible successor to Putnam. Frankfurter sent M a copy of his response, which supported the nomination. M first discussed the position in New York with Kent Keller, chairman of the House Committee on the Library of Congress, some two weeks before his initial meeting with Roosevelt.

8 Thomas Gardiner Corcoran (1900–1981) was a lawyer and Roosevelt's congressional liaison. He drafted many New Deal bills and saw them through Congress. The luncheon to which M refers was on May 24, 1939.

9 John Lomax (1867–1948) and Alan Lomax (1915–), American folklorists. Alan Lomax worked in the folksong and music area of the Library of Congress under M.

10 Keyes Metcalf, "Archibald MacLeish as Librarian of Congress," Pembroke (Bicentennial Issue) 7 (1976): 113–18. It is not clear if Metcalf was acting in any official capacity when he suggested M not accept the position. On May 28, 1939, M sent a letter to Roosevelt declining the appointment. He wrote a letter of acceptance four days later, on June 1, 1939. The appointment was announced by President Roosevelt on June 6.

11 M is correct; the school in Washington was St. Albans, an Episcopal private school affiliated with Washington Cathedral.

12 Auslander, an American poet, held the Chair of Poetry at the Library of Congress from 1936 to 1941. In a 1924 letter to Amy Lowell, M describes Auslander as one "who fancies himself as an imagist" (Letters, p. 140).

13 M removed Auslander from the poetry chair in 1941, but his replacement, Allen Tate, was not named until 1943. (Tate was also the first editor of the Quarterly Journal of the Library of Congress, launched by M.) Robert Penn Warren was the second incumbent (1944), and Louise Bogan was the third (1945). John Peale Bishop, as previously noted, served as Resident Fellow in Comparative Literature until his death in April 1944. Katherine Anne Porter was Resident Fellow in Regional American Literature and was one of the original Fellows of the Library of Congress in American Letters, a group of eight prominent American writers. Established largely by Tate, the group held its first meeting in May 1944. Porter served from 1944 to 1953. Others were Tate himself (1944–51), Carl Sandburg (1944–56), Mark Van Doren (1944–45), Van Wyck Brooks (1944–46), Katherine Garrison Chapin (1944–53), Willard Thorp (1944–51), and Paul Green (1944–53). M served as a Fellow of the Library of Congress in American Letters from 1949 to 1956, a year before the program was disbanded. Carl Sandburg, whom M mentions as someone he "would like to have had" in the post of consultant, was in fact invited to serve in that capacity by M in a letter of June 13, 1940. Sandburg declined the appointment.

14 Louise Bogan, "Books," New Yorker, December 16, 1939, p. 100.

15 The budget for the Library of Congress in 1939 was $3,000,000. In 1976, the appropriation for the Library was $116,000,000.

16 The Irresponsibles (New York: Duell, Sloan, and Pearce, 1940) was first delivered as an address before the American Philosophical Society on April 19, 1940. It created a furor in the press and among critics and writers. M makes further reference to this address, the circumstances of its delivery and publication, and one result of either or both in chapter 5.

17 The America First Committee, headed by Robert E. Wood, had been organized in the mid-thirties to argue against United States involvement in foreign wars.

18 M was named director of the Office of Facts and Figures on October 24, 1941. He
    served without pay and reported directly to the president.
19 The Office of Strategic Services, headed by William Donovan, operated from
    1942 to 1945. Donovan had been named coordinator of information by President
    Roosevelt in 1941.
20 Fiorello LaGuardia (1882–1947) was then director of the Office of Civilian Defense
    (1941–42). He was mayor of New York City from 1933 to 1945.
21 Missy Lehand and Grace Tully were secretaries to Roosevelt.
22 James Warburg (1896–1969) served as special assistant to the coordinator of in-
    formation (1941–42) and later as deputy director of the overseas branch of the Office
    of War Information (1942–44).
23 The group to which M refers was officially known as the Committee on Public
    Information, created by executive order in April 1917 and headed by George Creel.
24 M discusses the OFF situation, particularly the difficulties involved in getting in-
    formation from uncooperative or unwilling agencies (like the armed forces) in
    a "personal and confidential" letter to Frankfurter written April 9, 1942 (Letters,
    pp. 311–13).
25 Samuel I. Rosenman was the principal speech writer for Roosevelt.
26 Elmer Davis was a journalist, author, and radio news commentator. He was made
    director of the Office of War Information in 1942.
27 Franklin Knox (1874–1944) was secretary of the navy in Roosevelt's cabinet from
    1940 until his death. Adlai Stevenson (1900–1965) served during World War II as
    assistant to the secretary of the navy, and represented him on the Committee on
    War Information. John McCloy (1895–) served as assistant secretary of war from
    1941 to 1945. Wayne Coy (1903–57), radio and TV executive, served as special
    assistant to Roosevelt and liaison officer to the Office of Emergency Management
    from 1941 to 1943, and as assistant director of the Bureau of the Budget from 1942
    to 1944.
28 Bob Kintner (1909–80), TV executive, served in the United States Army during
    World War II and was stationed in Washington, D.C. Christian A. Herter (1895–
    1967) was overseer of Harvard (1940–44); member of the U.S. Congress (1942–53);
    secretary of state (1959–61); and governor of Massachusetts (1953–57). Barry
    Bingham (1906–), editor and publisher of the Louisville Times, was commander of
    the U.S. Naval Reserve (1941–45).
29 In 1943, M commented on the OFF mission and the powerful opposition he faced:
    "The American press won its fight against OFF, which was a good deal like a rail-
    road train winning its fight with a snail on the right of way. . . . the real victory was
    a victory for the proposition that all the people are entitled to is 'news' over the
    proposition that the people are entitled to know and to understand" (Letters,
    p. 320).
30 Elwyn Brooks (E. B.) White (1899–1985) was an American essayist and fiction
    writer noted for his children's stories. McGeorge Bundy was dean of Harvard during
    most of M's tenure there. Arthur Schlesinger, Jr., served with OWI (1942–43) and
    OSS (1943–45). He later taught history at Harvard. Henry Pringle was an American
    biographer and journalist who taught at the Columbia School of Journalism.
31 In a letter to Bundy (June 25, 1942), M cites the extraordinary "human warmth and
    reality" he had experienced at OFF (Letters, p. 314).
32 One of the major projects undertaken by OFF was This Is War, a series of radio

programs proposed by the major radio networks. The series, which began in February 1942, was designed to "put the fundamental facts before the country" (*Letters*, p. 319).

33   Russell (Mitch) Davenport was managing editor of *Fortune* in 1937. Wendell L. Willkie (1892–1944) was the Republican candidate for president in 1940 and unofficial envoy for Roosevelt during World War II.

34   In September 1940, the United States gave Great Britain fifty over-age destroyers in return for the right to lease bases for ninety-nine years in Bermuda, Newfoundland, and the British West Indies.

35   Arthur Krock was Washington correspondent for the *New York Times* from 1932 to 1953.

36   M describes OFF as "a little government agency of two or three hundred overworked, devoted, and bloody-headed human beings" (*Letters*, p. 320).

37   Anthony Eden (1897–1977) was British secretary of state for foreign affairs (1940–45; 1951–55). He later served as prime minister (1955–57).

38   *The American Story*, a series of ten plays, was broadcast on NBC in February, March, and April 1944. M was present for at least the first broadcast, which took place in New York on February 5, 1944. M's scripts were published in December 1944 by Duell, Sloan, and Pearce as *The American Story: Ten Broadcasts*.

39   Edward Stettinius (1900–1949) was secretary of state from December 1944 to June 1945.

40   James Reston is a columnist for the *New York Times*.

41   John Dickey served in the State Department as director of the Office of Public Affairs under M until he left to assume the presidency of Dartmouth in April 1945.

42   The Dumbarton Oaks Conference was held from August to October 1944 in Washington, D.C. It brought together delegates from the United States, Great Britain, and the Soviet Union to establish ways to maintain international peace. Most provisions were later made part of the United Nations Charter.

43   Hiss served in the State Department from 1936 to 1947. In 1948 he was accused by Whittaker Chambers, a senior editor of *Time*, of having acted as a Soviet spy. After one hung jury, he was retried, convicted of perjury, and sentenced to five years in prison.

44   Mary McLeod Bethune (1875–1955) was the daughter of former slaves. She served as an adviser on minority affairs for Roosevelt, and in 1935 founded the National Council of Negro Women.

45   Although M submitted his resignation on April 13 (Roosevelt died April 12), it did not become official until August 17. He was working on the ratification of the United Nations Charter during the summer, in addition to his work on UNESCO. This work continued through the following year when he headed the American delegation to UNESCO's first general conference in Paris.

46   The San Francisco Conference was held in 1945 for the purpose of organizing the United Nations. The United States delegation was led by Secretary of State Edward Stettinius.

47   Dulles (1888–1959), an American lawyer and diplomat, was secretary of state under Eisenhower from 1953 to 1959.

48   The seven months after the fall of Poland in 1939 were referred to as the *sitzkrieg* or "phony war."

49 The first step toward formation of the United Nations was the January 1, 1942, meeting of leaders of the United States, Great Britain, China, and the Soviet Union. This meeting produced a document supplementing the Atlantic Charter that was called the "Declaration by the United Nations."
50 Theta Sigma Phi was a communications association renamed Women in Communication, Inc., in 1972.
51 *Give 'em Hell, Harry* was a one-man Broadway show current at the time of this interview.
52 General George C. Marshall (1880–1959) served as chief of staff during World War II.
53 General Dwight D. Eisenhower was the United States Army commander in North Africa and Europe during World War II. In 1944 he was named Supreme Commander of the Allied Forces for the channel invasion of Europe.
54 Bernard Law Montgomery was commander of the British Army during World War II.
55 Henry Morgenthau, Jr., was secretary of the treasury under Roosevelt (1934–45).

4. THE HARVARD YEARS

1 James B. Conant, who became president of Harvard in 1933, had offered M a position with Harvard University Press in 1935. He was also responsible for bringing M to Harvard as Curator of the Nieman Foundation in 1938. (See chapter 3.)
2 Harry Levin (1912–) was professor of comparative literature at Harvard. The chairman of the English Department M mentions later was Gere Whiting.
3 F. O. Matthiessen (1902–50), a member of the English Department at Harvard, had written to M after his appointment as Boylston Professor of Rhetoric and Oratory at Harvard. The appointment was announced May 10, 1949, effective July 1.
4 M's writing course at Harvard was English S. His lecture course on poetry was Humanities 130.
5 Anne Morrow Lindbergh (1906–) is a poet and essayist. She was the wife of Charles Lindbergh, and it was their daughter, Anne, who was a student of M's at Harvard.
6 The poetry course demanded "a full working day per lecture—at least the way I work" (*Letters*, p. 371).
7 Rainer Maria Rilke (1875–1926) was a German lyric poet.
8 Donald Hall, a poet, essayist, teacher, and editor, graduated from Harvard in 1951.
9 Edward Hoagland (1932–) is an American novelist and essayist.
10 John Bunyan (1628–88), the author of *Pilgrim's Progress*. Alfred's play was published in *Botteghe Oscure* II, April 1953, pp. 249–353—the same issue in which M's play *This Music Crept By Me Upon the Water* first appeared (pp. 172–225).
11 M served as acting master of Eliot House for the academic year 1954–55.
12 Jill Conway (1934–) served as president of Smith College from 1975 to 1985.
13 J. Robert Oppenheimer (1904–67), an American physicist, was leader of the group that designed and built the first atomic bomb. M had met him at Antigua in the winter of 1953.
14 Edwin Muir (1887–1959), Scottish poet and prose writer; Paul Hindemith (1895–1963) was a German composer who settled in the United States in 1939 and taught at Yale University.

15 *The Trojan Horse*, which Houghton Mifflin published in a limited paperback edition (1952), was a revision of the play produced by the B B C in January of that year.

16 Nathan Pusey, Conant's successor as president of Harvard, served in that office from 1953 to 1971.

17 Adlai Stevenson, a Washington colleague of M's (as noted previously), had asked M to help draft the first speech of his campaign as the Democratic presidential nominee in 1952. The speech was delivered on August 27 at the American Legion convention in New York. M also became involved in Stevenson's 1956 run for the presidency.

18 "Ann's potatoes" is the play's penultimate line. It calls the characters back to the reality of dinner.

19 In 1951 the MacLeishes purchased property at the Mill Reef Club on Antigua in the British West Indies and built a house there. Most of the twenty years' residence on the island to which M refers must have postdated the writing of the play.

20 Seymour Rudin (1922–) was professor of English at the University of Massachusetts in Amherst from 1954 to 1985. He participated in the MacLeish Symposium (1982, see Afterword and note) at Greenfield Community College as reader of *Songs For Eve* in a presentation of that work composed and conducted by Alice Parker and performed by soloists Jane Bryden, Lucy Shelton, John Aler, and Bruce Fifer and the Manhattan String Quartet.

21 Richard Wilbur (1921–), a translator, poet, critic, and teacher at Smith College, lives in Cummington, Massachusetts, a town near Conway.

22 *J.B.* was published in March 1958 and was first performed at Yale a month later, on April 22. Its New York premiere was December 11, 1958. On May 6, 1958, M wrote to McGeorge Bundy requesting a leave of absence for the 1958–59 academic year because of the "frenzied pressures of production" of *J.B.* (*Letters*, p. 408). Apparently, a different accommodation with Harvard was arrived at, because on September 30, 1958, he wrote to Hemingway that he and Ada were "living in New York those months" and he would be "commuting up here [Cambridge] teaching one course" (*Letters*, p. 412).

23 F. Curtis Canfield (1903–) was chairman of the drama department at Yale from 1953 to 1955 and dean of the newly created School of Drama there from 1955 to 1966.

24 Robert Brustein (1927–), founder and artistic director of the Yale Repertory Theatre (1966–80), later became director of the American Repertory Theatre at Harvard.

25 Sets for the Yale production were designed by Donald Oenslager. Incidental music was composed by Samuel Pottle.

26 Brooks Atkinson (1894–1984) was drama critic for the *New York Times* from 1925 to 1942 and from 1946 to 1960.

27 Alfred "Delly" de Liagre (1904–), a stage and film director and producer.

28 William Elliot Norton (1903–) was, at the time of the Yale production of *J.B.*, drama critic of the *Boston Daily Record* and *Boston Sunday Advertiser*.

29 Elia "Gadg" Kazan (1909–) is an award-winning director of both stage and screen, as well as an actor and novelist.

30 "The Staging of a Play," *Esquire*, May 1959.

31 Lorraine Hansberry (1930–65), *A Raisin in the Sun* (New York: Random House, 1959).

32 R. P. Blackmur, "A Modern Poet in Eden," *Poetry* 28, no. 6 (1926).

33 David Amram had written the music for the New York production of *J.B.*

5 . THE LATER YEARS

1 The producer of *The Eleanor Roosevelt Story* was Sidney Glazier. There was no single photographer; a number of photos from various periods were used.

2 George Seferis (1900–1971) was a Greek poet and statesman.

3 In 1964, one year before its premiere, M wrote to Gerald Murphy that he had "been struggling for five years with a play about Herakles" (*Letters*, p. 420).

4 The play opened October 27, 1965, at the University of Michigan's Mendelssohn Theatre and ran through November 7. The play was co-produced by the University of Michigan Professional Theatre Program and the APA Repertory Company in New York. Rosemary Harris played the role of Megara.

5 W G B H planned a series of broadcasts of M's verse plays. Four of them were recorded in 1980.

6 Ezra Laderman composed the music for *The Magic Prison,* which was first produced on June 12, 1967.

7 Anne Draper played Emily Dickinson.

8 The essay was published on October 18, 1967.

9 *An Evening's Journey* was written by M in response to a request by the bicentennial committee of Conway. M's reading was in the town hall of Conway on Friday, October 1, 1976. "I'm going to get Spence (Chaloner Spencer), who wrote the music for it," he told us on September 28, 1976, "and who has a recording of the music and I will read it and we'll try to bring the music in at the right places. . . . I think it's going to have its laughable moments. But I discovered this morning it's also going to have the opposite. I was telling Ada that I'm not sure I can read that play. It's tremendously emotional for me. My feelings about the town are emotional. And there are two or three places in that play in which just sitting there at my desk and reading . . . I began to wonder what's going to happen."

10 Boylston Adams Tompkins was a classmate of M's at Yale.

11 At that time, Elliot Norton was drama critic for the *Boston Record American* and *Boston Sunday Advertiser.*

12 Adolph Ochs (1858–1935) was the publisher of the *New York Times* until 1935. Arthur Ochs Sulzberger was named publisher in 1963, and it seems probable that it was he who wrote M.

13 The date of the Pittsburgh production was April 1975. M says he worked "ten months without interruption" on the play (*Letters*, p. 436).

14 No recording was ever released by C B S.

15 Julian Boyd, librarian at Princeton, was M's first choice as his successor at the Library of Congress.

16 On April 19, 1940, M delivered the Richard A. F. Penrose, Jr., Lecture at the conclusion of the American Philosophical Society's Symposium on American Culture. A misunderstanding arose over publication of the address. The society wished to print it in the proceedings of the American Philosophical Society, but made clear to M it would do so only if it had not appeared elsewhere. Before the proceedings were published, however, the paper appeared in *Nation* (May 18, 1940) as "The Irresponsibles." A slightly revised version of the article was later published as a book by Duell, Sloan and Pearce (1940). It is not clear from the text if the row M refers to related to the issue of publication or to the highly controversial content of the address.

17 "The Colloquy" was presented at Yale on October 15, 1976, in commemoration of Yale's 275th anniversary.
18 Maxwell Perkins was Fitzgerald's editor at Scribners', a function, as noted in chapter 2, he also performed for Hemingway.
19 Saul Bellow received the Nobel Prize for Literature in 1976. His acceptance speech was delivered in December of that year.
20 Aaron Latham, "Books," *New York Times*, October 16, 1977, sect. 6, p. 52.
21 *Islands in the Stream* (New York: Charles Scribner's Sons, 1970).
22 Roy Winnick, editor of *Letters of Archibald MacLeish, 1907 to 1982*.
23 M did not write a new essay on the years in Paris. The essay entitled "Autobiographical Information," in the section of the same name in *Riders on the Earth*, was originally presented as an address entitled "Conversations with the Moon" to the Cosmos Club, Washington, D.C., in 1977.

AFTERWORD

1 Mark Kramer, *Three Farms* (Boston: Little, Brown and Co., 1980).
2 The University of Massachusetts at Amherst.
3 See chapter 5, n. 5.
4 The Hemingway Papers were dedicated at the Kennedy Library in Boston on July 18, 1980.
5 M addresses William Heyen, Anthony Piccione, and Alfred A. Poulin, Jr., members of the English faculty at the State University of New York at Brockport, as "the three young poets of Brockport" (*Letters*, p. 449).
6 The American Branch of International Artists Collaborative, Inc. (ABIA), based in Greenfield, Massachusetts, produced *Panic* in an outdoor setting in the center of that town in July 1980. The director was Marilyn Tobin.
7 "The Conquest of America" was originally published in August 1949 and was reprinted in the *Atlantic Monthly*, March 1980, pp. 35–42. When the article first appeared it prompted Luce to write M praising it. For M's response, see *Letters*, p. 348.
8 The Iranian crisis referred to is the seizure of the American Embassy in Iran and the taking of American hostages on November 5, 1979.
9 "Picasso: A Painter's Diary," a three-part documentary on Picasso produced by WNET/New York, was broadcast in 1980.
10 *Transition*, an international quarterly for creative experiment edited by Eugene Jolas, was published in Paris from 1927 to 1930. M's five poems were published under the group title M indicates in *Poetry* 137, no. 2 (1980). They are reprinted in MacLeish, *Collected Poems, 1917–1982* (Boston: Houghton Mifflin, 1985).
11 Richard McAdoo was M's last editor at Houghton Mifflin and is currently his literary executor.
12 The Stone House, a small unheated structure located across a field from the main house, was, as M says later, his principal place of work for many years.
13 Kennedy spoke at the dedication of Amherst College's Frost Library on October 26, 1963.
14 "The coach of that famous Harvard Freshman Team . . . announced . . . that I was, without question, the dirtiest little sonofabitch of a center ever to visit Cambridge, Massachusetts" ("Moonlighting on Yale Field," *Riders on the Earth*, p. 296).
15 Wallace Nutting (1861–1941) devoted himself from 1905 on to pictorial representa-

tion of landscapes and early American life. Among his books are *Massachusetts Beautiful* and *Furniture Treasury.* He was also the owner and director of a factory in Framingham, Massachusetts, that made copies of antique furniture.

16　The Cornwalls are located in northwestern Connecticut.

17　Kevin White was then mayor of Boston. M first read "Night Watch in the City of Boston" at the Boston Public Library on April 16, 1975. It appears in M's *New & Collected Poems, 1917–1976* (Boston: Houghton Mifflin, 1976) and in *Collected Poems, 1917–1982.*

18　Perry Miller was a former colleague of M's at Harvard (see chap. 4). Samuel Eliot Morison (1887–1976), a writer, historian, and Harvard lecturer, wrote *Admiral of the Ocean Sea* in 1942, for which he was awarded the Pulitzer Prize.

19　See chapter 1, n. 1.

20　"Art is man's highest possibility but it is nevertheless *man's* highest possibility and without the man the work of art is a vocable. You cannot take them apart. And any critic who undertakes to do so inflicts, not on the work of art but on himself, the self-defeating wound." M wrote this to Ilona Karmel, Radcliffe College (Class of 1952), a student in his writing course, where she had begun her widely acclaimed first novel, *Stephania* (*Letters*, p. 353).

21　Richard Calhoun, Clemens University, spoke on "Archibald MacLeish's *J.B.—* Religious Humanism in the '80's"; Michael Cavanagh, Grinnell College, " 'Conquistador'—An American Epic"; Helen Ellis, "MacLeish and the Nature of Women"; Philip Gardner, Memorial University of Newfoundland, "Verse Plays for Radio"; Judson Jerome, poetry editor, the *Writer's Digest*, "Archibald MacLeish: The Last of the Moderns"; Edward Mullaly, University of New Brunswick, "The Beginnings of Archibald MacLeish"; Alice Parker, "Setting 'Songs for Eve' to Music"; Richard F. Somer, Hamilton College, "The Public Man of Letters"; Barry Wallenstein, City College of New York, "*Poetry and Experience*"; and Thomas Walters, North Carolina State University, "A Look at Selected New Lyric Poems." Joseph Langland, poet, was a long-time faculty member at the University of Massachusetts; Paul Mariani, poet, biographer, and teacher at the University of Massachusetts; William Meredith, a poet, is from Connecticut College; Theodore Morrison is a former Harvard professor; Richard Wizansky is a member of the English faculty at Greenfield Community College.

I N D E X